Voices from Madagascar | Voix de Madagascar

This series of publications on Africa, Latin America, and Southeast Asia is designed to present significant research, translation, and opinion to area specialists and to a wide community of persons interested in world affairs. The editor seeks manuscripts of quality on any subject and can generally make a decision regarding publication within three months of receipt of the original work. Production methods generally permit a work to appear within one year of acceptance. The editor works closely with authors to produce a high-quality book. The series appears in a paperback format and is distributed worldwide. For more information, contact the executive editor at Ohio University Press, Scott Quadrangle, University Terrace, Athens, Ohio 45701.

Voices from Madagascar
Voix de Madagascar

AN ANTHOLOGY OF CONTEMPORARY FRANCOPHONE LITERATURE

ANTHOLOGIE DE LITTERATURE FRANCOPHONE CONTEMPORAINE

Edited by Jacques Bourgeacq

and Liliane Ramarosoa

Ohio University Center for International Studies

Research in International Studies

African Series No. 75

Athens

Works appear courtesy of the authors except as noted:

The poems "Cris d'île," "Avocats," "Mort aux rats," and " Les égouts" by Jean-Claude Fota; "Un pays comme le mien" by Lila Ratsifandriamanana; and "Une paix" and " Ile!" by Jean-Luc Raharimanana, which appeared in Liliane Ramarosoa's *Anthologie de la littérature malgache d'expression française des années 80*, appear courtesy of L'Harmattan.

Dox's poem "Loin d'Iarive" appears courtesy of his heirs.

David Jaomanoro's short stories appear courtesy of Radio France International. "Le petit os" received the 1991 RFI-ACCT Prix du Printemps Culturel du Valenciennois, unpublished short story category. "Funérailles d'un cochon" was awarded the 1993 RFI-ACCT Grand Prix des Inédits.

Jean-Joseph Rabearivelo's poem beginning "O ma mère. . ." was originally published in his *Poèmes* (Hatier, 1990) and appears by permission of Groupe Hatier International.

Jacques Rabemananjara's excerpt from *Antsa* and L.-X. M. Andrianarahinjaka's poem "Printanière" appear by permission and with the contribution of Editions Présence Africaine. Copyright Présence Africaine (1956, 1966).

Jean-Luc Raharimanana's short stories "L'enfant riche" and "Affaire classée," taken from the collection *Lucarne*, appear by kind permission of Le Serpent à Plumes, 20 rue des Petits Champs, 75002 Paris. Copyright Le Serpent à Plumes, 1995.

Narcisse Randriamirado's short story "Grand-mère" was originally published in *Variété* 2 (Bulletin de liaison de l'Alliance Française, 1990) and appears courtesy of the Alliance Française of Madagascar.

Alice Ravoson's short story "Aux cimes des *aloalo*" was originally published in *Nouvelles* (Editions du Centre Culturel Albert Camus, 1995) and appears courtesy of the Centre Culturel Albert Camus, Antananarivo.

Pen and ink drawings by A. Rajaonarivelo appear courtesy of the artist. The silk drawing of Malagasy street children by Marcel Razanakotoarison appears courtesy of the artist.

Ohio University Press, Athens, Ohio 45701

Printed in the United States of America

Ohio University Press books are printed on acid-free paper ♾

09 08 07 06 05 04 03 02   5 4 3 2 1

Library of Congress Cataloging-in-Publication Data

Voices from Madagasacar : an anthology of contemporary francophone literature = Voix de Madagascar : anthologie de littérature francophone contemporaine / edited by Jacques Bourgeacq and Liliane Ramarosoa.

p. cm. – (Monographs in international studies. Africa series ; 75)

Texts in English and French.

Includes bibliographical references and index.

ISBN 0-89680-218-3

1. Malagasy literature (French)–Translations into English. 2. Malagasy literature (French) I. Title: Voix de Madagascar. II. Bourgeacq, Jacques. III. Ramarosoa, Liliane. IV. Series.

PQ3985.5.E5 V65 2001

840.8'09691'09045–dc21   2001016341

Contents

Acknowledgments

We wish to thank all those who contributed to making this project a reality:

- The J. William Fulbright Foreign Scholarship Board, whose grant enabled Jacques Bourgeacq to conduct research in Madagascar in 1996 and to meet Malagasy scholars and writers on location.
- The members of the Council for International Exchange of Scholars (CIES), for their special assistance in preparing for this research trip. Special thanks go to Lilee Perera and Ann Martin.
- David J. Skorton, Vice President for Research at the University of Iowa, whose generous grant covered translation costs for the literary texts included in this anthology.
- Our colleague and friend, Professor Emeritus John T. Nothnagle, for his support, and for the time and professional expertise he generously provided in reading the whole manuscript. Jack is a Renaissance scholar with special knowledge of the history and travel literature of the Indian Ocean.
- All the writers in Madagascar who allowed us to translate and print their unpublished texts. (The texts were col-

lected by Professor Liliane Ramarosoa, who knows these writers personally and has followed their literary careers.)

- Marjolijn de Jager, who translated most of the texts, both prose and poetry, in this anthology. Marjolijn needs no introduction, as she is well-known in the world of literary translation, in particular for Francophone texts. We are deeply gratified that she undertook this project.
- Our thanks also go to three other dedicated translators, each of whom translated one short story: Professor Jacques Dubois (University of Northern Iowa), Dr. Gertrude Champe (Translation Laboratory, University of Iowa), and Lanscom, s.a.r.l. (Antananarivo, Madagascar).
- Finally, we wish to thank Sharon Rose, Ohio University Press copyeditor, for her thorough reading of the manuscript. Her attention to detail more than compensated for Jacques Bourgeacq's "approximative" editing skills.

Introduction

We do not hear much about Madagascar on our side of the oceans. On those rare occasions when we do, we hear about its legendary species of lemurs and unique plants and butterflies; or about the deforestation posing a threat to the unique ecology of the world's largest island; or, more rarely still, the political and socio-economic ups and downs of this struggling nation.

So we do sometimes hear about Madagascar, but rarely from the Malagasy themselves. Why? One main reason is that, although the Malagasy do write about their country's problems, there are no publishers in Madagascar that distribute abroad: for the most part, texts are circulated and read in manuscript or makeshift form on the island, but rarely outside. For writers have only two options: publishing *à compte d'auteur* (at their own expense) or being read only by their immediate circle of friends. Invariably, their individual income precludes the first option. Except for a handful of writers (e.g. Michèle Rakotoson, Jean-Luc Raharimanana, Charlotte Rafenomanjato, Esther Nirina) who combine talent and literary connections in France, the current francophone literature of Madagascar is virtually unknown beyond its shores. With little hope that their voices may be heard elsewhere, Malagasy writers nevertheless continue to express their concerns in both of their languages, Malagasy and French. The purpose of this anthology is to break this silent

vicious circle and bring contemporary voices from Madagascar within the reach of the Western public, especially the English-speaking public (the French-speaking world has already slowly begun to discover this literature).

Aside from the four types of ancient oral literature—the *kabary,*[1] the *hainteny,*[2] the *antsa,*[3] and the *angano*[4]—the Malagasy people had a written literature long before the Négritude movement of the 1930s, which marked the beginning of francophone African writing.[5] Even before the nineteenth century, manuscripts written on tree bark, the *sorabe* (great texts), recorded genealogies and religious thoughts in the Malagasy language, using Arabic script. As early as 1828, and due to English Protestant missionary action and to manuscripts produced by a literate Malagasy elite, a printing house in Madagascar published the Bible, as well as the king's archives, chronicles, and ancestral proverbs and precepts, in Malagasy. Long before the beginning of colonization (1896), then, there was a press in Madagascar and a literary production (tales, poetry, short stories) in the local language. The first colonial governor of Madagascar, General Joseph Galiéni (1896–1905), in spite of his determination to impose French language and schooling on Malagasy society, nonetheless encouraged his French colonial staff to learn Malagasy language and culture and founded the *Académie Malgache* (1902) for the preservation of Malagasy heritage.[6]

The cultural and linguistic "love affair" between France and Madagascar has a long history. In fact, it began long before

colonization. By the end of the eighteenth century, after Etienne de Flacourt had produced his *Histoire de la Grande Isle* (1661) and *Dictionnaire de la langue de Madagascar* (1658), France maintained trading posts on the east coast of Madagascar. Soon there began an ongoing competition for converts between Catholic missions, who championed the French language, and their English Protestant rivals, who proselytized in Malagasy, in order to facilitate the individual reading of the Bible.[7] Over time, however, after the English had withdrawn from the island in the late nineteenth century and the French took over, the French language was to become the instrument of power, social prestige, and professional promotion for a growing westernized elite.

Meanwhile a colonial literature—written in French by French authors—had developed, initially in the form of travel accounts, and later of novels, tales, and short stories. Jean-Louis Joubert sees here the gradual making of an *"imaginaire de Madagascar,"* the construction of an exotic and erotic myth in French consciousness,[8] though the French were not the only ones fantasizing about this distant island. One may remember indeed Daniel Defoe's account of an English seaman stranded on the Malagasy coast.[9]

The Pre-independence Period

During the early part of the twentieth century, unlike the rest of the French African colonies, Madagascar became a hotbed of literary activity. While serving as a colonial administrator in Madagascar, the French critic and essayist Jean Paulhan studied traditional Malagasy literature and produced the first translations of Malagasy hainteny in French. Journals, created by other French intellectuals who were avid students of Malagasy

culture (such as Pierre Camo, Robert Boudry, Octave Mannoni, Camille de Rauville) proliferated during the period up to World War II.[10] Camo and Boudry were instrumental in promoting the literary careers of promising young Malagasy writers, notably the now famous poet Jean-Joseph Rabearivelo.[11] Some of Rabearivelo's first poems were published in the journal *Du côté de chez Rakoto* (Rakoto's way), whose editor was Robert Boudry.

Jean-Joseph Rabearivelo is generally acknowledged, at home and elsewhere, as Madagascar's greatest poet. Born at the turn of the twentieth century, he grew up in the first stage of the colonial period, caught between his will to remain profoundly faithful to his Malagasy roots—he always rejected the possibility of French citizenship, which may have earned him financial security—and the seductive power that French literature had over him.[12] An autodidact—his formal schooling ended at age fourteen—Rabearivelo avidly read both Malagasy and Western literatures (he had taught himself Spanish and even wrote a few poems in that language). Although of a noble caste, he was quite poor and had to hold a number of menial jobs (ironworker, lace designer, library clerk) to survive. Yet he spent much of what money he had buying books, and maintained a steady correspondence with many writers outside Madagascar, like André Gide and Paul Valéry. Literature, especially poetry, was like a religion for him. It is said that he often compared the events of his daily life with those of famous writers (Baudelaire, Rimbaud, etc.). But as he could not solve the inner conflict of forces that confronted him and lacked the proper degrees to advance professionally and achieve financial security for his family, he committed suicide in 1937 in his midthirties. He left an abundant literary production, mainly poetry, in both Malagasy (he had begun writing in his native language at age fourteen) and French. He also wrote two novels: *L'aube rouge* (Red dawn) in 1925 (yet unpublished) and *L'interférence* (Interfer-

ence) in 1928 (published in 1987),[13] numerous essays for regional literary reviews, and translations of Malagasy poetry into French. The surviving eighteen hundred pages of his personal journals, which he referred to as *calepins bleus* (blue notebooks), are in the hands of his descendants and may soon be published. Among his best-known and valued collections of poems are: *Presque-songes* (Near-dreams, 1934), *Traduit de la nuit* (Translations from the night, 1935), and *Chants pour Abéone* (Chants for Abéone, 1936).[14] (See, in the "Pioneers" section of this anthology, the first poem by Rabearivelo, written in the later part of his life, which seems to predict his imminent death.)

Jean-Joseph Rabearivelo's fame has only increased over the years, judging from several re-editions of his works and an international colloquium held at the University of Madagascar in 1987, on the occasion of the fiftieth anniversary of his death.[15]

Three other important literary figures dominated the pre-independence period after Rabearivelo: Jacques Rabemananjara and Flavien Ranaivo, who began their literary careers in the 1940s, writing mainly in French, and Jean Verdi Salomon Razakandrainy, better known as "Dox," whose prolific poetical production was almost entirely in Malagasy. The latter is also known for his translations of French classical plays (by Racine and Corneille) into Malagasy, and for one collection of poems written in French: *Chants capricorniens* (Chants from the [tropic of] Capricorn), published in 1991 by the Centre d'Information et de Documentation Scientifique et Technique (CIDST) in Antananarivo.[16]

Jacques Rabemananjara (born in Arivonimano in 1913), who had acquired from his grandfather a wealth of traditional knowledge, would also take the latter's advice and master the French language, the better to resist colonization. After studying in Catholic seminaries—often the road to success in the colonies—where he was a brilliant student, he began a career in

the colonial administration. At the same time, he participated in the organization of a union for Malagasy civil servants and in the foundation, with Régis Rajemisa-Raolison, of a journal dedicated to the preservation of Malagasy cultural authenticity within the French culture: *Revue des jeunes de Madagascar* (Journal of young Malagasy, 1935). In 1937, under French government auspices, he traveled to Paris, where for a short time he studied literature and law and met the African and Caribbean intellectuals of *Présence Africaine:* Alioune Diop, Aimé Césaire, and Léopold Sédar Senghor. From 1939 through the war, while pursuing a successful career as a "French" civil servant, Rabemananjara increasingly militated for Malagasy autonomy. So when, in 1947, the "insurrection malgache" broke out, followed by a bloody repression from the colonial government, Rabemananjara was among the first Malagasy leaders arrested and imprisoned.

Put on trial for treason (he was a "French" civil servant), he received a life sentence and did time in several prisons: in Tananarive (now Antananarivo); in Nosy Lava (an island on the west coast of Madagascar); and in Marseilles, France, where he continued to write. It was in his Tananarive prison cell in 1947, expecting soon to be executed (the news proved to be only a rumor), that he wrote his long poem *Antsa* (Chant, 1948), a chant indeed of freedom from foreign rule.[17] (See an excerpt from *Antsa* in the "Pioneers" section of this anthology.) He also wrote *Lamba* (Cloth or Shroud, 1950) during his incarceration. Pardoned in Marseilles in 1956, he remained in France until 1960, when he returned to Madagascar to take office in the newly formed government of Madagascar's first president, Philibert Tsiranana. His life, like his poetry, has been one of political involvement and social commitment. Rabemananjara continued to write poetry until the late 1980s.

Among the pre-independence poets, Flavien Ranaivo was

the least prolific. Although his poetic production amounts to little more than a hundred pages in three short collections, he is considered a major poet in Malagasy literary history.[18] His poetry, written in French, is said to be the closest of all to Malagasy inspiration and esthetics, particularly to the traditional *hainteny* (whose features are the dialogue form, the accumulation of images, love applied to other themes, and alternately brutal and mild imagery). Ranaivo, who for his poetic inspiration admits his debt to Jean Paulhan's work,[19] also published essays in *Présence Africaine* and *Revue de Madagascar* on traditional Malagasy poetry and the hainteny in particular. About his poetry, Jean-Louis Joubert states: "If one compares Ranaivo's poems with acknowledged translations of hainteny (for instance Rabearivelo's *Old Songs from Imerina Land),* one is struck by their peculiar tonality. Ranaivo's style stands out by its bareness, its elliptical tendency, its search for violent contrasts. One senses a real attempt to capture in French the subtleties of the Malagasy language."[20] (See two poems by Ranaivo in the "Pioneers" section of this anthology.)

If Dox (1913–78) had not written his *Chants capricorniens* in the French language, his name would perhaps not have appeared in this anthology. Dox is regarded at home as *the* great twentieth-century poet in the Malagasy language. He had long claimed that writing in French would have been for him "grafting his poetry to a tree where it could bloom only malignantly." And yet, a few years before his death in 1978, the news was out: Dox was preparing a volume of poetry in French! For Rémi Andriamaharo, who wrote the preface to the volume, Dox, "an authentic artist," had always been a master at "integrating foreign inspiration into the wealth of the Malagasy homeland."[21] According to Andriamaharo, this was simply the logical consequence of the poet's versatility. *Loin d'Iarive* (Far from Iarive), a French sonnet from *Chants capricorniens,* is presented in the

"Pioneers" section of this volume; Dox's vision of Antananarivo (Iarive), his tone and imagery, foreshadowed those of the next generation of poets (cf. the "Poetry" section of this anthology).

The Post-colonial Period:

In 1960, Madagascar declared its independence from France, with Philibert Tsiranana as President of the First Republic. The first twelve years of the newly and painfully earned liberty—a fictitious liberty, as Paris continued to pull the strings of Malagasy political life through the "Accords de Coopération"—were to be for Madagascar a period of soul-searching.

The long association with France had produced a Malagasy elite saturated with French culture:[22] for several generations, French had been the language spoken and written in schools from the first grade on, a situation that relegated Malagasy (though it possessed its own written literature) to a mere vernacular dialect. The literature studied in school was of course French literature. Although they did not deny the importance of traditional values and Malagasy language and literature, the French-educated Malagasy knew well that prestige had always been spelled in French. After the initial euphoria of independence, a new spirit of duality emerged, giving Malagasy culture and language their rightful place, although France and French were by no means rejected. As two Malagasy scholars recently stated: "During these years of groping, [Malagasy intellectuals] assumed a double culture, henceforth without bashfulness and false pride, basing their philosophy on a syncretic vision."[23] So, paradoxically, and much as was the case for Négritude in the 1930s, *malgachéité* (or the pride of being Malagasy and the enhancement of Malagasy values) did not discard the French language. Indeed Malagasy writers of the time seemed reluc-

tant to give up the international audience and the universalist discourse that the French language provided.

As one might expect, the prevalent themes of the post-independence era were: 1) the quest for an authentic Malagasy soul, often in the form of a strange blend of ancestral wisdom and Christian faith; 2) the vicissitudes of love; 3) the dual theme of woman and nature; and 4) other more specific themes, such as advice and exhortation to wisdom, exaltation of the family, the virtues of work, etc. Nevertheless, over the first twenty years that followed independence, literary production in French was somewhat disappointing: only a dozen writers and fewer than forty works were published, in the following genres: poetry (twenty volumes), novels and short stories (twelve), traditional tales (four), and plays (two). One might blame an inert publishing industry that continues even today to hamper the production of Malagasy literature. Rodin and Rakotoarivelo indicate, in any case, that except for Jacques Rabemananjara and Flavien Ranaivo, none of the writers of the two decades following independence show enough merit to be studied in schools today.[24]

Most often the literature of this period follows the classical forms of Western literature: sonnets, odes, etc. Its poets published in bilingual Malagasy/French journals such as *Tatamo* (Water lily), edited by Régis Rajemisa-Raolison and Elie Charles Abraham or *Ecrivains de Madagascar* (Writers from Madagascar). Régis Rajemisa-Raolison's anthology, *Les poètes Malgaches d'expression française,* selected the most representative poems of this period.[25] The only work distancing itself from this conventional production is that of L.-X. M. Andrianarahinjaka. The rhythm and fervor of his hymns to the native land share in the spirit of Négritude. Unsurprisingly, *Présence Africaine* published his poems, in particular *Terre promise* (Promised land), which celebrates newly recovered freedom and a renewed

pact with the ancestral land. (See L.-X. M. Andrianarahinjaka's poem *Printanière* [Of spring] in the "Pioneers" section of this anthology.)

Not until the mid-1970s did Madagascar turn over a new political leaf. Under the short-lived government of President Gabriel Ramanantsoa (1972–75), and especially with the advent of the Second Republic in 1975 under the Marxist leadership of President Didier Ratsiraka, Madagascar resolutely began to distance itself from France and assert its own destiny. With Ratsiraka began a policy of *malgachisation* in all aspects of Malagasy life. Most notably, Malagasy was reestablished in primary and secondary schools as the main language of instruction—it had remained an optional "foreign" language along with English and German! Malagasy literature finally took precedence over French literature. For better or worse, and whatever the political and economic consequences of its rupture from France would be, Madagascar was indeed embarking on a new course. For two decades (the 1950s and 1960s), Malagasy literature written in French had slowly declined. In the 1970s, Malagasy authors practically ceased writing in French.

The Contemporary Period:

Meanwhile, deep and sweeping political, economic, and cultural changes were affecting the whole planet and principally the peoples of the Southern hemisphere. These changes are reflected in Malagasy literature, as at the start of the 1980s a true "literary revolution" marked all the literatures of the "South." During that period, several special issues of the journal *Notre Librairie* focused on these changes.[26] In his work *Littérature Africaine,* Jacques Chevrier calls this period the *"pleurer-rire"* (weep-laugh) period, when a new generation of

writers describe in a tragi-comic vein the disillusionment that followed the euphoria of independence for African countries (362–365). This new generation drew a dreary picture of the newly independent states of the 1960s, Madagascar among them: politics marked by corruption and abuse of power; socio-economic situations marked by acute misery and flagrant injustice; and the near impossibility of reconciling traditional values with the needs of emerging modern societies.[27]

During the 1980s in Madagascar a new wave of writers appeared, ones who turned their backs on the traditionalism and sentimentalism of the previous two decades. With more pressing concerns, they reacted to the concrete, disheartening social realities that surrounded them; and they did so with particularly brutal language and imagery.[28] Liliane Ramarosoa eloquently sums up this new period in Malagasy literature, which extends to the present:

> In an intimist tone, or through a poetics of violence and the atrocious, through humor and burlesque, all these works show the absurdity of daily life, unveil the sordid social and political undercurrents, denounce the inexorable rules of traditional rites, violate the forbidden zones of passions and vices, and become a plea for man and the individual.[29]

As a whole, these writers' works present all the aspects of an initiatory quest, with emphasis on death and the descent into hell.[30] All genres are not equally represented, with poetry and the short story overshadowing the novel. Dramatic literature is mostly written in Malagasy and, when in French, remains largely unpublished.

Poetry overflows with barely contained revolt, trading the standard forms (types of poem, versification, rhyme, etc.) for a more spontaneous, rhythmic style, better suited to the expression of violent and often conflicting emotions. (See Jean-Luc

Raharimanana's *Poèmes crématoires* in the "Poetry" section for typical examples of this new tone.) There is scathing anger and irony in the poem *Profitez* (Thrive on it) by David Jaomanoro, disrupting the topography of verse. More serene, but no less grieving, is the poem by Lila over the fate of her beloved country (*Un pays comme le mien* [This country of mine]). With Esther Nirina, poetry takes a more philosophical turn: back in Madagascar after many years of self-imposed exile, she integrates memories of the ancestral land and her Malagasy childhood into a quest for "universal"—a word she relishes—sensitivity and values. Her sober style, often elliptical (not unlike the traditional hainteny), lends itself thereby to a multiplicity of meanings. Liliane Ramarosoa has called Nirina's poetry "a plowing magic," where language is the plow . . . or an oar as in one of her poems (see *La lumière ne serait pas* [Light would not be]). Esther Nirina's search for the universal can be tinged with a discrete sensuality (see *Ma main regarde* [My hand beholds]).

Many short stories in French have been written in Madagascar. This is probably due to literary contests and to prizes awarded annually to young francophone writers, like those of Radio France International (RFI) in Paris.[31] In fact, the short story is probably the most productive genre in Madagascar today. Also, through its concision, the short story is ideal for stressing with brevity a specific problem or theme. All these stories indeed present the same drama, where the individual is trapped between the order of the modern city and the demands of the traditions of an earlier age.

Even the folk tale, traditional in form, often assumes a committed role in its denunciation of current untenable situations (see for example Lila Ratsifandriamanana's *Dieu descendra sur la terre demain!* [God will come down to earth tomorrow!]).

The sum of this prose production faithfully depicts Malagasy contemporary life and society, with emphasis on the cruel urban

landscape and its daily realities, in an often deliberately shocking language that responds to the "violence" of the environment.

In contrast to the abundance of short stories, there are only fifteen Malagasy novels. Between the 1920s, when Rabearivelo wrote his two novels, and 1980, no novel really stands out.[32] In the early 1980s, however, two talented novelists appeared: Michèle Rakotoson was awarded the *Prix littéraire de Madagascar* in 1984 for *Dadabe*, the story of a young westernized Malagasy woman who finds her freedom by confronting an anguishing traditional past, haunted as she is by the presence of her grandfather (her *dadabe*). In 1988, she published *Le bain des reliques* (The relics' bath), the story of a human sacrifice in the present day, against the background of an age-old royal ritual (the *fitampoha* of the Sakalava people) and its connection with contemporary politics. Tradition and modernity are linked here in unexpected ways. In 1990's *Le pétale écarlate* (The scarlet petal), Charlotte Rafenomanjato recounts the life of a young woman pursued by a deadly spell, which is viewed through Malagasy astrological conceptions pertaining to birth and individual destiny *(vintana)*; once more, the traditional occult world and modern life and science are closely, and strangely, intertwined. In *Le cinquième sceau* (The fifth seal, 1993), by the same author, despotic regimes are severely denounced: under the sign of Saint John's Apocalypse, the action takes place in the slums of "some" capital city, where a slowly growing revolt against despotism and inequality seeks an end to the people's misery.[33]

Rakotoson and Rafenomanjato have also written plays in French, most of which remain unpublished. They have contributed much in fact to the recent revival of Malagasy francophone theater. By 1992, according to critic Danielle N. Andrianjafy, some twenty plays in French had been written by several authors and staged in Madagascar and abroad since the end of

the 1970s.[34] Unfortunately, until the date of her article (1992), only three scripts had found their way to the printing press: *La retraite* (The retirement) by David Jaomanoro, the highly ironic story of a destitute garbage digger who decides to retire from active life and begins a most lucrative career impersonating a blind beggar; *La maison morte* (The dead house) by Michèle Rakotoson, a drama of passion for power and of political corruption during a revolution in "some" third-world country; and *Un jour ma mémoire* (Some day my memory), also by Rakotoson.

* * *

Aside from obvious historical references and clear instances of traditional values woven into fictional situations, the past also crops up implicitly in other ways. Some familiarity with Malagasy culture and history allows the reader to recognize current realities that persist from the past, such as: the pervasive presence of the omnipotent ancestors in the minds of the living (the ancestors, when pleased, grant fertility and prosperity to their worthy progeny);[35] the numerous *fady* (taboos) still weighing heavily on modern life; the curious mixture of a profound Christian faith and ineradicable occult beliefs and practices.[36] In short, Madagascar's culture and literature offer a whole world to discover, a world in which a proud people is struggling for its material survival and the preservation of its soul. The story told by these texts is that of a challenge facing the Malagasy people—the same challenge that faces ex-colonies in Africa and elsewhere—in their quest for salvation: that is, how to invent a new nation that must step into the modern world while preserving the positive, nurturing forces of its tradition, wherein its soul lies.

* * *

And yet, the culture and literature of Madagascar remain largely unknown. Very few Malagasy literary texts have been translated

to English, they are not widely available in the French-speaking world, and even specialists in francophone studies tend not to be aware of them. We present this anthology with a double purpose: to bring recent texts from Madagascar in their original French to the attention of students of French and francophone studies and to address a larger English-speaking public interested in third-world literatures and in the issues confronting post-colonial societies today. It is our hope that the publication of these texts will contribute to ending the isolation which has stifled Malagasy voices to this day.

We have purposely avoided excerpts (from novels or plays), as such fragments often leave the reader unsatisfied. We preferred to focus on complete, manageable texts, such as short stories and poems, especially since the choice was greater in these two genres, which have attracted substantial artistic talent. Perhaps the texts presented in this volume will inspire further reading and eventually lead to the translation of longer works—several novels are worthy candidates—from Madagascar.

Finally, in order to guide readers through the texts presented in this anthology, endnotes, often of a cultural nature, have been provided. We hope these notes will facilitate the interpretation of the texts.

Jacques Bourgeacq
(With input from Liliane Ramarosoa)

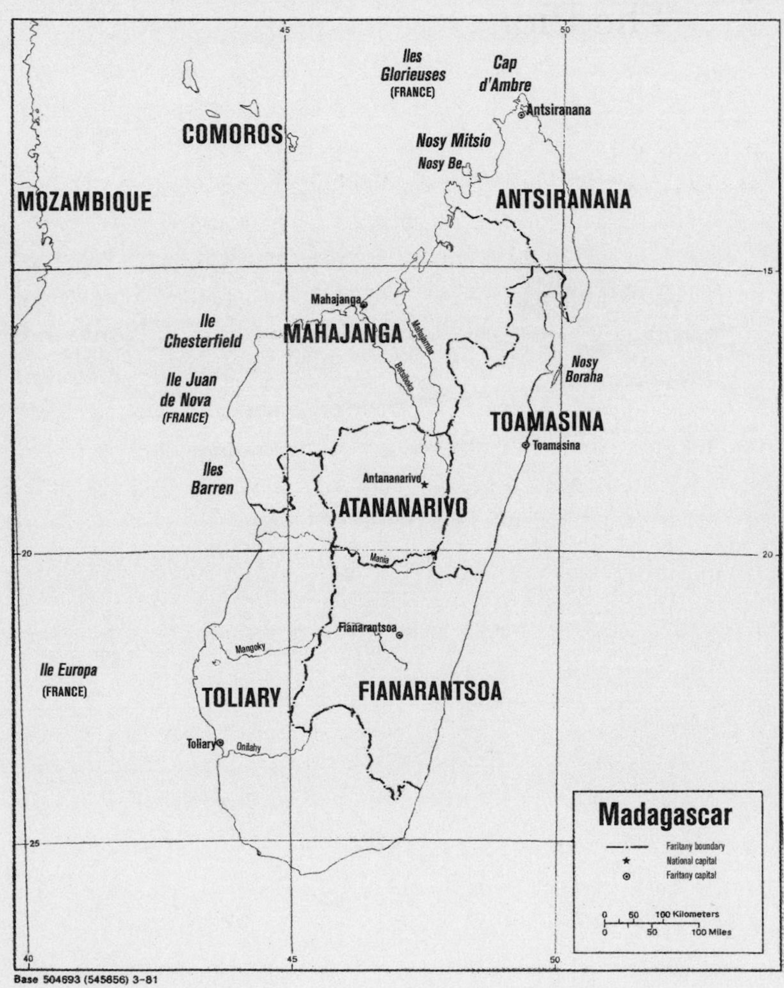

Base 504693 (545856) 3-81

The Pioneers / Les pionniers

Jean-Joseph Rabearivelo

O my mother, I awake from a melodious dream
whose ardor and tonality charmed me;
however, from that land not native to me
I return to you, my heart disenchanted!
I saw the blooming of resplendent dawns,
rosy as a child's lips, promised
to my ship, and rising out of loveliest Floridas,
and I felt, inflating the sky's empty goatskin, breezes
lavishing a savor of bliss and oblivion
into my cup where the regret of exile dissolved;
I saw myself facing a gulf filled with more flowers,
more melodies than a bursting garden in April;
but as my ship prepared to cast anchor,
beautiful as an altar boy serving mass on Sunday,
all collapsed, all faded! What inky
oil had spat on this white page?
And this evening, mother, I need your serene
brow, your arms, your soothing eyes:
the sole appeasing mirrors where the germinating
mirages of Departure will not appear!

(*excerpt from "Chants pour Abéone" in* Poèmes)

Poems in this section are translated from the French by Jacques Bourgeacq (The University of Iowa)

Jean-Joseph Rabearivelo

O ma mère, je sors d'un rêve musical
dont m'ont charmé l'ardeur et la tonalité;
pourtant de ce pays qui ne m'est pas natal,
je vous reviens avec un coeur désenchanté!
J'ai vu s'épanouir des aurores splendides,
roses comme une bouche enfantine, promises
à ma nef, et sortant des plus belles Florides,
et, gonflant de l'azur l'outre avide, des brises
donner une saveur de bonheur et d'oubli
à ma coupe où fondait le regret de l'exil;
je me suis vu devant un golfe plus fleuri
et chantant qu'un jardin où fleurit tout avril;
mais comme mon navire allait jeter son ancre,
beau comme enfant de choeur officiant dimanche,
tout se désagrégea, tout s'estompa! Quelle encre
huileuse avait craché sur cette page blanche?
Et j'ai besoin, ce soir, mère, de votre front
tranquille, de vos bras et de votre regard:
seuls miroirs apaisants où point ne s'offriront
les mirages déjà suscités du Départ!

(*"Chants pour Abéone,"* Poèmes)

Jacques Rabemananjara

    One word, Isle
    And you vibrate!
One word, Isle
And you leap up
Ocean rider!

The word of our desires!
The word of our chains!
The word of our lament!

It shines
in the tears of widows,
in the tears of mothers
and of proud orphans.

It germinates
with the flower of tombs
with the insomnia
and the pride of the enslaved.

Isle of my Ancestors,
this word *is* my salvation.
This word *is* my message.
The word flapping in the wind
on the highest peak!

One word.

From the middle of the zenith,
a drunken papango[1] plunges
hisses
in the ears of the four spaces:
Freedom! Freedom Freedom! Freedom!

(Antsa)

Jacques Rabemananjara

Un mot, Ile,
et tu frémis!
Un mot, Ile,
et tu bondis
Cavalière océane!

Le mot de nos désirs!
Le mot de notre chaîne!
Le mot de notre deuil!

Il brille
dans les larmes des veuves,
dans les larmes des mères
et des fiers orphelins.

Il germe
avec la fleur des tombes,
avec les insomnies
et l'orgueil des captifs.

Ile de mes Ancêtres,
ce mot, c'est mon salut.
Ce mot, c'est mon message.
Le mot claquant au vent
sur l'extrême éminence!

Un mot.

Du milieu du zénith,
un papangue ivre fonce,
siffle
aux oreilles des quatre espaces:
Liberté! Liberté! Liberté! Liberté!

(Antsa)

Flavien Ranaivo

Regrets

Six roads
leave from the foot of the traveler's-tree:
the first leads to the village-of-forgetfulness,
the second is a dead end,
the third is the wrong one,
the fourth saw the beloved pass by
but did not keep track of her footsteps,
the fifth
is for him who is bitten by regret
and the last . . .
I do not know if it is passable.

(*Valette, ed.*, Flavien Ranaivo)

Old Merina Theme

Plants germinate
spurred by their roots
and I come to you spurred by my love.

At the top of the high trees, beloved
the bird ends its flight
My wanderings never end that I am not
near you.

Stumble, stumble
the Farahantsana[2] waters, dear
without a sprain;
fall, they fall without a break.

My love for you, beloved,
resembles waves on the shore:
I wait for them to dry up. More will come.

Flavien Ranaivo

Regrets

Six routes
partent du pied de l'arbre-voyageur:
la première conduit au village-de-l'oubli,
la seconde est un cul-de-sac,
la troisième n'est pas la bonne,
la quatrième a vu passer la chère-aimée
mais n'a pas gardé la trace de ses pas,
la cinquième
est pour celui que mord le regret,
et la dernière. . .
je ne sais si praticable.

(*Valette, ed.*, Flavien Ranaivo)

Vieux thème merina

Germent les plantes
poussées par les racines,
et je viens jusqu'à vous poussé par mon amour.

Aux cimes des grands arbres, chérie,
l'oiseau termine son vol:
mes courses ne s'achèvent que ne sois
près de vous.

Trébuchent, trébuchent les eaux de
Farahantsana, chéri
sans se faire d'entorses;
elles tombent, elles tombent sans se briser.

Mon amour pour vous, chérie,
ressemble à de l'eau sur la grève:
j'attends qu'elle tarisse, il en vient davantage.

Two loves grew up together,
because twin loves:
woe on him who betrays.

Farewell, dear, farewell:
foolish love is a trompe l'oeil,
indecisive love turns one mad . . .[3]

(*Valette, ed.*, Flavien Ranaivo)

Deux amours ont grandi ensemble,
car deux amours jumelles:
malheur à celui qui trahit.

Adieu chéri, adieu:
l'amour insensé trompe l'oeil,
l'amour indécis rend fou. . .

(*Valette, ed.*, Flavien Ranaivo)

Dox

Far from Iarive . . .

I came from afar, far from your borders
But can one forbid me, o cosmopolitan city
to love you, rot, and to love you, elite,
with sweet scents and nauseating stench?

I love you like a flower of poisonous grace
adorned as a courtesan on a mat, offered . . .
for so you appear on your green rice fields
offering vahinys[4] your bewitching embrace.

When I am far from you, morose and amorous,
The thirst for your kisses, aflame and languorous
Throws me back at your feet, drugged, in your fringe . . .

Far from you, at night, my blues turn into torment.
Violent is my nostalgia, like lovers' ache
And I dream alike of monster and angel.

(Chants capricorniens)

Dox

Loin d'Iarive...

Je suis venu de loin, loin de tes horizons
Mais peut-on m'interdire, ô ville cosmopolite
de t'aimer pourriture, et de t'aimer élite
aux parfums doux et rémugles nauséabonds?

Je t'aime comme une fleur au charme empoisonnant
parée en courtisane sur la natte, offerte...
car telle tu parais sur tes rizières vertes,
offrant aux vahiny tes baisers envoûtants.

Quand je suis loin de toi, morose et amoureux,
la soif de tes baisers ardents et langoureux
me rejette drogué, à tes pieds, dans ta frange...

Loin de toi, mon cafard, la nuit, tourne en tourments.
Ma nostalgie est vive comme celle des amants
et je rêve du monstre aussi bien que de l'ange.

(Chants capricorniens)

L.-X. M. Andrianarahinjaka

Of Spring

Music I name you. Primordial silence identical to night:
and the feverish rise of time through my limbs
my eurhythmic peace.
This season remains ineffable
with purity and plenitude which restored to silence
the limpidity and resonance of light. [. . .]

Again here I stand,
quivering with emotion as on the very first day
on the threshold of this same landscape
that long ago had revealed to me the splendor of Spring.
Land flooded with light that I rediscovered at the bend
of my memory.
Flower bed in the garden of ecstasy where my heart has
never ceased
to search for all future springs. [. . .]

This morning, my youth reaches to the dawn of the
world,
and my hope seizes in a single embrace
all the days yet to come.
I salute this morning and its rites that forever initiated
me
to the old ritual of Joy and of Immutable Hope.

(*Terre promise* [Promised land])

L.-X. M. Andrianarahinjaka

Printanière

Musique je te nomme. Silence primordial identique à la
nuit:
et la montée fiévreuse du temps à travers mes membres
ma paix eurythmique.
Demeurant cette saison-ci inénarrable
de pureté et de plénitude qui a restitué au silence
la limpidité et la résonnance de la clarté.[. . .]

Or me voici de nouveau debout,
tremblant d'émoi comme au tout premier jour
au seuil de ce même paysage
qui m'avait jadis révélé les fastes du Printemps.
Paysage inondé de clarté que j'ai revue une fois au
détour de ma mémoire.
Parterre au jardin de l'extase où n'a cessé mon coeur de
se rendre
à la rencontre de tous les printemps futurs.[. . .]

Ce matin, ma jeunesse s'étend jusqu'à l'aube du monde
et mon espoir embrasse d'une seule étreinte
tous les jours encore à venir.
Je salue ce matin et ses rites qui m'ont à jamais initié
au vieux cérémonial de la Joie et de l'Immuable
espérance. . .

(Terre promise)

Short Stories / Nouvelles

David Jaomanoro

Born in 1953, David Jaomanoro is a high school teacher. In May 1987, he received the first prize for poetry on the occasion of the fiftieth anniversary of the death of Madagascar's foremost poet, Jean-Joseph Rabearivelo. He is the author of an unpublished volume of poems (Quatram's j'aime ça), *several other short stories* (Peau de banane, L'appel de la nuit, Une belle victoire, *and* Docteur parvenu), *and two plays* (Le dernier caïman *and* La retraite). *Jaomanoro was voted Literature Laureate during the third* Jeux de la Francophonie *(Antananarivo, August 1997) for his short story* Jaombilo. *He now lives in the Comoro Islands. Presented below are two of his short stories:* Funeral of a Pig *and* Little Bone.

Funeral of a Pig

He did come. That's true.

It was raining that day. He was caked with mud, and so was his soul. This child of my womb was unrecognizable. I didn't know him. He was still puny. In the place of the Saint Christopher medal his godfather gave him hangs a medal of a skull. His beautiful smile which, as a child, made him look so cute even when his face was covered with mango juice, has disappeared, replaced by a sneer that exposes his teeth. He is still just a kid, but old beyond his years and not far from the grave.

It is said that shaking is the partner of fear. My stomach was all knotted up. I leaned against the post of the adjoining room.

"Don't! Stand up straight!" he cried. I stepped away from the post as if it were a venomous snake.

He and his fellow druggies were on assignment in the area. Supposedly one of their men had deserted with knowledge of an important secret. They had to find him and dispose of him. They went to all the villages, searching all the houses. They

Translated from the French by Jacques Dubois (University of Northern Iowa)

David Jaomanoro

Né en 1953, David Jaomanoro est professeur de lycée. En mai 1987, il obtint le premier prix de poésie à l'occasion du cinquantième anniversaire de la mort du grand poète malgache Jean-Joseph Rabearivelo. Il est aussi l'auteur d'un volume de poésie, Quatram's j'aime ça, *de plusieurs nouvelles* (dont Peau de banane, L'appel de la nuit, Une belle victoire, Docteur parvenu), *ainsi que de deux pièces de théâtre* (Le dernier caïman *et* La retraite). *Récemment, Jaomanoro a été élu lauréat du Concours de littérature des IIIèmes Jeux de la Francophonie (Antananarivo, août 1997) pour sa nouvelle* Jaombilo. *Il réside aux Comores depuis 1998. Deux de ses nouvelles,* Funérailles d'un cochon *et* Le petit os, *sont reproduites ci-dessous.*

Funérailles d'un cochon

Il est venu, oui.

Un jour de pluie. Crotté de boue, le corps. Crotté de boue, l'âme. Il était enfant sorti de mes entrailles méconnaissable. Je ne le reconnaissais pas. Gringalet, toujours. Mais la médaille de Saint Christophe à lui offerte jadis par son parrain remplacée par une tête de mort. Mais le sourire qui, gosse, enjolivait son visage barbouillé de jus de mangue, déchiré par un rictus qui lui dévoilait le bout des dents. Gosse, toujours, mais un gosse vieilli. Déjà mort de vieillesse.

Le tremblement est époux de la trouille. La trouille sciait mes tripes. Je me suis appuyée au poteau de la porte de séparation.

— Non! Droite! a-t-il crié. Je me suis écartée du poteau comme d'un serpent venimeux.

Avec des "cam" il effectuait une "mission" dans les parages. Un cam aurait déserté la Bande, porteur d'un terrible secret. Le trouver coûte que coûte et le régler. Ils ont fait tous les villages, fouillé toutes les cases. Violer toutes les femmes, tuer tous les hommes, mais trouver le déserteur. Utiliser tous les

raped all the women, killed all the men. They had to find the deserter. Anything that could help convince or dissuade was acceptable. All the women and young girls had fled with the children. All the men had taken cover in the forest. You could try to reason with kids, but not with the Kalachs,[1] nor with their grenades. I stayed behind, having convinced myself that he wouldn't dare do anything. He wouldn't do this to his own father, his own brothers and sisters.

My father, he is the captain
My mother, she is the commando
My brothers and sisters, the druggies

When the 4x4 came to a screeching halt in the middle of the village square, I recognized his voice.

"We've been had. The village is abandoned!"

The blood froze in my veins. It was him! I wanted to go out but I could already hear his steps across the floor of the big cabin where I was. He came in. He stopped and stared at a photograph of his father in a French uniform. You could read the envy in his eyes. Although a soldier himself, his brand new combat uniform was much too big for his skinny physique. A wide belt encircled his effeminate waist. The silk scarf around his neck gave him the appearance of a *oiseau-des-îles,* a colorful bird. His legs were slightly bowed, probably because of the many days I carried him on my back when he was a child. His feet were bare in his leather sandals. He was still so cute. I felt a twitch in my stomach.

—Son! My son!

He turned around slowly. His eyes glowing, burning a hole right through my clothes, giving me the impression that I was standing there naked. I started to go toward the other room of the big cabin.

—Stop! Don't move!

He held a large-caliber pistol in each hand pointing them at my stomach. Bulges in his pockets suggested that they contained

moyens de persuasion et de dissuasion. Toutes les femmes et filles avaient fui, avec les enfants. Tous les hommes se sont réfugiés dans la forêt. On pouvait raisonner des gosses, mais des Kalach' non; des grenades, non. Je suis restée. Je me suis dit non il n'osera pas. Il n'oserait pas avec son propre père, avec ses propres frères et soeurs.

Mon père, c'est le Capitaine
Ma mère, c'est le Commando
Mes frères et soeurs les Cam

Quand leur quatre-quatre a freiné brutalement au milieu de la place du village, j'ai reconnu sa voix.

— On nous a eus, le village est vide!

Mon sang s'est coagulé dans mes veines. Lui! J'ai voulu sortir, mais ses pas craquaient déjà le plancher de la case-grande où je me trouvais. Il est entré. Il tomba en arrêt devant la photo de son père quand il était dans l'armée francaise. Ses oreilles remuaient de convoitise. Lui-même était soldat, mais sa tenue de combat flambant neuve flottait autour de son corps maigre. Un gros ceinturon de cuir rayait sa taille efféminée. A son cou un foulard de soie qui le faisait ressembler à un oiseau-des-îles. Jambes légèrement arquées, sans doute à cause des longues journées qu'il avait passées sur mon dos. Pieds nus dans des sandales de cuir. Terriblement mignon. Mon ventre a remué.

— Fils! Mon fils!

Il s'est retourné lentement. Ses yeux étincelaient, brûlant mes pagnes, me mettaient à nu. J'ai fait un mouvement vers l'autre pièce de la big cabin.

— Stop! Bouge pas!

Il tenait maintenant dans chaque main un "gueule-puante" de gros calibre; il les braquait sur mon ventre. Les bosses de ses poches trahissaient les fameuses grenades qui vous soufflaient votre case comme un tas de feuilles mortes. Un moment j'ai cru qu'il allait tout abandonner, tout laisser tomber et se jeter dans

those famous grenades capable of blowing up a house like a pile of leaves. For an instant I thought that he was going to have a change of heart, drop the whole thing, and throw himself into my arms like he used to, as recently as three months ago. Or that he would call me Mom knowing that I liked it, talk about Mbe, his studies, and about girls who interfered with his school work. I expected him to inquire if there were any *ampango*[2] left in the pot; he was crazy about *ampango*. He was staring at my heart, between my breasts. A chill ran down my spine.

Then a smile came across his face.

—Where is Jinoro?

—You want to see your father, he went into the forest.

I was not surprised by the harshness of his voice. The insolence of his stare did not upset me. I was powerless, two pairs of holes threatening both my life and my virtue; one pair in the middle of his face, the other firmly held in his hands. I felt a chill. I crossed my arms across my chest, covering my breasts.

—Drop your arms!

I obeyed. He took a few steps toward me. I walked backward into the other room of the big cabin, right into mother and father's room. Off limits to children once they have reached puberty. He followed me. I yelled for him to stop. He did, his chest heaving, his eyes staring at my chest, his handguns still pointing at my stomach.

—Where is Jinoro?

—Your father is in the forest.

—You're lying! Jinoro is here and you are going to turn him over to me. Or else. . .

—Listen, he is your father, and you owe him love and respect.

I was trying to regain control of myself and of him.

—I don't have any respect for pigs! I hate bastards!

He whistled. Four of his cohorts burst in the big cabin, kids, all of them, barely the age of puberty, just like him. They

mes bras comme autrefois. C'est à dire il y a trois longs mois. Qu'il allait m'appeler maman comme je l'aimais, qu'on allait parler de Mbe, de ses études, des filles qui les confondaient. Demander s'il restait un peu d'ampango au fond de la marmite, il raffolait d'ampango. Il regardait fixement mon coeur, entre mes seins. Tous mes poils se sont dressés.

Puis il a souri.

— Où est Jinoro?

— Tu veux voir ton père, il est allé dans la forêt.

La dureté du ton ne m'a pas surprise; l'insolence du regard ne m'a pas froissée. J'étais subjuguée par les deux paires de trous qui menaçaient ma vie autant que ma vertu: une paire sur son visage, une autre dans ses mains fermes. J'ai eu froid. J'ai croisé les bras sur mes seins.

— Baisse les bras!

J'ai fait. Il s'est avancé de quelques pas. J'ai reculé dans l'autre pièce de la case-grande. La pièce de père et mère. Interdite aux enfants à partir de la puberté. Il m'y a suivie. J'ai crié arrête! Il s'est arrêté, haletant, les yeux rivés sur ma poitrine, les revolvers braqués sur mon nombril.

— Où est Jinoro?

— Ton père est dans la forêt.

— Tu mens! Jinoro est ici, et tu vas me le livrer. Sinon. . .

— Ecoute, c'est ton père, tu lui dois respect et amour.

J'essayais de reprendre mon autorité, de le reprendre.

— Je ne respecte pas les cochons, je hais les cons!

Puis il a sifflé. Quatre de ses cam ont fait irruption dans la case-grande, tous des gosses, à peine pubères. Comme lui. Revolvers aux poings et grenades en poches. Il m'a désignée avec le canon de son gueule-puante. Les cam se sont rués sur moi en salivant. J'ai vu leurs pupilles dilatées. Le mot cochon tourbillonnait dans ma tête pendant qu'ils déchiraient mes pagnes, lacéraient ma peau, mordaient à pleines dents dans ma viande.

entered, gun in hand, their pockets filled with grenades. He pointed at me with one of his black holes. The druggies pounced on me as if famished. Their eyes had a hollow look. The word pig was still spinning in my head as they ripped my clothes, bruised my flesh, and devoured me. They were drinking my blood. While they were having their way with me, Ntsay uttered to me, his voice breaking up from sobbing:

—I'm not a pig! Nor is Mbe! My brother is not a pig!

* * *

Ntsay had a twin brother who looked as much like him as two eyes on the same face. As is the case with all twins, the first born is the younger of the two. His name was Ntsay, and the last born, the elder, was called Mbe. I loved them more than anything in the world. Specially since, according to the midwife, I couldn't have any more children.

Then there was no more room for them at the primary school of the neighboring village, nor at the middle school in Anivorano. They left for Diego-Suarez.[3] They were big boys, they were fourteen. After that Mbe became ill. A stomach ailment probably related to disobeying some taboo. Young city dwellers don't have taboos. We sold off a lot of our cattle. We brought him back to the village. He died on the way. It is as if I had lost one of my eyes or that I was a legless stump.

During the five-day-long funeral, our "kin" carried themselves in exemplary fashion. They were led by their father himself, the old Zaidy.

The sons of Zaidy chopped down the two trees which were carved out for the two pieces of the *tamango*[4] coffin: the bottom, the female part, and the lid, the male part. The hardness of the wood required three whole days of nearly uninterrupted work. The sons of Zaidy contributed three of the five cows that were eaten and sixty-two cans of rice that Zaidy's daughters crushed

Ils buvaient mon sang. Tandis qu'ils me faisaient, Ntsay me lança d'une voix brisée par les sanglots:

— Je ne suis pas un cochon! Mbe non plus n'est pas un cochon! Mon frère n'est pas un cochon!

* * *

Ntasy était jumeau d'un frère qui lui ressemblait comme les yeux du même visage. Comme tous les jumeaux le premier sorti était le cadet, il s'appelait Ntsay, et le dernier sorti, l'aîné, s'appelait Mbe. Je les chérissais plus que tout au monde. D'autant que je ne pouvais avoir d'autres enfants selon les dires de l'accoucheuse.

Puis il n'y a plus eu de place pour eux à l'école primaire du village voisin, ni au collège d'Anivorano. Ils partirent à Diégo, ils étaient grands, ils avaient quatorze ans. Puis Mbe tomba malade. Une maladie du ventre, sans doute consécutive à une transgression de tabou. Les jeunes citadins n'ont pas de tabous. On a vendu des boeufs et des boeufs. On l'a ramené au village. Il est mort en route. J'étais comme éborgnée, ou devenue fesse-sans-jambes.

Pendant les cinq jours qu'ont duré les funérailles de Mbe, nos parents à plaisanterie se sont comportés de manière exemplaire. Ils étaient conduits par leur père en personne, le vieux Zaidy.

Les fils de Zaidy ont abattu les deux arbres où on a creusé les deux pièces du cercueil tamango: l'auge femelle et le mâle couvercle. Bois dur qui a nécessité trois jours pleins de travail presque ininterrompu. Les fils de Zaidy ont fourni au total trois boeufs sur les cinq qu'on a mangés; soixante-douze bidons de paddy que les filles de Zaidy pilaient le matin avant toute autre corvée. Les fils de Zaidy ont amassé la rondelette somme de quatre-vingt mille francs, le salaire mensuel d'un instituteur. Pour ces "zivas" exemplaires, cet adage Njoaty était loin d'être caduc: "Quand pourrit la chair, il reste l'os pour

every morning before doing their chores. Zaidy's sons also collected the tidy sum of eighty thousand francs,[5] the equivalent of a teacher's salary for a month. In the case of these model *zivas*[6] the old Njoaty adage was very appropriate: "When the flesh has rotted away, the bone is still there to hold everything together." The rotten flesh was represented by the Njoaty,[7] Mbe, whose stench overpowered the village; the bone for support were the Antankandrefas,[8] Zaidy's sons, *zivas* of the Njaoty.

The kinship between Njoatys and Antankandrefas went back to a rather vague period when boats, called *"boutres,"*[9] ventured across the Big Blue to stock up on slaves on the Morima[10] coast. They made a pact of mutual help and support, and solidarity in happy times as well as in hard ones. The Njoatys could use the cattle, the land, and even the harvest of the Antankandrefas without fear of retribution and vice versa. On the other hand, they could insult each other, if they so desired, without any danger of committing an act deemed socially improper.

The day of the burial was buzzing with activity. The large coffin was glistening under a thick coat of beef suet. Underneath, the sun shone in a large pool of pus, Mbe's pus. All the utensils had been washed in hot water, the branch shelter removed. Chosen for their "kinship," Zaidy's sons fastened two long poles to the side of the malodorous, fly-covered coffin with vines made supple in the fire. Some called for the last word. Rum was flowing abundantly. A large crowd was there to witness this moment of disgrace.[11] My son Ntsay was lying on the lap of his uncle, Zaman'i Tsay. The old Zaidy got up to pronounce the customary *kigny*[12] to prepare the deceased for his ultimate voyage. The women began their wailing. Many of those who had attended the putrefaction of Mbe passed out—they had eaten and slept next to his decomposing body for five days.[13] For a moment the sobbing noise stood out above the stench of Mbe. Then a man's voice boomed out amid Zaidy's sons.

la supporter". La chair pourrie c'était le Njoaty, mon fils Mbe dont la putréfaction étouffait le village, et l'os pour le supporter, l'Antankandrefa, les fils de Zaidy, ziva du Njoaty.

La parenté à plaisanterie entre Njoaty et Antankandrefa remonte à une époque nébuleuse où les boutres malgaches affrontaient la Grande Bleue pour aller se ravitailler en esclaves sur les côtes du pays Morima. Ils ont conclu un pacte: entr'aide, solidarité, soutien mutuel dans la joie comme dans le malheur. Le Njoaty pouvait utiliser les boeufs, les terres et même les récoltes de l'Antankandrefa en toute impunité, et vice versa. En revanche, ils pouvaient s'injurier réciproquement, consciencieusement, sans être inquiétés par les règles de la convenance.

Effervescence des préparatifs le jour de l'enterrement de Mbe. Le grand cercueil luisait de graisse de boeuf. Dessous brillait une nappe importante de pus. Le pus de Mbe. On a fini de laver les ustensiles à l'eau chaude, on a détruit l'abri de branchages. Les fils de Zaidy en tant que parents à plaisanterie attachèrent deux longs balanciers au cercueil couvert de mouches et de puanteurs avec des lianes assouplies au feu. Quelqu'un a appelé l'ultime discours. Le rhum circulait. Une foule immense assistait à la disgrâce. Mon fils Ntsay était pâmé sur les genoux de son oncle, Zaman'i Ntsay. Le vieux Zaidy s'est levé pour prononcer le kigny d'usage par lequel il préparait le défunt à l'ultime voyage. Les femmes s'ouvrirent en lamentations. Beaucoup de celles qui avaient veillé la putréfaction de Mbe se sont évanouies—elles avaient mangé et dormi pendant cinq jours près du corps en décomposition. Le fracas des pleurs a dominé un moment l'odeur de Mbe. Puis une voix d'homme a fusé du milieu des fils de Zaidy.

— Ne pleurez pas, femmes, c'est un cochon qu'on va enterrer!

Ntsay a jailli des genoux de son oncle. Il a hurlé comme un taureau castré à blanc. Imperturbable, le vieillard accroupi près du cercueil qui lui renvoyait l'image d'un peuple endeuillé et

—Do not cry, women, we are about to bury a pig!

Ntsay jumped up from his uncle's lap. He screamed like a bull being castrated. Unflappable, the old man, crouched down next to the coffin where he could see the reflection of his drunken and mournful people, went about his farewell speech. The jokester was now standing next to the coffin. He raised one leg and straddled it.[14]

—If you are not a pig, Mbe, speak up! You see, Mbe didn't say anything, it is just a pig. We are going to bury a pig. One of Zaidy's daughters added:

—Mbe is a pig, but you are a sorcerer riding a wild pig in broad daylight!

Her words were welcomed by loud laughter. Then the *ziva* imitated a possessed rider, slapping wildly at the male part of the coffin: —HIA! ARR'ti! HIA! An old toothless *ziva* addressed the corpse rider:

—At that pace, your mount is not going to last very long. You can't see, but it is leaving huge droppings behind you!

More laughter and hoots followed. The rider turned to the old lady and said:

—When my mount is through, I will eat its testicles with my morning *ampango*. Meanwhile, I. . .

He didn't finish his sentence. Ntsay's club had struck him in the temple. He fell face first. A silence fell over the crowd. Ntsay was trembling from emotion. His uncle walked up to him:

—Just because you know how to scribble your name on a scrap of paper doesn't give you the right to trample our customs!

He slapped Ntsay with such force that his skinny body reeled backward against the coffin, unconscious. A voice shouted to the pallbearers: "Let's go!"

The men rushed to the coffin. Twelve swearing, drunken men raised the enormous coffin toward the sky, oblivious of the passed-out child who fell face first in the pool of pus. Gruff

saoûl, continuait son discours d'adieu. Le plaisantin était maintenant debout tout contre le flanc du grand cercueil. Il leva une jambe et se mit à califourchon dessus.

— Si tu n'es pas un cochon, Mbe, eh bien, dis-le! Vous voyez, Mbe ne dit rien, c'est un cochon, on va enterrer un cochon! Une des filles de Zaidy surenchérit:

— Mbe est un cochon, mais toi, tu es un sorcier, qui montes un cochon sauvage en plein jour!

Un tonnerre d'éclats de rire a salué cette boutade. Alors le ziva mima une cavalcade endiablée, administrant de puissantes claques sur le mâle couvercle du cercueil: "HIA! HIA! ARR'ti! HIA!" Une vieille ziva édentée lança à l'endroit du monteur de cadavre:

— A cette allure, fils, tu vas crever bientôt ta monture. Tu ne vois pas mais elle fait déjà d'énormes crottes derrière toi!

Rires en cascades, huées. Le cavalier s'est tourné vers la vieille:

— Quand le cochon aura fini de crotter, je lui mangerai les couilles avec mon ampango du matin. En attendant, je. . .

Il ne termina pas. Le gourdin de Ntsay l'a atteint à la tempe. Il piqua du nez. Cet acte jeta la consternation dans l'assistance. Ntsay tremblait d'émotion. Son oncle s'approcha de lui:

— Ce n'est pas parce que tu sais griffonner ton nom sur un chiffon de papier que tu vas fouler aux pieds nos coutumes!

Il asséna à Ntsay une gifle qui propulsa son corps maigre contre le cercueil. Evanoui. A ce moment, on cria l'appel des porteurs. "Nous partoooons!"

Les porteurs se ruèrent sous les balanciers. L'énorme cercueil fut soulevé de terre par douze gaillards vociférants, imbibés d'alcool, indifférent à l'enfant évanoui qui tomba le nez dans la mare de pus. Le plaisantin fut tiré sans ménagement, mis debout, puis entraîné dans le tourbillon des chanteurs de gouma. Alors seulement j'ai pu répondre au remous de mon sang, à

hands pulled the jokester up, got him to stand up and ushered him behind the swarm of *gouma*[15] singers. Then, and only then, was I able to answer the call of my blood, of my womb. With the help of a few women, *zivas* for the most part, still wearing the smell of my child, I ran to my son. A large colony of ants was drinking from the pool of pus. They soon abandoned the putrid blood of the elder for the fresher one of the younger. Before long Ntsay's body was covered with large puffy marks. I washed his face with my clothes. I cried for a long time, my head nestled in his neck, as I caressed his ant bites. As I whispered his name in his ear, I slowly brought him back to life.

—Mom, Mbe is not a pig. My brother is not a pig, is he, Mom?

—Of course, o fruit of my womb. Mbe is not a pig.

—Mbe is not a pig. Mbe is not a pig. Mbe is not a pig.

As he repeated that over and over, I felt the umbilical cord being severed.

That is how he became a Federal.[16] After the ablution, he packed his bags like someone bent on never coming back. He took everything with him. He was gone three months. In three months the Federals transformed my son into a monster. One day I received some mail with a photograph of my only son, at the wheel of a 4L.[17] Subsequently I learned that young Federals drive without a license and are given candy which kills their hunger and their hearts before sending them out on assignment. He informed me in his letter that he was a soldier. He had enlisted in the *Bande.* He was getting intensive military training. He had been sworn in and vowed to obey all the orders from his Captain. Rumors have it that druggies drink the blood of their victims.[18] It is probable that Ntsay had already done that. He said in his letter that the day would come when he would return and take care of his slap-happy uncle. He would also wipe out the Zaidy clan to the last man. He repeated that

l'appel de mon ventre. Je me suis précipitée avec quelques femmes, des zivas pour la plupart, imprégnées de l'odeur de mon fils. Une importante colonie de fourmis s'abreuvait à la mare de pus. Elles délaissèrent le sang pourri de l'aîné pour celui encore chaud du cadet. Bientôt le corps de Ntsay fut couvert de boursouflures. J'ai nettoyé son visage avec mes pagnes. J'ai longtemps pleuré dans son cou en caressant les morsures de fourmis. Je l'ai ramené à la vie en murmurant son nom dans son oreille.

— Maman, Mbe n'est pas un cochon. Mon frère n'est pas un cochon, n'est-ce pas, Maman?

— Bien sûr, ô morceau de moi-même. Mbe n'est pas un cochon.

— Mbe n'est pas un cochon. Mbe n'est pas un cochon. Mbe n'est pas un cochon.

Tandis qu'il répétait, j'ai senti le cordon ombilical qui se rompait.

C'est ainsi qu'il est devenu fédéré. Après les ablutions il a fait ses bagages, comme quelqu'un qui part sans espoir de retour. Il a tout emporté. Il est resté absent trois mois. En trois mois les fédérés ont changé mon Ntsay en monstre. Un jour j'ai reçu un courrier avec la photo de mon unique. Au volant d'une 4L. J'ai appris par la suite que les jeunes fédérés conduisent sans permis. Qu'on leur distribue des bonbons qui tuent la faim et les coeurs avant de les envoyer en mission. Il me disait dans sa lettre qu'il était soldat. Il s'était enrôlé dans la Bande. Il suivait une formation militaire accélérée. Il avait prêté serment, juré une obéissance aveugle au Capitaine. Des rumeurs disent que les cam boivent le sang de leurs victimes. Ntsay avait sans doute déjà bu. Il disait dans sa lettre qu'il viendrait un jour régler son gifleur d'oncle. Qu'il exterminerait le clan de Zaidy jusqu'au dernier. Il repétait Mbe n'est pas un cochon. Le cochon, c'était Zaidy qui avait tout reçu du grand-père de Ntsay: boeufs, rizières, femme, dignité. A son arrivée dans le pays,

Mbe was not a pig. That Zaidy, who had gotten everything from Ntsay's grandfather: cattle, rice paddies, wife, dignity, was the real pig. When he arrived in the region, Zaidy had, as his sole possession, his earth-red colored loincloth. He survived by scraping the leftover ampango from the bottom of the pot of Dadin'i Mbe, the twins' grandmother. As far as Ambiloma, called Loma the corpse rider, was concerned, he planned to bury him alive. I could never bring myself to finish reading the letter.

—Where is Jinoro?

—Where is Jinoro?

I found myself fourteen years back, in our new big cabin. I was short of breath. A sharp pain was ripping my insides. Walk, walk, the midwife kept repeating. I was walking in a puddle of a whitish liquid. My eyes were popping out. Now lie on your back. Part your legs. Bend your knees. Squeeze. Squeeze. Tearing, savage ripping followed. Several times in a row in spite of my contractions. Free! Free! Twins! Four of them! Their names will be Mbe the elder, Mbe the younger, Ntsay the elder, Ntsay the younger. I never screamed once. No scream in the world could have expressed the pain of the moment. The druggies wiped themselves off with my clothes. I was covered with their slobber and their bite marks. Even after the noise of their 4x4 had disappeared down the muddy road, I remained lying there for a long time.

They had poked my other eye out.

Yes, Captain, he did come. I am worried for Jinoro's sake. I am not filing a complaint about the other stuff. The other stuff is not important. It didn't happen. The child of the earth returns to the earth. My son returned to the womb that protected him for nine months. He has not been born yet. I never had twins. I only imagined having them. Please Captain, find my husband and prevent him from being buried alive.

Zaidy possédait en tout et pour tout son pagne couleur latérite. Il se nourrissait d'ampango gratté au fond de la marmite de Dadin'i Mbe, la grand-mère des jumeaux. Et Ambiloma, dit Loma, le monteur de cadavre, il l'enterrerait vivant. Je n'ai jamais pu lire la lettre jusqu'au bout.

— Où est Jinoro?

— Où est Jinoro?

Je me suis retrouvée quatorze ans plus tôt. Dans la case-grande neuve. J'avais le souffle gros et court. Une douleur atroce me fouillait le ventre. Marchez, marchez, répétait l'accoucheuse. Je marchais dans une flaque de liquide blanc. Les yeux sortis de leurs trous. Maintenant mettez-vous sur le dos. Ecartez les jambes. Relevez les genoux. Crispez. Crispez. Ecartèlement. Déchirement sauvage. A plusieurs reprises, malgré mes crispations. Libérée! Libérée! Des jumeaux! Quatre! Je les appellerai Mbe-Aîné, Mbe-Cadet; Ntsay-Aîné et Ntsay-Cadet. Je n'ai pas crié une seule fois. Aucun cri au monde ne pouvait rendre ma douleur de cet instant. Les cam se sont essuyés avec mes pagnes. Mon corps était couvert de leurs baves et de leurs morsures. Je suis restée longtemps étendue après que le bruit de leur quatre-quatre s'est fondu dans la boue de la piste.

On m'a crevé le deuxième oeil.

Oui, il est venu, Monsieur le Commissaire. Je m'inquiète pour Jinoro. Je ne porte pas plainte pour le reste. Le reste ne compte pas. N'a pas eu lieu. L'enfant de la terre retourne à la terre. Le fils a réintégré la poche qui l'a protégé neuf longs mois. Il n'est pas né. Je n'ai jamais eu de jumeaux. Je les ai seulement pensés. Commissaire, retrouvez mon mari et empêchez qu'il soit enterré vivant.

Little Bone

(by David Jaomanoro)

Someone's coming to this House of Cold.[1] It must be the Dancing Women.[2] Don't worry, Masinera, if it's the Dancing Women, they're not coming for you. And as for me, I'm not a Dancer. Their love potions and charms are nothing but spells. *Mosavy* witchcraft[3] that draws them out at night. They can't help themselves.

I am here for something else, though. Back when you left us, I was holding on to old scores against you.[4] Maybe you were doing the same against me. Scores like that can't be washed out, not even by the final sprinkling.[5] I couldn't settle them with your family and you couldn't settle them with my family. I hadn't taken anything from your family, nor you from mine.

But first, the Dancing Women have to move on by. They feel me here in the House of Cold. Wait!

—Alive or dead?

—In between.

—One of ours or one of theirs?

—Yours.

—What's your name?

—Masizara.

—Where you from, Masizara?

—I'm Masizara from Ampasimaty.

—Come around the Houses of Cold with us?

—Um, no, not today.

—Go back with us afterwards?

—Sure. Stop by for me.

—Good dancing.

Translated from the French by Gertrude Champe (The University of Iowa)

Le petit os

(David Jaomanoro)

Des êtres s'approchent de la Maison-Froide. Sans doute des Danseuses. Rassure-toi, Masinera, si ce sont des Danseuses, elles ne viennent pas pour toi. Et puis, moi, je ne suis pas une Danseuse. Elles, leurs philtres d'amour et leurs charmes ont dégénéré en sorcellerie. Mosavy qui les entraîne hors de chez elles la nuit. Malgré elles.

Moi, je suis venue pour tout autre chose. Au moment de ton départ, j'avais gardé des restes contre toi, et peut-être aussi toi contre moi. De tels restes, l'aspersion d'eau, l'ultime, ne pouvait les laver. Je ne pouvais les rendre à la famille-tienne, ni toi les rendre à la famille-mienne. Je n'avais rien pris à ta famille, tu n'avais rien pris à la mienne.

Mais il faut d'abord que les Danseuses s'éloignent. Elles ont senti ma présence dans la Maison-Froide. Attends.

— Un être vivant ou un être mort?

— Entre les deux.

— Des nôtres ou des leurs?

— Des vôtres.

— On s'appelle comment?

— Masizara.

— Masizara d'où?

— Masizara d'Ampasimaty.

— On fait le tour des Maisons-Froides avec nous?

— Euh. . . Non. Pas aujourd'hui.

— On rentre ensemble avec les amies quand on a fini?

— Sûr. Passez me prendre.

— Danse bien.

Donc, me voilà. Je suis Masizara, tu te souviens? Ça m'étonnerait que tu m'aies oubliée en si peu de temps. Quatre ans, ce

So here I am. I'm Masizara, don't you remember? I'd be surprised if you didn't, it hasn't been that long. Four years isn't an eternity. Especially not for someone who lives in a House of Cold, covered by Immobility and shrouded in Silence. I've broken the taboo of the Cold,[6] the taboo of Immobility, the taboo of Silence. I bring you a little Warmth, a little Movement, a little Voice. And now, I'll get rid of the scores I've held against you in spite of customary advice.

Forgive her, for she is leaving. Passing through the Narrow Gate, she goes from among us. She borrowed from you; ask her family, gathered here, to give it back.

You didn't borrow anything, you stole something from me. My Besoa. My man.

When I rid myself of this Heavy Load—not the one the young ones labor under to carry it to its last home, this House of Cold—but my grudge.

Let me strike a match so I can admire your eyes, as my Besoa loved to do. Fires that blazed, back then, four years ago, that tormented my Besoa with all the wounds of burning passion. Two chasms where today I can plumb the infinite uselessness of your arrogance gone by. Two holes in the abyss of Forgetting. I put my fingers in and shiver from the cold of their absence.

Haiko mason'ny tie zaho
Selaka indraiky tsy manindroe
Balagna an-tendro-maso
Mahay misaha
I Masinera

He sang that chant. Forgotten now. Forgotten by the man who "knew you loved him, just by looking into your eyes." Forgotten by the man you knew how to "bewitch with a single flutter of your eyelids." From now on, no one will dare to sing about your eyes.

n'est pas l'éternité. Surtout quand on habite une Maison-Froide, quand on se couvre d'Immobilité et quand on s'entoure du Silence. J'ai franchi le tabou du Froid, le tabou de l'Immobilité et le tabou du Silence. Je t'apporte un peu de Chaleur, un peu de Mouvement et un peu de Voix. Par la même occasion je me débarrasserai des restes que j'avais gardés contre toi malgré les recommandations d'usage:

Pardonne-lui, car elle s'en va. Elle va franchir la Porte-Etroite et cesser d'être parmi nous. Elle vous a emprunté des choses, réclamez-les à la famille-sienne réunie ici.

Tu ne m'avais pas emprunté une chose, tu m'avais volé ma chose. Mon Besoa. Mon homme.

Quand je me serai déchargée de mon Lourd-Fardeau—pas celui que les jeunes gens enlèvent de terre en ahanant pour aller le déposer dans sa dernière demeure, cette Maison-Froide—mais ma rancune.

Permets-moi de craquer une allumette, pour admirer tes yeux comme mon Besoa aimait à les admirer. Des brasiers qui tourmentaient mon Besoa de toutes les brûlures de la passion, jadis; il y a quatre ans. Deux gouffres où je peux sonder l'infinie vanité de tes arrogances passées, aujourd'hui. Deux trous dans l'abîme de l'Oubli. J'y introduis mes doigts et je frissonne du froid de leur absence.

Haiko mason'ny tie zaho
Selaka indraiky tsy manindroe
Balagna an-tendro-maso
Mahay misaha
I Masinera

C'était un chant. Maintenant oublié. Oublié de l'homme qui "se savait aimé de toi rien qu'en regardant tes yeux". Oublié de l'homme que tu savais "envoûter d'un seul battement de la peau de tes yeux". Tes yeux, désormais, personne n'osera les chanter.

If death's going to carry me off
I'd rather bring it on myself,
Impaled on your piercing breasts.

Breasts, there was no lack of them at Ampasimaty! And not just *assegais* that cut through the heart and destroy the will. There were papayas, grapefruit, lemons, guavas, mangoes, pumpkins. Yes, and there were pillows, cushions, pads, waves, waterfalls. Breasts. Besoa preferred the warrior knives. But weapons like that, they always end up dull, no matter how hard the iron of their tongues. Four years in the shadow of the House of Cold has ruined your charms, Masinera. When your breasts were *assegais,* my breasts were *zebu* tongues, too long, too soft. Today, they're a delight again. And yours are blades dashed against the stone, with all the might of Fate.

Masinera-Boy's-Haircut, you shocked us, kindled our envy. The rest of us did our hair with home-made coconut oil after we worked with the vanilla flowers. But you used perfumed oil that Besoa brought you from town with money that came from my sunburned back, my bramble-torn skin, my tortured nails. And after all, my hair was better than yours, but yours had perfume on it. Now the hair is gone from your head. Not even your insolent brow could make it stay. Surely, that hair will grow again, thicker than before, on your bed of plaited bamboo. After all, euphorbia grows on harder ground than a bed of plaited bamboo. Your skull is smooth and round like the stone of the hair braiders. No weight to it anymore, your skull, it's hollow, it rings. I'll take it, if you don't mind, to hear in it the Hell-dwellers cackling and grinding their teeth, those sounds our catechist talks about all the time. Husband stealers go down there, you know.

No songs from your mouth now. It's filling up with earth, with your own earth. When we were little, we played hide and seek behind the Great Falls. Your voice rang with the thousand notes of the Falls. It's true, your voice wasn't grating. Except

Si la mort doit m'emporter
Je préfère me l'apporter moi-même
En m'empalant aux sagaies de tes seins.

Des seins, il y en avait pourtant à Ampasimaty. Et pas que des sagaies qui transpercent le coeur et tuent la volonté. Il y en avait, des papayes, des pamplemousses, des citrons, des goyaves, des mangues, des citrouilles. Il y en avait, des oreillers, des coussins, des tampons, des vagues, des cascades. Des seins. Besoa préférait les sagaies. De telles armes, aussi dur que puisse être le fer de leurs langues, finissent toujours par s'émousser. Quatre années à l'Ombre de la Maison-Froide ont détruit tes charmes, Masinera. Au temps de tes sagaies, Masinera, mes seins étaient des langues de zébu, trop longs, trop souples. Aujourd'hui, ils sont redevenus délicieux. Tandis que les tiens des sagaies lancées contre le roc, de toutes les forces du Destin.

Masinera-Coupe-Garçon.

Tu choquais et allumais l'envie. Nous autres, nous nous coiffions à l'huile de coco que nous fabriquions nous-mêmes après le travail des fleurs de vanille. Toi tu mettais des huiles parfumées que Besoa te rapportait de la ville, avec l'argent qui était le fruit des brûlures du soleil sur mon dos, des écorchures de ma peau par les ronces, et de mes ongles retournés. Mes cheveux étaient bien meilleurs que les tiens, mais les tiens étaient parfumés. Maintenant ils ont quitté ta tête. L'insolence de ton front n'a su les retenir. Ils repousseront sûrement, plus dru que jadis, sur ton lit de bambous tressés. Les euphorbes poussent sur bien plus dur qu'un parterre de bambous tressés! Ton crâne est lisse et rond comme la pierre des tresseuses de nattes. Il ne fait plus le poids, ton crâne, il est creux, il sonne creux. Je vais le prendre, ne t'en déplaise, pour y entendre les ricanements et les grincements de dents des habitants de l'Hadès dont parle souvent notre catéchiste. Celles qui volent l'homme des autres vont peupler l'Hadès.

when you walked by in front of our place some mornings and called to Bozivelo across the street. You shouted to her so that my Besoa could hear where you were going, what you felt like eating, what you were going to do that day. And Bozivelo, that hellion, answered you at the same pitch, said the two of you together were the even-footed zebu: you were the front legs and she, the hind legs. Bozivelo shouted to you that she would eat from the cleft between your breasts and drink from your cupped hand. We haven't heard that refrain for four years now. Your mouth, your breast, your hands have turned into the dust of the earth. Your arms, so quick to close about another woman's man, your belly sprinkled with honey,[7] home of his every sated desire: dust of the earth. You're nothing now but a forest of white reeds growing sideways in this Cold Place where your disgrace as a man thief goes to ground.

I was there when they did you up. To see the beginning of the Inexorable with my own eyes. Apathy had already molded the shape of your face, unyielding to the old biddies who tried to knead it into a smile. You were bloated, it was Decay knocking at your gates. Hot water couldn't unloose your rigid limbs. They sat you up on your discolored hams. They wanted to braid your hair, but that didn't work because of your boy cut. Then they dressed you in your most beautiful clothes, one dress atop the other. A doll stuffed with bran. They laid you back down. They washed their hands with hot water and soap. Then they cried, and that's when the men were supposed to come and get you, to put you in your little resting place. With my *pagne* carefully pulled up to cover my face, I gathered spittle and slathered it all over my cheeks, my chin, and my chest to mark my mourning. And all the time I was moaning and sniffling, very loud. An old mother hugged me to her breast to comfort me. "Life's like that," she said. "The young shoots disappear and the useless old stock remains." She thought I must

Ta bouche ne chante plus. Elle se remplit de terre, de ta propre terre. Petites nous jouions à cache-cache derrière la Grande-Chute. Ta voix avait les mille timbres de la Grande-Chute. Je reconnais qu'elle n'était pas désagréable, ta voix. Sauf quand tu passais devant chez nous certains matins et interpellais Bozivelo, en face. Tu criais à Bozivelo, à l'intention de mon Besoa, où tu allais, ce que tu avais envie de manger, ce que tu ferais dans la journée. Et Bozivelo, la bandite!, te répondait sur le même ton qu'à vous deux vous étiez le zébu au pas égal: les pieds de devant c'était toi, et, elle, les pieds de derrière. Bozivelo te criait qu'elle mangerait dans le creux de ta gorge et boirait dans le calice de ta main. Ce refrain, on ne l'entend plus depuis quatre ans. Ta bouche, ta gorge, tes mains sont devenues de la poussière de terre. Tes bras prompts à se refermer sur l'homme d'autrui, ton ventre saturé de miel où il assouvissait jusqu'au moindre de ses désirs: de la poussière de terre. Tu n'es plus qu'une forêt de roseaux blancs qui poussent à l'horizontale dans ce Lieu-Froid où tu terres ta honte de voleuse d'homme.

J'ai assisté à ton ultime toilette. Pour voir de mes yeux le commencement de l'Inexorable. L'Indifférence avait déjà sculpté ton visage, malgré les efforts des vieilles mères qui tentaient d'y modeler un sourire. L'Immonde montait à l'assaut de ton édifice, par des boursouflures. L'eau chaude n'a pu chasser la Raideur déjà logée dans tes jambes. Puis on t'a assise sur tes fesses décolorées. On a voulu te faire des tresses, mais ça n'a pas marché à cause de la coupe-garçon. Puis on t'a mis tes plus belles robes, les unes sur les autres. Poupée de son. On t'a recouchée. On s'est lavé les mains à l'eau chaude et au savon. Puis on a pleuré, les hommes devaient venir à cet instant pour te prendre et te mettre dans ta loge. Le visage soigneusement caché derrière mon pagne, j'ai puisé une quantité de salive que j'ai répandue avec prodigalité sur mes joues, mon menton, sur ma poitrine. En gémissant et en reniflant très fort. Une vieille mère m'a prise sur

have loved you with all my heart to be in such a state. But I was young, she told me, I'd forget soon.

> Like a song you heard
> That you don't hear now
> That's the roar of a crocodile who's
> Dead.

Outside the young people were waiting. The Old One, the *Sojabe*,[8] reminded you of the rules. You were leaving, weren't coming back. Your mother was not your mother. Your father, brothers, sisters were not your father, brothers, sisters. Your real family was where they were taking you. From now on your rivals, if you had any, were your rivals no more. . . .

The young people took up that Heavy Burden, in a storm of howls and lamentations. I went with the *gouma*[9] singers, half walking, half dancing behind the bearers. The farther we got from the village, the closer the *gouma* came to frenzy.

Oh, the whole world owed you everything, but you don't even have the right to come back to the village now to get anything, no matter what it is.[10] You have no right to show yourself to the little girls going to the spring for water or to the boys collecting dead wood in the forest. And you were such a flirt. Seeing your bones bleach on this bed of touchless dust, it's hard to believe that you danced the *masevy*[11] at the zebu fair. The flask of rum for your last journey has gone dry. The ants made quick work of your eyes, covered with honey to sweeten your Solitude. The chewing tobacco is mingled with the earth dust that is you.

Don't be afraid, Masinera, I'm not one of the Dancing Women. I'll never be one. You see, I haven't even gotten undressed. What good does it do to get undressed in the presence of Nakedness? I've come in the middle of the night because broad daylight is no time to visit a dweller in Nothingness.

son sein. C'était comme ça, la vie. Les jeunes pousses partaient tandis que les vieilles souches inutiles restaient. Je t'aimais sans doute très fort pour me trouver dans cet état. Mais j'étais jeune, j'oublierais vite!

Tel un chant qu'on entend
Puis qu'on n'entend plus
Telle la gueule d'un caïman
Mort.

Dehors les jeunes gens attendaient. Le Sojabe t'a rappelé les consignes. Tu partais pour ne plus revenir. Ta mère n'était plus ta mère; ton père, tes frères et tes soeurs n'étaient plus ton père, tes frères et tes soeurs. Les vrais parents étaient là où l'on t'emmenait. Désormais tes rivales, si tu en avais, cessaient d'être tes rivales. . .

Les jeunes gens enlevèrent le Lourd-Fardeau, sous une averse de hurlements et de lamentations. Je me suis mise avec les chanteurs de Gouma mi-marchant mi-dansant derrière les porteurs. Plus on s'éloignait du village, plus le Gouma devenait frénésie.

O Celle à qui tout le monde devait tout, tu n'as même plus le droit de retourner au village pour réclamer quoi que ce soit. Tu n'as plus le droit de te montrer aux fillettes qui vont puiser de l'eau à la source, ou aux garçons qui vont chercher du bois mort dans la forêt, toi qui étais si coquette. A voir tes os blanchir froidement sur ce lit de poussière impalpable, j'ai du mal à croire que tu as dansé le Masevy à la foire aux zébus. Evaporé, le flacon de rhum qu'on t'avait donné pour ton ultime voyage. Les fourmis ont vite fait de manger tes yeux avec le miel destiné à t'adoucir la Solitude. Le tabac à chiquer s'est mélangé à la poussière de terre que tu es devenue.

Rassure-toi, Masinera, je ne suis pas une Danseuse et ne le serai jamais. Tu vois, je ne me suis même pas déshabillée. A quoi

The Dancing Women come despite themselves. I came, and I'll leave, of my own free will.

From now on, the possessor, the mistress of Besoa is me. I've only come to tell you that. Now I have no more leftover grudges against you. For me, the leftovers are not the quarters of meat we throw away after the funeral: that's a waste. We only eat beef at funerals and then we throw the leftovers to the dogs. Unconscionable! To me, the leftovers are hearts we keep turned against others. And today, I've rid myself of that.

It's getting late. My thick kapok mattress is waiting for me. My place, close against Besoa's side. Oh, and I almost forgot. Let me carry away a bit of dust from your body, a little hair. And a little bone from your foot. Dog hair and boar hair will be easy enough to get.[12] And so will your tie with Besoa be, the tie between your shade and his spirit: like the dog's with the boar, like the tie of the flesh to the bone when it turns to dust and falls off in little heaps.

Maybe I'll come back. Now that I've broken the taboo of Silence there's nothing to stop me from coming as many times as I want.

There are the Dancers again, behind the House of Cold. I'm going back with them. After all, why not! Still, we don't have anything that binds us. I'm going.

—Alive or Dead?

—In between.

—One of ours or one of theirs?

—Yours.

—And they call you?

—Masizara. Masizara from Ampasimaty.

—We're in a hurry to leave this place. It's time to go back.

It's a good thing these Dancer friends came by. I wouldn't have been able to return alone by night. My clothes, I have to take off my clothes.[13]

bon se déshabiller devant la Nudité. Je suis venue en pleine nuit, parce qu'on ne rencontre pas une habitante du Néant en plein jour. Les Danseuses viennent malgré elles, je suis venue, moi, et je repartirai de mon plein gré.

Désormais la propriétaire et la maîtresse de Besoa, c'est moi. Je suis venue uniquement pour te le dire. Maintenant je n'ai plus de restes contre toi. Pour moi, les restes, ce ne sont pas les quartiers de viande que l'on jette après l'enterrement: c'est du gaspillage. On ne mange des boeufs que pendant les funérailles, et après on jette les restes aux chiens! Inconscience. Les restes, pour moi, ce sont les coeurs que l'on garde contre autrui. Aujourd'hui je m'en suis débarrassée.

Il se fait tard. Mon épais matelas de kapok m'attend. Ma place, tout contre le flanc de Besoa. Ah! j'oubliais. Tant qu'à faire, permets-moi d'emporter un peu de la poussière de ta chair, un peu de tes cheveux. Et aussi un petit os de ton pied. Les poils de chien et les poils de sanglier seront faciles à se procurer. Ainsi seront tes rapports avec Besoa, les rapports de ton fantôme avec son esprit: comme ceux du chien avec le sanglier; comme ceux de la chair avec l'os quand elle est devenue poussière qui tombe et se tasse.

Je reviendrai peut-être. Maintenant que j'ai franchi le tabou du Silence, rien ne m'empêche de revenir autant de fois que je veux.

Voilà de nouveau les Danseuses, derrière la Maison-Froide. Je vais me joindre à elles pour rentrer. Au fait, pourquoi pas! Pourtant je n'ai rien de commun avec elles. Je te quitte.

— Un être vivant ou un être mort?

— Entre les deux.

— Des nôtres ou des leurs?

— Des vôtres.

— On s'appelle comment?

— Masizara. Masizara d'Ampasimaty.

* * *

—Masizara! Sweet Masizara! Wake up, the sun's high in the sky. People are going to say I don't let you sleep when decent people do.

—My husband?

—Get up, I say. The vanilla flowers won't wait for the shiftless.

Besoa stood in the door. Masizara was lying across the thick kapok mattress on the ground. Sun poured into the little hut.

—You were lazing around so long I've eaten up all my *habobo.*"[14]

The young man was chewing on a little bone. He had found it at the bottom of the pot. He only noticed it when he put it in his mouth in the spoon full of curds. Masizara was definitely getting really careless: to find a chicken bone from a week ago in the milk pot!

—Darling Besoa, come help me get up.

—No, no. forget it. You're going to try to keep me here again. It's indecent to be in bed at this hour if you're not sick.

—That's just it. I'm sick for you.

—Little flirt. I've got your cure.

Besoa spit out the bone. Or rather, the pieces of bone. For he had cracked it between his teeth to suck out the marrow. The curds had an aftertaste like *kitoza,*[15] badly dried and spoiled.

The door was pulled shut and fastened behind him.

(St. Denis de La Réunion, May 4, 1991)

— On se dépêche de sortir. C'est l'heure de rentrer.

Quelle chance que ces amies Danseuses. Je n'aurais pas eu la force d'affronter seule la nuit du retour. Mes vêtements, il faut que j'enlève mes vêtements.

* * *

— Masizara! chérie, Masizara! Réveille-toi, le soleil est haut. On va finir par raconter que je t'empêche de dormir aux heures décentes.

— Mon époux?

— Lève-toi, je dis. Les fleurs de vanille n'attendent pas les fainéantes.

Besoa se tenait dans l'entrebâillement de la porte. Masizara était couchée en travers de l'épais matelas-kapok posé à même le sol. La petite case était inondée de soleil.

— Pendant que tu fainéantes, j'ai eu le temps de manger mon habobo!

Le jeune homme mâchouillait un petit os. Il l'avait trouvé au fond de la marmite. Il s'en était rendu compte seulement une fois qu'il l'eut porté à sa bouche dans la cuiller pleine de lait caillé. Décidément, Masizara devenait de plus en plus négligente: du poulet qu'ils avaient mangé une semaine plus tôt, on retrouvait un os dans la marmite à lait!

— Chéri, Besoa! viens me mettre debout!

— Ah non, ça va! Tu vas encore essayer de me retenir. C'est indécent d'être couché à cette heure. A moins d'être malade.

— Justement, je suis malade de toi.

— Petite coquine. Je vais te guérir à l'instant.

Besoa a recraché l'os. Ou plutôt les morceaux de l'os. Car il l'avait broyé entre ses molaires pour en sucer la moëlle. Le habobo avait un arrière-goût de viande kitoza mal séchée, avariée.

La porte fut tirée et attachée derrière lui.

(Saint-Denis de la Réunion, 4 mai 1991)

Jean-Luc Raharimanana

Born in 1967, Jean-Luc Raharimanana is a high school teacher in Paris, France. He received the second prize for poetry on the occasion of the 50th anniversary of the death of Malagasy's foremost poet, Jean-Joseph Rabearivelo. He was also awarded in 1989 the Tardivat prize (Radio France International, 1989) for his short story Le lépreux (The leper), *and the second prize for his play* Le prophète et le président *(Radio France International, 1990). He is also the author of a volume of twelve short stories,* Lucarne *(Paris: Le Serpent à Plumes, 1992), that includes the two texts reproduced below. His volume of poetry,* Poèmes crématoires, *is yet unpublished (see "Poetry" section).*

The Rich Child

What is suffering?

A terrifying desire to up and die so that living will no longer be anyone's lot.

A song. . .

Everything sings, except there, there where the notes of the *valiha*[1] could have vibrated, could have fused with all cries, those cries that exist just to be in harmony.

Cries. . .

The cry of some animal, the call of a woman in heat, and more and more.

Everything sings.

The heart hangs suspended, then takes off again in a faltering beat. A child is running—dirty, almost naked—stumbling on the stone steps. There are alleys and more alleys, alleys that rise steeply, keep rising. You see the *Rova*[2] as your gaze wanders at random managing to avoid the screen of immense walls, of houses packed tightly one against the other.

Translated from the French by Marjolijn de Jager

Jean-Luc Raharimanana

Né en 1967, Jean-Luc Raharimanana est professeur de lycée à Paris. Il reçut le second prix de poésie à l'occasion du cinquantième anniversaire de la mort du grand poète malgache, Jean-Joseph Rabearivelo. On lui a aussi décerné en 1989 le prix Tardivat (Radio France International, 1989), pour sa nouvelle Le lépreux, *ainsi qu'un second prix pour sa pièce de théâtre,* Le prophète et le président *(Radio France International, 1990). Il est également l'auteur d'un recueil de douze nouvelles,* Lucarne *(Paris: Le Serpent à Plumes, 1992), dont deux sont reproduites ci-dessous. Enfin, son volume de poésie,* Poèmes crématoires, *est encore inédit. (Voir la section "Poésie".)*

L'enfant riche

Souffrir, qu'est-ce?

Une effroyable envie de crever pour que vivre ne soit plus le lot de personne.

Un chant. . .

Tout chante, sauf là, là où les notes de la *valiha* auraient pu vibrer, se mêler à tous les cris, cris existant pour être harmoniques.

Cris. . .

Le cri d'un quelconque animal, l'appel d'une femme en rut, et tout et tout.

Tout chante.

Le cœur se suspend, puis repart dans un battement balbutiant. Un enfant court—sale, presque nu—, trébuche sur les marches de pierre. Il y a des ruelles et des ruelles, des ruelles qui montent, montent. On aperçoit le *Rova* au hasard des regards qui parviennent à éviter l'écran des murs immenses, des maisons serrées les unes contre les autres.

L'Enfant. . . il est là, mains au bas-ventre, faussement intéressé, comme ébloui devant une affiche publicitaire. L'image de la gitane réfléchie dans la mare. La mare n'est pas due à la pluie

The Child . . . is there, hands on his lower belly, feigning interest, as if thrilled before an advertising poster. The picture of the *gitane*[3] reflected in the pool. The pool was not caused by yesterday's rain. The drunk pisses here, the "gentleman" as well, the "lady" looks furtively around in the evening, raises her skirt, and so on. The Child follows suit.

The pool is a small lake thanks to everyone's contributions. It is the fruit of good people's cooperation. Little plants grow there, very green lichens, already rising to attack the poster—a poster streaked with filthy trails, a poster on which the gypsy wriggles through her veil of smoke!

Everything dances.

The Child is done. He shakes a bit, small drops falling in the pool. He looks to see if anything is showing from his badly sewn little pants; in front of the poster he tilts his head a bit. Is the gypsy laughing? His zipper is still holding his fly together.

A Coca-Cola bottle on the ground. The Child picks it up. There's a bit of water in it, water from the pond? No matter. . . The bottle will bring him a few more francs for the things one swallows, a few more coins with which to visit the hovel of a very dear cousin. A hovel where it doesn't smell very good, a very dear cousin who's always gone and for whom you leave an important message. Oh! You don't have to be literate, it's enough to leave a mark on a crumpled piece of paper. He'll understand. "I've eaten," he'll read. His name is William, sometimes Claude as well, or sometimes you simply forget what his name is, but never his presence, never his call. NEVER!

"Mister!"

The Child shows the Coke bottle. The counter is very high and the Chinese is talking business again on the telephone.

Grey light inside an unusual setting: "Dragons all over the walls!"

"Mister. . ."

d'hier. L'ivrogne y pisse, le "monsieur" aussi, la "madame" guette le soir, lève la jupe, etc., etc. L'Enfant imite.

La mare est un petit lac grâce à la contribution de tout un chacun. Elle est le fruit de la coopération des bonnes gens. Des petites cultures y poussent, des lichens bien verts, qui déjà montent à l'assaut de l'affiche—affiche striée de traînées sales et sur laquelle la gitane se trémousse à travers son voile de fumée!

Tout danse.

L'Enfant a fini. Il secoue un peu, petites gouttes qui tombent dans la mare. Il regarde si rien ne dépasse de sa petite culotte mal cousue; là devant, il penche un peu la tête. La gitane rit-elle? La braguette tient encore le coup.

Une bouteille de Coca traîne. L'Enfant la ramasse. Il y a dedans un peu d'eau, l'eau de la mare? Qu'importe. . . La bouteille lui ferait quelques francs de plus pour ces choses que l'on avale, quelques sous de plus pour pouvoir visiter la masure d'un très cher cousin. Une masure qui ne sent pas très bon, un très cher cousin toujours absent et à qui on laisse un message significatif. Oh! Pas besoin d'être lettré, il suffit de laisser une trace sur le papier froissé. Il comprendra. "J'ai mangé", lira-t-il. William qu'il s'appelle, quelquefois aussi Claude, ou bien on oublie carrément son nom, mais jamais sa présence, jamais son appel. JAMAIS!

— M'sé!

L'Enfant montre la bouteille de Coca. Le comptoir est très haut et le Chinois parle encore affaires au téléphone.

Lumière grise dans un décor insolite: "Des dragons plein partout le mur!"

— M'sé. . .

Tchuing, tchang, pling, plong, bonzour-sava. Les Chinois ont un rhume terrible. Et tout le temps!

— M'sé?

— Hmm?

— Coca, dit l'Enfant en tendant la bouteille.

Tchung, tchang, pling, plong, hullo-howzthings. The Chinese have terrible colds. And all the time, too!

"Mister?"

"Hmm?"

"Coke," the Child says, handing him the bottle.

He's a nice man but you shouldn't come as a group. One by one, very nice, very dirty, very alone!

100 FMG![4]

Outside: heaven! A river of delight that will bring, will bring. . . oh fragrance! In sight, well-cooked rice and then burps. . .

"Thanks mister!"

Leave. His heart jumping, his belly is warming up without any apparent reason. A small dog suddenly is running at the heels of the Child. The animal has one of those sharp noses. No wonder he is so healthy!

Wishing he were a dog!

Cars pass by, all those lovely shiny cars. Inside, beautiful ladies wearing *lambas*[5]—such elegance!—A 505[6] . . . Another one, a red Volvo: superb! A Toyota—what make? . . .—A Mercedes with a little dog on the back seat, a well-combed, well-washed, nice and clean little dog, a pretty ribbon around its neck. Little dog that never barks, has all its dignity in check. Of course, when you ride in a Mercedes, you have no right to recall where you came from, that would ruin the effect. You're quite simply middle-class, human! It would only take a bit more for the little dog to start talking. He sinks into the seat, pretends to be asleep. A ray of light illuminates the vermilion red of his ribbon.

The Child is in no hurry, his mind is at peace, and he has 100 FMG in his pocket. He's not yet going to his grave, not today. The only and unique eye of the day still shines: oh sun across the innumerable leaves of the jacaranda tree. The Child's gaze

L'homme est gentil mais il ne faut pas venir en groupe. Un par un, bien sage, bien sale, bien seul!

100 fmg!

Dehors: paradis! Rivière de délice qui emporterait, emporterait. . . ô senteur! Le riz bien cuit, des rots en perspective . . .

— M'si m'sé!

Sortir. Le cœur tressaute, le ventre se réchauffe sans raison apparente. Un petit chien court aussitôt aux talons de l'Enfant. L'animal a un de ces flairs. Pas étonnant qu'il soit aussi vigoureux!

Envie d'être chien!

Des voitures passent, toutes des belles voitures reluisantes. Dedans, des belles dames qui portent des *lamba*—qu'elles sont chics!—Une 505. . . Encore une autre, une Volvo rouge: superbe! Une Toyota—quelle marque?. . .—Une Mercedes avec un petit chien sur la banquette arrière, petit chien bien peigné, bien lavé, bien propre, un joli ruban autour du cou. Petit chien qui n'aboie jamais, qui garde toute sa dignité. Pardi, quand on roule en Mercedes, on n'a pas le droit de rappeler ses origines, cela ferait mauvais effet. L'on est tout simplement bourgeois, humain! Pour un peu, le petit chien se mettrait à parler. Il s'affaisse sur la banquette, fait semblant de dormir. Un trait de lumière illumine le rouge vermeil de son ruban.

L'Enfant n'est pas pressé, il a paix en l'esprit et 100 fmg dans la poche. La tombe n'est pas encore pour aujourd'hui. Brille toujours le seul, l'unique œil du jour: ô soleil à travers les feuilles innombrables du jacaranda. Le regard de l'Enfant suit la taille de l'arbre: immense! Immense malgré la plaque métallique clouée sur son tronc. Y sont inscrits quelques caractères, quelques lettres: le nom d'un prince sûrement. Les princes aiment rappeler leur présence partout.

Soleil ô soleil!

follows the height of the tree: immense! Immense despite the metal plaque nailed on its trunk. Inscribed are a few characters, a few letters: the name of a prince, for sure. Princes like to have their presence remembered everywhere.

Sun oh sun!

Other kids like himself are playing in the street, skillfully kicking a lemon. The lemon is their soccer ball. Here a chest trap, a kick, the lemon flies toward another player. Headed, the shot is returned. The lemon is flying, flying, never touching the ground.

The Child clutches the coin in his hand. Reassuring that coin, uplifting . . . He moves away. A hole in the seat of his pants: giving his butt over to the sly approaches of the wind, pleasure when he feels the cool air coming in.

Sun oh sun!

Strolling.

The dust colors his feet yellow with a touch of black. Yellow stands for madness. Black for death. The Child walks. The little street dog is still following him, circling him, runs ahead, goes off to water, to wash a public bench that cleanliness has abandoned.

Songs, voices . . .

He walks faster. A crowd has gathered around a group of *mpihira gasy.*[7] They are singing in their guttural voices, their voices badly adapted to song, voices that shriek rather than sing. But the Child is excited. He is holding his money in his fist. The little dog is sniffing at the dancers. The crowd is laughing. Everybody is happy. They're throwing coins. The Child does, too. His only coin.

He applauds!

The good people seemed a bit lost but they were smiling. Eyes were shining: fires that could not be extinguished but that came from within themselves, leaving their masters cold, indifferent,

D'autres gosses pareils à lui jouent dans la rue, font des tours d'adresse avec un citron. Le citron remplace le ballon de foot. Par-là un amorti de la poitrine, un coup de patte, le citron vole vers un autre allié. Par-ci des têtes, un retourné. Vole, vole le citron, ne jamais toucher terre.

L'Enfant serre sa pièce dans sa main. Rassurante la pièce, euphorisante. . . Il s'éloigne. Trou dans le cul de sa culotte: donner ses fesses aux entrées sournoises du vent, plaisir quand il sentait frais l'air s'y infiltrant.

Soleil ô soleil!

Flâner.

La poussière colore ses pieds en jaune un peu noirâtre. Le jaune, c'est la folie. Le noir, la mort. L'Enfant marche. Le petit chien des rues le suit toujours, tourne autour de lui, le précède, va arroser, laver un banc public déserté par la propreté.

Des chants, des voix. . .

Accélérer le pas. Une foule s'entasse autour d'un groupe de *mpihira gasy*. Ils chantent de leurs voix gutturales, de leurs voix mal adaptées au chant, des voix qui hurlent plutôt. Mais l'Enfant est enthousiasmé. Il tient son argent dans son poing. Le petit chien vient renifler les danseurs. La foule rit. Tout le monde est content. On jette des pièces. L'Enfant aussi. Son unique pièce.

Il applaudit!

Les bonnes gens semblaient un peu perdues mais ils souriaient. Les yeux brillaient: des feux que l'on ne pouvait éteindre mais qui partaient d'eux-mêmes, laissant leurs maîtres froids, indifférents, sans vie. Les yeux se détachèrent peu à peu des *mpihira gasy*, se reportèrent sur les façades des grands établissements. Un homme sortit des rangs de la foule, bouscula. L'Enfant tomba sous le heurt. L'homme partit, n'ayant rien aperçu.

Mal aux fesses!

Du coup, l'Enfant sentit la faim cogner à son ventre. Entre

lifeless. Bit by bit the eyes began to move away from the *mpihira gasy,* wandered back to the facades of large establishments. A man came out from among the crowd, pushing. The Child was knocked down. The man left, not having noticed a thing.

His butt hurt!

Suddenly, the Child felt hunger beating against his stomach. Between his fingers the warm presence of his money was gone, all there was were the lines in his palm, lines ending in bifurcations of fate. He threw himself on his coin. Right there in the middle of everyone else, at the dancers' feet. His face met with a well-aimed heel. He was pulled backwards. A kick between the thighs, in the lower belly, another to his back. His head hit the pavement. The Child put the coin in his mouth. Clenched his teeth. Someone tried to pry his jaws apart. He swallowed the coin and choked. The blows stopped.

"The bastard!"

"Son of a bitch!"

A final kick to the back of his neck and the Child sank into unconsciousness. The crowd moved away, the dancers picked up their coins. Only the little dog stayed. The Child was lying in the middle of the road. Legs went by, looks dwelled briefly, compassions rose up only to disappear like leaves in a violent wind. Staying is no good. You would rot. Pass, pass as life itself does so well. Pass . . . Bitch of a life.

He was hoping for night to fall, hoping to sleep—to sleep oh little death that nibbles at the flesh, at the soul—hoping to sink away and silence that burning inside his entrails. He was hungry, he was in pain. Pain, hunger, two calls to life.

"Mamma . . . !"

The little dog turned around. The Child felt the coin in his belly. To be able to eat with this coin, with this coin!

His head seemed light to him, so light. . . His feet, heavy as lead, were glued to the ground—top and bottom were pulling

ses doigts, il n'y avait plus la présence chaude de son argent, il n'y avait que les lignes de sa main, des lignes s'achevant sur des fourches de fatalité. Il se précipita sur sa pièce. Là, au milieu des autres, au pied des danseurs. Son visage rencontra un talon bien ajusté. On le tira en arrière. Un coup entre les cuisses, au bas-ventre, un autre dans le dos. Sa tête heurta le sol goudronné. L'Enfant porta la pièce dans sa bouche. Serrer les dents. Quelqu'un essaya de lui desserrer les mâchoires. Il avala la pièce et suffoqua. Les coups s'arrêtèrent.

— Le salaud!

— Fils de putain!

Un dernier coup de talon derrière la nuque et l'Enfant sombra dans l'inconscience. La foule se dispersa, les danseurs ramassèrent leurs pièces. Seul le petit chien resta. L'Enfant gisait au milieu de l'allée. Des jambes passaient, quelques regards s'attardaient, quelques pitiés voltigeaient pour disparaître comme des feuilles au vent violent. Rester n'est pas bien. L'on pourrirait. Passer, passer comme le fait si bien la vie. Passer. . . Salope de vie.

Il espérait la nuit, il espérait dormir—dormir ô petite mort qui grignote dans la chair, dans l'âme—sombrer et faire taire cette brûlure dans les entrailles. Il avait faim, il avait mal. Le mal, la faim, deux appels à la vie.

— Maman. . . !

Le petit chien se retourna. L'Enfant sentit la pièce dans son ventre. Pouvoir manger avec cette pièce, avec cette pièce!

Sa tête lui semblait légère, légère. . .Ses pieds, lourds comme du plomb, collaient au sol—le haut et le bas s'entre-tirent, au milieu, il y avait la pièce. Elle, si présente, comme seule existant . . .

Une fontaine.

Les seaux alignés ressemblaient à n'importe quelle queue. Les fillettes qui y attendaient étaient des statues quelconques.

away from each other, and in the center there was the coin. So present, as if it alone existed . . .

A fountain.

The lined-up buckets looked like any other line. The little girls waiting there were statues like any other. The Child wanted to drink, drink a lot. He looked at the little girl filling up her bucket.

"No!"

Her mouth formed a little pout, her eyelids closed slightly, her head turned away: a seedling of small womanhood . . . Already!

The water is running.

The Child is drooling

The little girl went away, her water bucket on her head. The Child rushed toward the free faucet. The others cried out, pulled at his rags, at his pants and tore them. Now they were laughing. He looked at his bit of clothing in the hand of one of these furies. Something more than his butt was out in the open. His pride was dangling and he stared at it in astonishment. They were still laughing.

And all that water running!

The Child wanted to laugh, too—stupidly—but the coin turned over in his stomach. The burning, even more intense . . . Ignore the laughter, bend over . . . Drink! They watered his behind, which stuck out uncovered.

The Child held his breath, his belly was swelling up. He jumped up and down to listen to the coin rolling inside his belly. It was ringing out. The little dog barked.

He hopped some more, holding what remained of his pants around his hips tightly knotted end to end.

"Get out! Get out of my belly!"

The coin thoughtlessly rolled around, not thinking that a life depended on it. At the end of the street, a door opened. Oh the fine smell of well-seasoned meat. . .

L'Enfant voulait boire, beaucoup boire. Il regarda la petite fille remplissant son seau.

— Non!

La bouche fit une petite moue, les paupières se fermèrent un peu, la tête se détourna: une graine de bout de femme. . . Déjà!

L'eau coule.

L'Enfant bave.

La fillette s'en alla, son seau d'eau sur la tête. L'Enfant se précipita sur le robinet libre. Les autres s'écrièrent, tirèrent sur ses hardes, sur sa culotte qui se déchira. Maintenant, on riait. Il regarda le bout de son linge dans la main d'une de ces furieuses. Quelque chose de plus que ses fesses était en l'air. Son orgueil pendait et il le contemplait étonné. On riait toujours.

Et l'eau qui coulait!

L'Enfant voulut aussi rire—bêtement—mais la pièce se retourna dans son ventre. La brûlure, encore plus intense. . . Faire fi des rires, se pencher. . . Boire! On arrosa son derrière qui pointait découvert.

L'Enfant se tenait de respirer, son ventre gonflait. Il sautilla pour écouter la pièce clapoter dans son ventre. Ça résonnait bien. Le petit chien aboya.

Il sautilla encore, retenant bien sur ses hanches ce qui restait de sa culotte nouée bout à bout.

— Sors! Sors de mon ventre!

La pièce clapotait sans réfléchir, sans penser que d'elle dépendait une vie. Au bout de la rue, une porte s'ouvre. Oh, la bonne odeur de la viande bien assaisonnée. . .

Freiner le pas, faire semblant d'être plus innocent qu'un condamné à mort, marcher dans les ruisseaux comme si l'on jouait comme tout enfant digne de l'être. A l'intérieur, la radio proférait des sottises, des choses révolutionnaires et censurées. Atteindre la porte mal fermée, s'apprêter à s'y faufiler souplement. . . ô bonne l'odeur de la viande. Le petit chien passa entre

Slow down your step, pretend to be more innocent than a man condemned to die, walk in the ditch as if playing like any child worthy of being one. Inside, the radio was spouting nonsense, revolutionary and censored items. Reach that badly closed door, get yourself ready to slink in there gingerly. . . oh the fine fragrance of the meat. The little dog slipped between the Child's legs, pushed the door open noisily, that door of hope that was fast becoming a door of hell.

Noises in the house: dogs barking, broken glasses, swear words . . . The man sure knows his way around words of abuse.

The little dog came out running, a piece of meat in his mouth. The Child was exultant. He ran after the animal. The animal ran after solitude. Where he would be alone with his appetite. Two small beings moving away quickly into the darkness of the silent alleyways. . . .

A "gentleman" in front of the poster. The picture of the gypsy quavers in the pool. Could she be afraid of the "gentleman," of the waterfall pouring into the pool?

Two small beings, two dots quickly coming closer to each other in the silence of the dark alleys.

"Here!"

The Child shrieks. The little dog runs.

The "gentleman". . . He's done. He tilts his head a little, shakes. The Child collides with him. The picture of the gypsy is no longer visible in the pool: a "gentleman" sprawled in his full length in a strange little lake, a confused child watching an animal disappear behind a house.

Hungry!

Hunger and an aching head, an aching back, an aching behind, an aching belly, pain everywhere.

Pain! Pain!

The Child was sobbing, a whirlwind of violence swept him up. Everything becomes a blur. Everything is weeping. He

les jambes de l'Enfant, poussa avec fracas la porte, cette porte d'espérance qui maintenant devenait une porte d'enfer.

Bruits dans la maison: aboiement de chien, des verres cassés, des injures. . . L'homme se connaît en matière d'injures.

Le petit chien sortit en courant, un morceau de viande est dans sa gueule. L'Enfant exultait. Il courut après l'animal. L'animal courut après la solitude. Là où lui seul serait avec son appétit. Deux petits êtres s'éloignent rapidement dans l'obscurité des ruelles silencieuses. . .

Un "monsieur" devant l'affiche publicitaire. L'image de la gitane tremblote dans la mare. Aurait-elle peur du "monsieur", de la cascade d'eau qui se déverse dans la mare?

Deux petits êtres, deux points s'approchent rapidement dans le silence des ruelles obscures.

— Ici!

L'Enfant hurle. Le petit chien court.

Le "monsieur". . . Il a fini. Il penche un peu la tête, secoue. L'Enfant le heurte. L'image de la gitane n'est plus dans la mare: un "monsieur" étalé de tout son long dans un petit lac singulier, un enfant confus regardant un animal disparaissant derrière une maison.

Faim!

Faim et mal à la tête, mal au dos, mal aux fesses, mal au ventre, mal partout.

Mal! Mal!

L'Enfant sanglotait, une bouffée de violence le soulevait. Tout s'embrouille. Tout pleure. Il lança son poing dans le visage de l'homme.

— Salaud, voleur, sorcier!

Il reçut en retour ce qu'il avait donné, mais en plus nombreux, en plus généreux. . . percutant.

L'Enfant gisait une fois encore.

Des voix:

punches the man in the face.

"Bastard, thief, evildoer!"

What he dished out he now got back, but more of it, with interest . . . and hard-hitting.

The Child was once again sprawled out.

Voices:

"What's that?"

"A poor starving kid."

"And all that blood?"

". . . !"

Get up, snivel. Blood was running from his mouth. The lovely red of the sun. The blood was flowing. Salty, it was salty. The Child licked his cracked lips. The blood ran underneath his tongue. He swallowed it. He swallowed again, again. . . His hunger abated. He wanted this flow never to stop. His calves were trembling. He pulled his pants up a little. He felt like pissing.

Piss.

He moved along walking up against the walls, his bladder was burning, his belly also, and his lips. Everything was burning. He let go without having the reflex of lowering his pants. He felt a hot thread drip down his thighs. It felt good.

"Mamma!"

Alleyways have a nice echo, too.

He leaned hard against the wall, then slid down slowly, his back scraping the rough cement, very slowly.

Sit down.

He clasped his stomach with both his hands, with his fingertips he probed for the spot where the coin might be: 100 FMG!

The little dog had come back, nibbled at the soles of his feet. The coin was there. He stood up. Drink, drink a lot. And then spit everything out again. Would the coin follow?

— C'est quoi ça?

— Un pauvre gosse affamé.

— Et ce sang?

— . . . !

Se lever, pleurnicher. Du sang coulait de sa bouche. Un beau rouge couleur de soleil. Le sang coulait. Salé, c'était salé. L'Enfant lécha ses lèvres fendues. Le sang fila sous sa langue. Il l'avala. Il avala encore, encore. . . Sa faim s'apaisa. Il voulut que cet écoulement n'en finisse jamais. Ses mollets tremblaient. Il remonta un peu sa culotte. Il avait envie de pisser.

Pisser.

Il allait marchant contre les murs, sa vessie lui brûlait, son ventre aussi, ses lèvres. Tout brûlait. Il se libéra sans avoir eu le réflexe de baisser sa culotte. Il sentit un filet chaud descendre le long de ses cuisses. Cela lui fit du bien.

— Maman. . . !

Les ruelles ont aussi de bons échos.

Il s'appuya fortement contre le mur, puis s'affaissa lentement, dos raclant le ciment rugueux, très lentement.

S'asseoir.

Il serra son ventre de ses deux mains, chercha du bout des doigts à deviner la pièce: 100 fmg!

Revenu, le petit chien lui mordilla la plante des pieds. La pièce était là. Il se leva. Boire, beaucoup boire. Et après recracher le tout. La pièce suivra-t-elle?

Il n'y avait personne près de la fontaine. Le soir descendait. Lâcher un soupir: un soupir filant comme un vent hagard. . .

Boire, beaucoup boire.

Il appuya sur son ventre. Vomir, vomir. La salive seule vint. Il s'enfonça un doigt dans la bouche, dans la gorge. Dégobiller!

De l'eau gluante, seulement cette eau gluante. La pièce reposait impitoyable au fond de ses entrailles. Sa culotte glissa de ses hanches. Ne pas s'en apercevoir. Tout nu, l'Enfant se mit à

There was nobody near the fountain. Night was beginning to fall. Heave a sigh: a sigh rushing out like a dazed wind . . .

Drink, drink a lot.

He pressed on his stomach. Vomit, vomit. Only saliva came out. He stuck a finger in his mouth, down his throat. Puke!

Slimy water, just this slimy water. The coin lay resting mercilessly at the bottom of his entrails. His pants slid down his hips. Do not take any note. Completely naked, the Child began to go forward, forward toward the sun, toward that setting sun seen between the rooftops, at the end of the alleyways. . . He, too, would have liked to topple over behind the horizon, topple into the void.

Naked Child, his skin moist with sweat, sweat or water from hell dripping shamelessly.

In the distance, the bells of the cathedrals were ringing. Good people were praying to the Son of God and sporting their newest outfits. Upon my word! You have to be properly dressed before Christ, that will bring him a change from those sober and honest angels. What won't they do to lighten the godhead's wretchedness?

Hunger!

Collapse.

The smell of the earth rises to his brain. It is like a rough thrust that compresses every nerve. Close the eyelids. Hold yourself motionless, belly on the ground. Mosquitoes attack. Fine, that's just fine like that. The bites cause the muscles to contract. The contraction calls for strength. Strength is like desire, it gives you the wish to live, to survive. He got up painfully.

100 fmg!

Strange smile, a grimace? Laugh! The Child was laughing, pretended to laugh, not to be what he is: a wreck in rags! He took on a deputy's stance: belly thrust out, his arms spread wide, his short legs up very high.

avancer, avancer droit vers le soleil, vers ce soleil couchant entrevu sur les toits, au bout des ruelles. . . Il aurait aimé aussi, comme lui, basculer dans l'horizon, basculer dans le vide.

Enfant nu à la peau tiède de sueur, sueur ou eau des enfers qui dégouline sans pudeur.

Au loin, les cloches des cathédrales résonnaient. Les bonnes gens priaient le fils de Dieu et arboraient leurs nouvelles parures. Dame! Il faut être bien mis devant le Christ, cela le changera de ces anges sobres et intègres. Que ne fera-t-on pour adoucir la misère du dieu?

Faim!

S'effondrer.

L'odeur de la terre monte au cerveau. C'est comme une poussée brutale qui compresse tous les nerfs. Clore les paupières. Se tenir immobile, ventre à terre. Les moustiques assaillent. Bien, c'est bien ainsi. Les piqûres provoquent une contraction des muscles. La contraction appelle la force. La force est comme le désir, elle donne envie de vivre, de survivre. Il se releva péniblement.

100 fmg!

Sourire bizarre, une grimace? Rire! L'Enfant riait, fit semblant de rire, de n'être pas ce qu'il est: une loque! Il prit une démarche de député: ventre en avant, bras écartés, courtes jambes lancées très haut.

— Ha! Ha!

Il riait.

Transe!

Le monde rapetissait. . . Lui, il grandissait. Ah! Grandir! Le ciel descendait, la ruelle glissait sous ses pieds. Combien de folie, combien de délire pour pouvoir sentir ce qu'il éprouvait, lui?

Dégobiller! Dégobiller!

100 fmg!

— Salauds! J'veux mourir, crever!

"Ha, ha!"

He was laughing.

Trance!

The world was shrinking. . . He, he was growing. Ah! Grow! The sky was coming down, the alleyway was slipping underneath his feet. How much madness, how much delirium to be able to feel what he was feeling?

Puke! Puke!

100 fmg!

"Bastards! I wanna die, kick off!"

Why does the world exist? Why is it called a privilege to be alive?

"Mister!"

"No."

"Mister!"

"No."

The Child was holding out his hand. He is now a true beggar, with 100 FMG in his belly to boot! Money taking shape with him! Life in person sits in his entrails and nobody will be able to take that away from him, not even the President of the Republic!

(Lucarne)

Pourquoi le monde est-il ? Pourquoi vivre est appelé privilège?

— M'sé!

— Non.

— M'sé!

— Non.

L'Enfant tendait la main. Il est maintenant un mendiant en bonne et due forme, avec en plus 100 fmg dans le ventre! De l'argent qui fait corps avec lui! La vie en personne est dans ses entrailles et nul ne pourra la lui reprendre, pas même le président de la République!

(Lucarne)

Case Closed

(by Jean-Luc Raharimanana)

The woman stopped crying and opened up her dead baby's stomach. The knife tore into the skin, sunk itself into the flesh, already blue. No blood flowed. She pulled out the entrails. Cut. Pulled out the small heart, dissected the veins. The lungs shriveled up with a hiss of air. She emptied the body. The tears were like acid on her cheeks. Again, her hiccupping and shaking began. She threw the organs into the garbage can. Her hands were sticky, the rotten flesh had secreted a gluey and nauseating liquid. She put the child into the bath-tub, washed the empty body. She took her bag, fished out the sachets, stuffed the child's stomach and stitched up the skin. She injected some formalin into the split veins. She dressed the body. No one would think to find any drugs in there.

She went out. She didn't know it was night. Everything was already completely black. Everything was already so dark. She didn't hear the sea caressing and groaning on the beaches. She didn't hear the waves, licking the hulls of the boats. All she saw was this light, shining over there, on the small *boutre.*[1] She marched straight ahead, clasping the small body against hers.

She boarded the dhow, unaware of her precarious balance. She climbed down into the cabin. The man was waiting for her there.

"Is it done?"

She cried and cried. The dead baby rolled down to the floor of the boat. You might have thought it to be a carved stone doll, a sculpture out of silver, gold, or copper. The woman groaned, curled up, bent double. She wanted her tears to turn

---

Translated from the French by Lanscom, s.a.r.l. (Antananarivo, Madagascar)

Affaire classée

(Jean-Luc Raharimanana)

La femme cessa de pleurer et ouvrit le ventre de son enfant mort. Le couteau déchira dans la peau, s'enfonça dans la chair déjà bleue. Le sang ne coula pas. Elle tira les entrailles. Elle coupa. Elle arracha le petit coeur, cisailla les veines. Les poumons se recroquevillèrent dans un chuintement d'air. Elle vida le corps. Les larmes étaient comme de l'acide sur ses joues. Elle se remit à hoqueter, à trembler. Elle jeta les organes dans le sac à poubelles. Ses mains collaient, la chair pourrie avait secrété un liquide gluant et nauséabond. Elle mit l'enfant dans la baignoire, lava le corps vide. Elle prit son sac, sortit les sachets, bourra le ventre de l'enfant et recousit la peau. Elle injecta le formol dans les veines éclatées. Elle habilla le cadavre. Personne ne songerait à y trouver de la drogue.

Elle sortit. Elle ne savait pas que c'était la nuit. Tout était déjà si noir. Tout était déjà si obscur. Elle n'entendait pas la mer qui se caressait et geignait sur les plages. Elle n'entendait pas les vagues qui léchaient les coques des bateaux. Elle ne voyait que cette lumière qui brillait là sur le boutre. Elle marchait droit devant elle, serrait le petit corps contre elle.

Elle monta sur le navire, ne prit pas conscience de son précaire équilibre. Elle descendit dans la cabine. L'homme l'y attendait.

— C'est fait?

Elle pleura. Elle pleura. L'enfant mort roula sur le plancher du boutre. On aurait dit une poupée de pierre, une sculpture d'argent, d'or ou de cuivre. La femme gémissait, lovée sur son propre corps. Elle voulut que ses pleurs fussent de pointes et de sagaies. Elle voulut s'empaler sous les lames de ses larmes.

L'homme empoigna sa chevelure et lui releva la figure. Elle ne le voyait pas. Elle ne voyait rien. Rien. Rien. Rien. Rien. . .

into spearheads and assagais. She wanted to gore herself on the blades of her tears.

The man seized her hair and lifted up her face. She couldn't see him. She saw nothing. Nothing. Nothing. Nothing. Nothing. . . .

NOTHING!

She was knocked down by the blows, she fell down under his spitting. The man tied her under the bunk and left. The woman stifled her tears but saw, at the same level as her face, the dead child's body, rolling to the rhythm of the boat's pitching. She burst out howling, shattering her throat and her conscience. She howled and blood flowed from her nose, blood flowed from her eyes. She howled and felt her temples tearing and burning. There, she delivered her soul and became insane.

It was beneath this same bunk that she had delivered her child. Her stomach had almost touched the bunk's planks. She had wanted to raise her legs to open up her vagina and let the child out. She had wanted more space. She had groaned, called for help. Her wrists were grazed from her bonds while she felt her bones shattering. The child no longer wanted her womb, the child forced itself out. She pushed and pushed. She cried. Her child's life was weakening inside her. She had felt its breathing getting weak and ebbing out of its heart. She didn't want it to. No, she didn't want it to. With all her soul. With all her love. She thumped her head against the bunk. She didn't stop howling. She was hurting. The child no longer moved. She panicked and rapped her feet on the planks.

This was when the man had reappeared. He had quickly understood. He had put his hands inside her, caught hold of the child's head. He pulled. He had pulled like an absolute madman. The woman didn't want to. She knew that the life had gone out of the child. She had closed up her legs again. She contracted all her muscles to swallow the child into the very depths of her

RIEN!

Elle tomba sous les coups, elle tomba sous les crachats. L'homme la rattacha sous la couchette et s'en alla. La femme étouffa ses pleurs, mais vit à la hauteur de son visage l'enfant mort qui roulait au plaisir des tanguements du boutre. Elle hurla à s'en éclater la gorge et la conscience. Elle hurla et le sang coula de ses narines, le sang coula de ses yeux. Elle hurla et sentit à ses tempes comme un déchirement fulgurant. Elle y délivra son âme et devint folle.

C'était également sous cette couchette qu'elle avait délivré son enfant. Son ventre touchait presque la planche de la couchette. Elle aurait voulu remonter les deux jambes pour ouvrir son vagin et sortir l'enfant. Elle aurait voulu avoir plus d'espace. Elle gémissait, appelait au secours. Ses mains s'écorchaient sous ses liens tandis qu'elle sentait tous ses os se briser. L'enfant ne voulait plus de son giron, l'enfant forçait le passage. Elle poussa. Elle poussa. Elle pleurait. La vie de l'enfant faiblissait en elle. Elle sentait que son souffle se rétrécissait et se retirait doucement de son coeur. Elle ne voulait pas. Non, elle ne voulait pas. De toute son âme. De tout son amour. Elle cogna sa tête contre la couchette. Elle ne cessait de hurler. Elle avait mal. L'enfant ne bougeait plus. Elle paniqua et tapa du pied sur le plancher.

C'était à ce moment que l'homme réapparut. Il avait vite compris. Il entra ses mains en elle, rattrapa la tête de l'enfant. Il avait tiré. Il avait tiré comme un dingue. La femme ne voulait pas. Elle savait que la vie avait quitté l'enfant. Elle referma les jambes. Elle contracta tous ses muscles pour ravaler l'enfant au plus profond de son ventre. Elle hurlait. Elle criait qu'il ne fallait pas, qu'il ne fallait pas. . . L'enfant ne doit pas s'en aller. Elle criait. L'homme l'assomma d'un coup sec dans la gorge.

Quand elle reprit conscience, l'enfant gisait à ses côtés. Au ras du sol. Sur le plancher. Le boutre tanguait. Dehors, un vent

stomach again. She had screamed. She had cried that she mustn't, she mustn't . . . She couldn't let the child go. She had yelled. The man knocked her out with a single blow to her throat.

When she came around again, the child was lying at her side. On the ground. On the floor. The sailboat was swaying. Outside, a wind was building up. The waves were angry. The water seemed so dark that one would think the whole dark sky had been poured right there. The woman knew nothing of all this. She saw nothing except the naked baby, tinged with blood. She saw nothing except the little human being without life, who still had "vaginal grasses" in its mouth and the long umbilical cord from its tummy. It was a little girl, with sleek smooth hair, with skin almost white, an island flower, a tropical half-caste. The woman cried. The woman shut down her conscience and forgot it was her child. She was still crying, that's all she did. She wasn't rich. All she did was to corrupt further a country already lost in misery and oblivion. She was black. She was a slave,[2] a zombie's daughter, possessed by djinns . . .

The man came back. He threw a bag on the floor. The woman understood. It wasn't the first time he had done this: bringing her his bag, and she . . . she . . .

Sometimes, the man would come back from town with the corpse of some child in rags, some kidnapped child, some adopted child. And they would proceed with their dirty work. Never had the man attended "surgery." Never had the man seen her hands plunged into entrails. The man was "civilised." She would knock back liters of alcohol. She would let herself be swayed by the rhythm of the sailboat. Then she would call the spirit of the dead child. Then she would call the wandering spirits to take possession of her being. She would dance in a trance. She would drain all her loathing and disgust. She would become like a big bird crossing the seas. She would become like a large bird of prey, cleaving the air. She would give herself up entirely

s'était levé. Les vagues étaient en colère. L'eau semblait si noire que l'on aurait cru que tout le ciel obscur s'y était versé. La femme ne savait rien de tout cela. Elle ne voyait que l'enfant nu et sanguinolent. Elle ne voyait que le petit être sans vie qui avait encore dans la bouche les herbes vaginales, et sur le ventre le long cordon ombilical. L'enfant était une petite fille, les cheveux lisses, la peau presque blanche, fleur des îles, métisse des tropiques. La femme pleura. La femme bloqua toute sa conscience et oublia que c'était son enfant. Elle pleurait toujours, elle ne faisait que cela depuis sa naissance. Oui, elle ne faisait que cela. Elle n'était pas riche. Elle ne faisait que corrompre un pays déjà perdu dans la misère et dans l'oubli. Elle était noire. Elle était esclave, une fille de zombi, une possession des djinns. . .

L'homme rentra. Il jeta un sac sur le sol. La femme comprit. Ce n'était pas la première fois qu'ils faisaient ainsi: lui apportant son sac, et elle. . . elle. . .

Des fois, l'homme revenait de la ville avec dans les bras le cadavre d'un enfant en guenilles, un enfant recueilli, un enfant adopté. Et ils procédaient à leur sale besogne. Jamais l'homme n'avait assisté à la "chirurgie". Jamais l'homme n'avait vu ses mains plonger dans les entrailles. L'homme était un civilisé. Elle ingurgitait des litres d'alcool. Elle se laissait balancer au rythme du boutre. Puis elle appelait l'esprit. Puis elle appelait les âmes errantes pour prendre possession de son être. Elle dansait en transe. Elle évacuait sa répugnance. Elle devenait comme un grand oiseau traversant la mer. Elle devenait comme un grand rapace qui fendait l'air. Elle se délivrait de tout et fondait alors sur le corps à vider. Elle n'appartenait plus à ce monde. Elle n'existait plus dans cette dimension.

Le boutre quittait ensuite le port, gagnait le large. Les garde-côtes ne s'étonnaient jamais de la présence de ces enfants qui se succédaient à bord, enfants sages et plein de sommeil, enfants

and would then start on the body to be emptied. She would no longer belong to this world. She would no longer exist in this dimension.

The sailboat would then leave the port and get out to the open sea. The coast-guards would never be surprised by the presence of these different children on board, good sleeping children, well brought up children. The coast guards would never closely examine these sleeping angels. The exchange would often take place as the sun went down. A motorboat would come up alongside them, the crew would load the packages, the man would pick up the money. The sailboat would come back to the port. The horizon would be purple all over and the ocean an immense dazzling sailcloth. Red, the color of kings.[3] Red, the color of sovereigns. Red, the color of Revolution.

Afterwards the man had taken her. Then the man had made her pregnant, he was a madman. He had tied her under the bunk, arms crossed, legs apart. She only came back to reality the day when the man threw the bag down in front of her, in front of her dead baby. . .

The woman had been mad for a long time but she didn't know it. The child growing inside her had maintained her clear-mindedness. There was the fetus turning into a human being, water becoming its body, a reprieve for her sanity, some kind of countdown until she gave birth.

The man had untied her. She wrapped the child in some canvas which stank of fish. She got down onto dry land, ran, cried.

"Is it done?"

"It's done."

She yelled in the streets and people turned their heads as she went by. She hailed a rickshaw. Got on and watched the strong man who was pulling the vehicle. She was crying. The man carefully avoided the enormous potholes in the asphalt. One

très bien élevés. Les garde-côtes n'avaient pas à scruter ces sommeils des anges. L'échange se faisait souvent au coucher du soleil. Un hors-bord les abordait, l'équipage embarquait les colis, l'homme recevait l'argent. Le boutre revenait au port. La couleur était pourpre sur tout l'horizon et l'océan était une immense voile éclatante. Rouge, couleur des rois. Rouge, couleur des souverains.

Puis l'homme l'avait prise. Puis l'homme l'avait engrossée, était devenu fou. Il l'avait attachée sous la couchette, les bras en croix, les jambes écartées. Elle ne descendit plus à terre que ce jour où il avait jeté le sac devant elle, devant son bébé mort. . .

La femme était folle depuis longtemps, mais elle ne le savait pas. Il y avait l'enfant grandissant en elle qui maintenait sa lucidité. Il y avait le foetus qui se faisait homme, il y avait l'eau qui se faisait corps, un sursis pour sa raison, un compte à rebours.

L'homme l'avait détachée. Elle emballa l'enfant dans une toile qui puait le poisson. Elle descendit à terre, courait, pleurait.

— C'est fait?

— C'est fait.

Elle hurlait dans les rues et les gens se retournaient sur son passage. Elle héla un pousse-pousse. Elle monta, regarda l'homme robuste qui tirait sa voiture. Elle pleurait. Elle pleurait. Le tireur évitait avec soin les nids de poules qui trouaient l'asphalte, on aurait dit un char des dieux, un esquif de sirènes. . .

Puis elle était arrivée, avait monté les marches pourries, avait poussé la porte défoncée. Avait tranché, charcuté, bourré, recousu.

L'enfant roulait toujours sur le plancher de la petite cabine du boutre. La femme n'avait plus ses pensées. La femme n'avait plus ses regards. Elle était complètement folle.

L'homme faisait tous les bars du port. L'homme se soûlait comme le typhon s'énivrait de vent et de tourbillon. L'homme

would have thought a chariot of the gods or a skiff of the sirens . . .

Then she arrived, climbed the rotten steps, pushed the broken-down door. She sliced, butchered, stuffed, stitched up again.

The child was still rolling about on the deck of the sailboat's small cabin. The woman no longer had control over her thoughts. The woman no longer saw with her eyes. She was completely insane.

The man did his rounds in all the bars in the port. The man got drunk as a typhoon gets drunk on the storm and the whirlwind. He told the whole of his story to his drinking buddies. The man was raving. The man spewed up the story of his life as an old mercenary and lost legionnaire. He landed in a police station, confessed everything. He was found the next morning, his throat slit, lying stranded in the gutter.[4]

The dhow burned mysteriously in the dilapidated port. The madwoman. The bastard child.

The case is closed.

(Lucarne)

racontait toute son histoire à ses compagnons de bouteille. L'homme délirait. L'homme dégueulait sa vie de vieux mercenaire et de légionnaire perdu. Il atterrit dans un commissariat, avoua tout. On le retrouva, le matin venu, la gorge tranchée, gisant dans les rigoles.

Le boutre brûla mystérieusement dans le port délabré. La folle. L'enfant bâtard.

Affaire classée.

(Lucarne)

Christiane Ramanantsoa

Born in 1953, Christiane Ramanantsoa is a high school teacher in Antananarivo, Madagascar. Director of the Atelier Théâtre (Theater Workshop) of the Alliance Française in Antananarivo, she has produced several Malagasy plays in French, among them: Sambany *and* Un jour ma mémoire *(Some day my memory) by Michèle Rakotoson and* Le prophète et le président *by Jean-Luc Raharimanana. She is also the author of several unpublished short stories:* Soa, Le canapé *(The sofa), and* Grand-mère *(Grandma), whose translated text is reproduced below.*

Grandma

Grandma tucked the child in bed. He was a bit touchy this evening.

"Tell me—are ghosts real?" She replied:

"No. Don't be afraid of anything."

She gently stroked his brow. He fell asleep. She got up cautiously from the bed where she had been sitting to reassure him. She heard the echoes of the night vigil dirges. She, however, had been entreated to go up and rest, as she needed to spare herself in her old age. She made her way to the room's skylight. She clung to this opening. Listened.

The wind brought her distant howls in short blasts.

It was a full moon[1] . . .

. . . The women were shining under the full moon, naked.[2] And slippery. Before gathering, the women had all smeared themselves with oil or fat at home so as to be able to give the slip if "someone" tried to catch them.

There they were, at the side of this ring road, where the houses were few and far between, roads bordered with trees and hard grasses.

Translated from the French by Lanscom, s.a.r.l. (Antananarivo, Madagascar)

Christiane Ramanantsoa

Née en 1953, Christiane Ramanantsoa est professeur de lycée à Antananarivo, Madagascar. Elle dirige l'Atelier Théâtre de l'Alliance Française à Antananarivo, où elle a mis en scène plusieurs pièces malgaches en français, parmi lesquelles Sambany *et* Un jour ma mémoire *de Michèle Rakotoson, ainsi que* Le prophète et le président *de Jean-Luc Raharimanana. Elle est elle-même l'auteur de plusieurs nouvelles encore inédites:* Soa, Le canapé, *et* Grand-mère, *qui est présentée ci-dessous.*

Grand-mère

Grand-mère borda l'enfant. Ce soir, il était un peu nerveux:

— Dis, est-ce que les fantômes existent? Elle répondit:

— Non. Ne crains rien.

Elle lui massa doucement le front. Il s'endormit. Elle se leva avec précaution du lit où elle était assise pour le rassurer. Elle entendait des échos de la veillée funèbre. Mais elle, on l'avait priée de monter se reposer, car son grand-âge avait besoin d'être ménagé. Elle se dirigea vers la lucarne de la chambre. Elle s'agrippa à cette ouverture. Ecouta.

Le vent lui apporta, par rafales, des hurlements lointains.

C'était la pleine lune. . .

. . . Elles étaient nues, brillantes sous la pleine lune. Et glissantes. Avant de se rassembler, chacune de son côté s'était enduite d'huile ou de graisses, de façon à pouvoir glisser si jamais "on" cherchait à les attraper.

Elles étaient là, au bord de cette route périphérique aux rares maisons, route bordée d'arbres et d'herbes dures.

Elles s'étaient toutes mises à quatre pattes, à la queue leu leu, à la suite de celle qui semblait être la chef. Elles suivaient, en hurlant et ricanant, le chien bâtard et hirsute qui s'était trouvé là par hasard.

Les rares voitures qui passaient accéléraient à leur vue.

They had got down on all fours, tail-to-tail, following the one who seemed to be their leader. They followed, howling and giggling at the bastard shaggy dog who had found himself there by accident.[3]

The few cars that passed by accelerated at their sight.

They were the masters of this lunar world. Nobody ever dared to approach them. They were terrifying. Everyone would flee at their sight.

They were the masters of this lunar world.

It wasn't yet midnight. They had time. They had the whole night in front of them.

They knew that sooner or later their victim would come.

Sooner or later, they would catch the rash passerby, who had dared to come home late, who would inevitably be coming back from an over-alcoholized celebratory evening, or who had come from some clandestine meeting. Woe to him who dares to have a good time at night and goes home ALONE.

They also had a well-defined itinerary and destination. They took their time getting there. It wasn't yet midnight. They had time.

They were masters of this lunar world. They were masters of time.

So on they went, mooching about for now, rolling themselves in the dust, pushing each other about like schoolchildren.

Only their long, wild, wind-swept, disorderly manes of hair clothed them somehow; these were the only bible-black stains on their brown gleaming backs and their brown gleaming backsides.

All of a sudden, they were quiet.

Dense silence.

Then the noise of hasty footsteps. Panting.

Someone in a hurry.

They scattered instantly, unbelievably fast. Without making the slightest noise.

Elles étaient les maîtres de ce monde lunaire. Personne n'osait les approcher. Elles faisaient peur. "On" fuyait à leur vue.

Elles étaient les maîtres de ce monde lunaire.

Il n'était pas minuit. Elles avaient le temps. Elles avaient toute la nuit devant elles.

Elles savaient que tôt ou tard viendrait leur victime.

Tôt ou tard, elles attraperaient le passant téméraire, qui avait osé rentrer tard, qui rentrait sûrement d'une soirée trop arrosée, ou qui venait d'une soirée clandestine. Malheur à celui qui avait osé s'amuser tard dans la nuit et qui rentrait SEUL.

Elles avaient d'ailleurs aussi une direction bien précise. Elles prenaient leur temps pour y aller. Il n'était pas minuit. Elles avaient le temps.

Elles étaient les maîtres de ce monde lunaire. Elles étaient les maîtres du temps.

Elles avançaient donc, baguenaudant pour le moment, se roulant dans la poussière, se poussant comme de jeunes écolières.

Seuls leurs cheveux longs les vêtaient un peu: échevelées, crinières aux vents, c'étaient les seules tâches bien noires sur leur dos brun et brillant et leur croupe brune et brillante.

Elles firent silence tout d'un coup.

Moment de silence épais.

Puis des bruits de pas rapides. Une respiration haletante.

Une personne pressée.

Elles s'égaillèrent à une vitesse rapide, incroyable. Sans qu'on entendit le moindre bruit.

Sauf les pas pressés de la personne pressée.

Puis un cri. Une chute. Des ricanements, des hurlements et des injures. Les injures les plus grossières énoncées par des voix de crécelles.

Elles lui avaient sauté dessus. L'une, d'un croc-en-jambe, l'avait fait tomber. Et elles s'entassèrent sur tout son corps.

Only the hasty footsteps of the hasty person.

Then a cry. Someone falling. Sniggers, howling and insults, the crudest insults uttered in rasping voices.

They had jumped on top of him. One of them brought him down with a rugby tackle. They piled up all over his body. They sat on his head. They crushed him with their torsos. They trampled on him.[4]

They were just an immense brown mass with hollows and humps.

They smeared him with all the filth they could amass there and then. They made him eat . . . he didn't dare think what. They tore his clothes, stripped him. . . .

He couldn't move. He was stone cold. Paralyzed. He couldn't really see, couldn't really feel anything . . . except the disgusting smell of crap, shit, rot, gluey flesh, slime, all flowing into one sticky substance.

He couldn't utter a single sound. Couldn't move.

And they had had it in for him. Threw him on the ground, to beat up and insult him, with all their hearts, all their rage, all their snarling, all their hate and their frustration.

He couldn't defend himself. He was paralyzed . . .

Then, a loud laugh: their leader's laugh. Release.

He suddenly found himself all alone: bloody, dirtied, and stinking.

They left, running and hooting. They followed a path bordered with trees. Sniggering.

They were the masters of this lunar world.

They arrived in front of an isolated house. A light was shining there. A song rose from the house: a funeral dirge.

A night vigil before burial.

They scattered to the four corners of the house . . .

And as if they had given each other a signal, they threw some stones on the house, all at the same time. Without a laugh,

Elles s'étaient assises sur sa tête. Elles l'avaient écrasé de leur ventre. Elles le piétinaient.

Elles n'étaient que masse brune avec des creux et des bosses.

Elles l'enduisaient de toutes les saletés qu'elles avaient pu amasser en un rien de temps. Elles lui faisaient manger. . . Il n'osait, il ne voulait y penser. Elles lui déchiraient ses vêtements, le dévêtaient. . .

Et il ne pouvait bouger. Il était glacé. Paralysé. Il ne voyait rien, ne sentait rien très distinctement. . . Mais des odeurs écoeurantes de crottes, de merde, de pourritures, de chair gluante, visqueuse, poisseuse, confondues.

Il ne pouvait crier. Il ne pouvait bouger.

Et elles s'acharnaient sur lui. Y mettaient, pour le tabasser et l'insulter, tout leur coeur, toute leur rage, leur hargne, leur haine et leur frustration.

Il ne pouvait se défendre. Il était paralysé. . .

Et puis, un rire éclatant: le rire du chef. La délivrance.

Il se retrouva soudain tout seul: sanguinolent, crotté et puant.

Elles étaient parties en hululant, tout en courant. Elles suivirent un sentier longé d'arbres. Elles ricanaient.

Elles étaient les maîtres de ce monde lunaire.

Elles arrivèrent devant une maison isolée. Une lumière y brillait. De cette maison s'élevait un chant: un cantique des morts.

Veillée funèbre.

Elles s'éparpillèrent aux quatre coins de la maison. . .

Et comme si elles s'étaient donné le mot, au même moment, elles lancèrent des cailloux sur la maison. Sans un rire, ni ricanement, ni hurlement. Les crépitement des cailloux résonnèrent sur les fenêtres et les portes. . .

Le chant s'arrêta.

Silence total, silence épais.

snigger or a howl. The doors and windows made a cracking noise as the stones landed . . .

The singing stopped.

Absolute, dense silence.

Then there was a cry from the house:

"Mpamosavy! At them! Witch-hunt! At them!"

They heard the cry. They hid. They disappeared into the night.

"They" didn't catch them.

The hunters didn't dare go too far from the house, otherwise they might go in and kidnap the body.

They were the masters of this lunar world. Masters of life. Masters of death.

At the hoot of an owl, they found themselves at the end of the path. They sat down on the ground for a moment. In silence. Then, without a word, without a single glance at each other, they got up and separated.

Dawn had just arrived.

One of them, the one who seemed to be their leader, came back along the path. She quickly made her way toward the house in mourning. She hugged the walls in order to get back via the back yard. She found the drain-pipe. Up she climbed, and went in through the open skylight of the roof.

She found herself in an attic room. A bed. A child in the bed. A bedcover. An undefinable piece of furniture, upon which there was a washbasin full of water.

She moistened a towel, cleaned herself, and braided her hair. She put on a flannel night dress: collar up to the neck, with long sleeves down to her wrists.

She got into bed, beside the child who was sleeping like a log.

Grandma soon fell asleep next to her grandson.

Once the sun was up, she would wash the child, take care of

Puis un cri dans la maison:

— Mpamosavy! Au sus! Chasse aux sorcières! Au sus!

Elles entendirent le cri. Elles se cachèrent. Elles se fondirent dans la nuit.

On ne les rattrapa pas.

Les chasseurs n'avaient pas osé trop s'éloigner de la maison, sinon elles se seraient risquées à y entrer, et kidnapper le cadavre.

Elles étaient les maîtres de ce monde lunaire. Maîtres de la vie. Maîtres de la mort.

Le hululement d'un hibou, et elles se retrouvèrent au bout du sentier. Elles s'assirent à même le sol un moment. En silence. Puis sans rien se dire, sans se regarder, elles se levèrent, se séparèrent.

L'aube commençait à poindre.

L'une d'elles, celle qui semblait être le chef, revint sur le sentier. Elle se dirigea rapidement vers la maison endeuillée. Elle rasa les murs pour parvenir à l'arrière-cour. Elle repéra la gouttière. Elle l'escalada, entra par la lucarne ouverte du toit.

Elle se retrouva dans une chambre sous le toit. Un lit. Un enfant dans le lit. Un tapis de lit. Un meuble indéfinissable. Sur ce meuble, une cuvette pleine d'eau.

Elle mouilla une serviette, se nettoya, se natta les cheveux. Elle se vêtit d'une chemise de nuit de flanelle: col au ras du cou, longues manches à poignets.

Elle se mit au lit, à côté de l'enfant qui dormait à poings fermés.

Grand-mère s'endormit très vite auprès de son petit-fils.

Au lever du soleil, grand-mère laverait l'enfant, s'en occuperait. Puis, elle présiderait honorablement, dignement l'enterrement du mort.

En attendant, Grand-mère dormait auprès de son petit-fils.

him. Then, honorably, with dignity, she would preside over the burial ceremony.

Meanwhile, Grandma slept beside her grandson.

She would reassure the whole family, her oldest son, her daughter . . ., that she had slept very well and would become properly indignant when told about the witches' dance. . . .

Elle rassurerait toute sa famille, son fils aîné, sa fille. . . , qu'elle avait bien dormi et s'indignerait comme il faut quand on lui raconterait la sarabande des sorcières. . .

Narcisse Randriamirado

Born in 1954, Narcisse Randriamirado is a high-school French teacher in Madagascar. He is the author of several comic plays: On ne vit que trois fois *(You live only three times),* Allons z'omlettes *(Rise little men), and* Mes femmes et tes maris *(My wives and your husbands). He has also written two short stories:* Dahalo, voleur de zébus *(Dahalo, cattle thief) and* Grand-mère *(Grandmother), whose translation is reproduced below. Both of these short stories were published in the bulletin of the Alliance Française in Madagascar,* Variété 2, *1990.*

Grandmother

Grandmother died at the cock's first crowing.

She had only two grandsons. Our parents died in an ordinary car accident now almost ten years ago. My brother is the older one: Monsieur Rakoto. He is married, had both a civil and a religious wedding, and has only two children.[1] He is a civil servant and earns quite a good living.

I am the younger one. I am married. A traditional marriage, that is to say, before the Creator, the ancestors, the sacred hill, and the village community. With the sacrifice of a white-headed zebu and rum galore. I have seven children. They call me Rainibe, or father of Be, the diminutive of Bertrand, my last child.[2]

Grandmother died at the cock's first crowing.

Our neighbors had stayed at her bedside all night long. A one-room house made of *falafa.*[3] They had been taking turns. Some were chatting outside and others were holding grandmother's hand in theirs. They were combing her hair. They were massaging her forehead and her legs. Coffee was being served.

For two months Grandmother had not stopped talking about her death, what they were supposed to do at her funeral.

Translated from the French by Marjolijn de Jager

Narcisse Randriamirado

Né en 1954, Narcisse Randriamirado est professeur de français au niveau secondaire à Madagascar. Il est l'auteur de plusieurs comédies: On ne vit que trois fois, Allons z'omlettes, *et* Mes femmes et tes maris. *Il a également écrit deux nouvelles:* Dahalo, voleur de zébus *et* Grand-mère, *dont le texte est reproduit ci-dessous. Ces deux nouvelles ont paru dans le bulletin de l'Alliance Française à Madagascar:* Variété 2, *1990.*

Grand-mère

Grand-mère est morte au premier cocorico.

Elle n'avait que deux petits-fils. Nos parents ont disparu dans un banal accident de voiture voilà bientôt dix ans. L'aîné, c'est mon frère: monsieur Rakoto. Il est marié, mariage civil et religieux, et n'a que deux enfants. Il est fonctionnaire et gagne assez bien sa vie.

Le cadet, c'est moi. Je suis marié. Mariage traditionnel, c'est-à-dire devant le Créateur, les ancêtres, la colline sacrée et la communauté villageoise. Avec le sacrifice de zébu à tête blanche et du rhum à gogo. J'ai sept enfants. On m'appelle Rainibe, ou le père de Be, diminutif de Bertrand, mon dernier enfant.

Grand-mère est morte au premier cocorico.

Nos voisins étaient restés à son chevet toute la nuit. Une case d'une chambre, en falafa. On se relayait. Les uns bavardaient à l'extérieur et les autres tenaient la main de grand-mère dans les leurs. On lui peignait les cheveux. On lui massait le front et les jambes. Le café circulait.

Grand-mère n'avait cessé de parler de sa mort depuis deux mois, de ce qu'on devrait faire lors de ses funérailles. Si bien que tout le monde était au courant. De plus, il y avait des signes précurseurs: j'ai rêvé qu'on m'extrayait ma canine. Cela voulait dire le "grand départ" d'une personne âgée dans la famille. Ma

So much so that everybody knew all about it. In addition, there had been prior signs: I dreamed that I had a canine tooth extracted. That indicated the "great departure" of an elderly person in the family. My wife had also dreamed that I was eating beef[4] and that there were many people present.

And yet, one week earlier, she was still in the rice fields pulling out weeds. She had still gone for clay in a neighboring village to make earthenware cooking pots. Roughly twenty kilometers on foot. Then came exhaustion. A little fever. The deteriorating illness, and death a few days later.

A week before her death, the village already knew that mourning would take place, that a member of society would soon "depart." At night, the village dogs would not stop howling in a very odd way as they looked up at the moon. The cat of the house had disappeared: rats leave the ship when it is about to sink.

Grandmother died at the cock's first crowing and I feel a little guilty. A fever? A few tablets or a quick injection and all is resolved. But try and tell grandmother that. Did she not know the secrets of herbal teas and plants? That is how she had grown old and lasted. For grandmother another science, another form of medicine, of logic, was needed. Half an hour after she had given birth to papa, she was bathing in the river, from head to toe.

Grandmother died at the cock's first crowing. When she returned from the rice fields a week earlier, she knew that she'd be leaving soon. As she was pulling weeds, she had seen her reflection in the water. It was paler than usual. The same was true for her eyes, and the half-light was darker . . .

Early in the morning, the village women were washing the body of the departed one, dressing and adorning it. Then they cleaned the house and prepared the meal. Huge pots and dishes were brought in . . .

When everything was ready, a woman began to weep. As

femme a aussi rêvé que je mangeais de la viande de boeuf et qu'il y avait beaucoup de monde.

Et pourtant, une semaine plus tôt, elle était encore à la rizière pour arracher les mauvaises herbes. Elle était encore allée chercher de l'argile dans un village voisin pour fabriquer des marmites de terre. Une vingtaine de kilomètres à pied. Et puis, la fatigue. Un peu de fièvre. La maladie qui empirait, et la mort quelques jours après.

Une semaine avant sa mort, le village savait déjà qu'un deuil se préparait, qu'un membre de la société "partirait" bientôt. La nuit, les chiens du village ne cessaient de hurler d'une drôle de façon en regardant la lune. Le chat de la maison avait disparu: les rats quittent le navire quand il va sombrer.

Grand-mère est morte au premier cocorico et je me sens un peu coupable. La fièvre? Quelques comprimés ou une petite piqûre et tout est résolu. Mais allez donc le dire à grand-mère. Ne connaissait-elle pas le secret des infusions et des plantes? C'est pour cela qu'elle est restée vieille. Pour grand-mère, il fallait une autre science, une autre médecine, une autre logique. Une demi-heure après avoir accouché de papa, elle se baignait dans la rivière, de la tête aux pieds.

Grand-mère est morte au premier cocorico. A son retour de la rizière, une semaine plus tôt, elle savait qu'elle partirait bientôt. En arrachant les mauvaises herbes, elle voyait son reflet dans l'eau. Celui-ci était plus pâle que d'habitude. Il en était de même pour les yeux, et la pénombre était plus sombre. . .

De bon matin, les femmes du village lavaient le corps de la disparue, l'habillaient et la décoraient. Après, elles nettoyaient la case et préparaient la cuisine. On apportait de grosses marmites, des assiettes. . .

Quand tout était prêt, voilà qu'une femme pleurait. Le plus fort possible. Un cri à fendre l'âme. Peu après, toutes les femmes l'imitaient: un étrange hululement de hibou. Puis le silence. Une

loudly as possible. A cry that would break your heart. Shortly thereafter, all the women followed her example: a peculiar sound like the hooting of an owl. Then there was silence. One way to let it be known that a death had occurred in this house. And so, within a radius of ten kilometers, everyone would know the news that was passed on by word of mouth. Every farmer in the area would abandon his daily work for at least a week.

One or more zebus would be killed depending upon the wealth of the grief-stricken family. The meat would not be salted.[5] People would bring rice, coffee, money, and plates.

Evening falls. Everyone is there and it is a celebration. Complete joyousness. They try to outdo one another with songs until the morning. Their themes touch upon every aspect of life: death, life, harvest time, sex. . . . The smell of grilled meat perfumes the air. Young girls prepare the coffee and bring rum which they carry in a bucket. They walk on their knees as a sign of greater politeness. Jokes are told and told very loudly so that everyone can enjoy them. Guffawing laughter from all those present. A good many of the men will be drunk this night. They will argue among themselves and they will weep over grandmother.

This night, there will be love in the air. Anyone may sleep with anyone else, provided there is no family relationship whatsoever between them.[6] For romantics, this is an idyllic opportunity that will end with a child, followed by a marriage.

Grandmother had demanded a traditional wake at her death. Every person there was to speak vulgarities before her inert body and insult her.[7] Obscenities; abject, vile, and sexual words. Everyone was to mime the act of procreation within an atmosphere of piety. What greater honor than this for the deceased?

Grandmother lived alone in the country and hated the city. Everything in her village had an emotional meaning for her. There she had lived her youthful years with grandfather.

Monsieur Rakoto and I live in the city. I on the outskirts and

façon d'annoncer que dans cette case il y avait un mort. Ainsi, dix kilomètres à la ronde, tout le monde était au courant de la nouvelle qui passait de bouche à oreille. Tous les paysans voisins délaisseront leur travail quotidien pendant au moins une semaine.

On tuera un ou plusieurs boeufs selon la richesse de la famille endeuillée. La viande ne sera pas salée. Les gens apporteront du riz, du café, de l'argent et des assiettes.

Le soir arrive. Tout le monde est là et c'est la fête. La gaîté totale. On rivalise de chants jusqu'au matin. Les thèmes touchent tous les aspects de la vie: la mort, la vie, la moisson, le sexe. . . Les grillades parfument l'air. Les jeunes filles préparent le café et apportent du rhum dans un seau. Elles marchent sur les genoux pour plus de politesse. On se raconte des blagues et on les dit très fort pour que tout le monde en profite. Rires à gorge déployée de toute l'assistance. Une bonne partie des hommes seront ivres cette nuit. Ils se disputeront entre eux et pleureront grand-mère.

Cette nuit, il y aura de l'amour dans l'air. Chacun peut se coucher avec n'importe qui, pourvu qu'il n'y ait aucun lien de parenté. Pour les romantiques, ce sera l'occasion d'une idylle, qui se terminera par un enfant puis un mariage.

Grand-mère avait exigé pour sa mort une veillée traditionnelle. Tous les gens prononceraient des gros-mots devant son corps inerte et l'insulteraient. Des mots obscènes, abjects, vils et sexuels. Tout le monde mimerait la procréation dans une atmosphère religieuse. Quel plus grand honneur pour la défunte?

Grand-mère habitait seule à la campagne et détestait la ville. Tout, dans son village, avait un sens affectif pour elle. Elle avait vécu là sa jeunesse avec grand-père.

Monsieur Rakoto et moi habitons en ville. Moi à l'orée et lui en plein centre. De temps en temps, grand-mère nous rendait visite. Elle restait trois ou quatre jours chez mon frère, et faisait de même chez moi.

he right in the center. From time to time, grandmother would visit us. She'd stay three or four days with my brother, then do the same with me.

She would always arrive at dinner time. That created a big problem because she had very specific tastes. She would only eat *brèdes,*[8] except on the anniversary of her first meeting with grandfather. Moreover, she didn't like food cooked over charcoal, oil, or gas. She wanted to eat sitting on the floor, for she was always afraid she'd fall off the chair. At night, she'd sleep on a mat spread out right on the wood floor and assure us that she was just fine that way.

Another problem arose from the fact that she was afraid of toilets. She would choke because of the smell and loathed locking herself in there. Besides, the fact that father and daughter would be doing their business in the same place was practically incestuous. What a pain in the neck it was to find a discreet spot for grandmother's small needs. . . .

The trouble didn't stop there. She didn't want any paper. She would use water: that was cleaner. So two or three children had to accompany grandmother to a proper place, armed with a small bucket of water, a tumbler, and a spade. In short, everything needed to attract attention.

My brother, Monsieur Rakoto, also would tear out his hair when grandmother was with him. He has a high position in society and his reputation is quite important to him. And there was grandmother doing her laundry—and what laundry!—in the public wash house of the neighborhood. And that while the house had a washing machine and two servants. In order to avoid this, my brother, Monsieur Rakoto, used to put grandmother's things in the machine while she was sleeping. It would make grandmother mad with rage. The machine ruins clothes. It is not careful with them. Panties are mixed in with headscarves. Everyone's underwear is in there, too. It is indecent. It is incestuous.

Elle arrivait toujours au moment du dîner. C'était tout un problème car elle avait des goûts précis. Elle ne voulait que des brèdes, sauf pour l'anniversaire de sa première rencontre avec grand-père. De plus, elle n'aimait pas les aliments cuits sur le charbon, le pétrole ou le gaz. Elle voulait manger à terre, car elle avait toujours peur de tomber de la chaise. La nuit, elle dormait sur une natte étalée à même le parquet, et nous assurait qu'elle était très bien comme ça.

Un autre problème venait du fait qu'elle avait peur des W-C. Elle y suffoquait à cause de l'odeur et répugnait à s'y enfermer. D'ailleurs, faire ses besoins dans un même lieu, pour le père et sa fille c'était pratiquement un inceste. Quel casse-tête de trouver un lieu discret pour les petits besoins de grand-mère. . .

L'ennui ne s'arrêtait pas là. Elle ne voulait pas de papier. Elle utilisait de l'eau: c'est plus propre. Alors, deux à trois enfants devaient conduire grand-mère dans un endroit propice, munis d'un petit seau d'eau, d'un gobelet et d'une pelle. Bref, tout ce qu'il fallait pour attirer l'attention.

Mon frère aussi, Monsieur Rakoto, s'arrachait les cheveux quand grand-mère était là. Il occupe une place distinguée dans la société et tient beaucoup à sa réputation. Et voilà que grand-mère lavait son linge—et quel linge!—au lavoir public du quartier. Alors que la maison avait une machine à laver et deux domestiques. Pour éviter cela, mon frère, Monsieur Rakoto, mettait les affaires de l'aïeule dans la machine pendant qu'elle dormait. Elle entrait dans une colère folle, la grand-mère. La machine abîme les vêtements. Ça ne fait pas attention. Les culottes y sont mêlées aux foulards. Les slips de tout le monde y sont mélangés. C'est indécent. C'est incestueux.

Parfois, elle vendait des pistaches, à même le sol, au marché du quartier et interpelait les clients. Elle chantait et racontait des blagues pour faire rire les gens. Elle ne passait jamais inaperçue.

Sometimes, sitting right on the ground, she would sell peanuts in the neighborhood market and shout at the customers. She'd sing and tell jokes to make people laugh. She would never go unnoticed.

The wash house and market were merely pretexts. That is where she found people to talk to. She would make new friends. There everyone speaks loudly, tells jokes, laughs without any hang-ups. The wash house and the market? Places to meet someone and to hear the news. Wasn't it at the village fair that she had met grandfather?

With her, you'd put in half an hour to bargain for a twenty-franc pile of peanuts. There is the human warmth this city lacks. And so, what difference does it make if she buys two hundred francs' worth of peanuts and resells them at a hundred francs having spent ten hours under the sun? Friendship first. Friendship has no price.

Grandmother died at the cock's first crowing.

She had demanded that at her burial everyone sing as they clap their hands. Everyone was to clown around. They were to do the crocodile dance and the warrior dance and imitate the walk of the duck. They would do a parody of the sex act. Her burial was to be held according to custom, and not in the manner of foreigners and city folk.

They would not carry any crosses, just the horns of zebus. There were not to be any flowers, just knives, chicken, tobacco, money, and plates to be put in her tomb and on top. *Brèdes* and a few seeds were not to be forgotten. The procession would move along amidst a roar of laughter and deafening, improvised songs, and not in the icy and hypocritical silence of the city. The sloppiest clothing should be worn, for grandmother's body was to be carried on the run. The elderly and the children were to stay in the village for they wouldn't be able to keep up with the young people running. The latter were to drink alcohol and smoke

Le lavoir et le marché n'étaient que des prétextes. Elle y trouvait des gens à qui parler. Elle y nouait des nouvelles amitiés. Là, tout le monde parle fort, dit des blagues, rit sans complexe. Le lavoir et le marché? C'est pour rencontrer quelqu'un et apprendre les nouvelles. N'était-ce pas à la foire du village qu'elle avait rencontré grand-père?

Avec elle, on mettait un quart d'heure à marchander pour un tas de pistaches à vingt francs. Voilà la chaleur humaine qui manque dans cette ville. Et alors, qu'est-ce que ça fait si elle achète deux cents francs de pistaches pour les revendre cent francs après dix heures passées sous le soleil? L'amitié d'abord. L'amitié n'a pas de prix.

Grand-mère est morte au premier cocorico.

Elle avait exigé que lors de son enterrement tout le monde chante en battant des mains. Tout le monde ferait le pitre. On jouerait la danse du crocodile et du guerrier, et on imiterait la marche du canard. On parodierait l'acte sexuel. Son enterrement devrait se faire selon la coutume, et non à la mode des étrangers et des citadins.

On ne porterait pas de croix, mais des cornes de zébus. Il n'y aurait pas de fleurs mais des couteaux, du poulet, du tabac, de l'argent et des assiettes qu'on mettrait dans sa tombe et par dessus. On n'oublierait pas les brèdes et quelques semences. Le cortège s'avancerait dans un fracas de rires et de chants assourdissants et improvisés, et non dans le silence glacé et hypocrite de la ville. On porterait la tenue la plus débraillée possible, car on porterait le corps de grand-mère en courant. Les vieux et les enfants resteraient au village car ils ne pourraient pas suivre la course des jeunes. Ces derniers boiraient de l'alcool et fumeraient du chanvre avant le départ. Sur le cercueil de grand-mère, on ferait asseoir ses arrière-petits-fils.

Grand-mère est morte au premier cocorico. Avant de mourir, un mois plus tôt, elle avait confié son testament, oral bien sûr, à

hemp before they took off. Grandmother's great-grandsons were to be seated on her coffin.[9]

Grandmother died at the cock's first crowing. A month before she died, she had entrusted her last will and testament, orally of course, to Monsieur Soja. Soja is the village chief, its most senior citizen and sorcerer at the same time; it is his grave task to find a woman for every stranger who spends the night in the village. Grandmother had given him the responsibility of putting her little radio in her tomb, when the time came. That way, she'd be able to listen to music.

And so, all grandmother's wealth was to go to my brother, Monsieur Rakoto. Her *falafa* house, five or six acres of land, about twenty head of cattle, about fifty heads of fowl, the kitchen utensils. . . . But she had not forgotten me. She told everybody that the best part of her inheritance was reserved for me. That it would be a very big surprise for me, her favorite grandson.

The big surprise lay in an enormous crate that measured almost a cubic meter. I could not take possession of it until after the burial.

So, afterwards, I followed Monsieur Soja to open the heavy crate. Inside the box was every last one of the now-dead batteries grandmother had used for her radio.

Grandmother didn't like solitude. That is why she used to sell pistachios in the market. That is why she used to go to the wash house to do her laundry. At night, it was the radio that kept her company. Without batteries, "those magic and talkative stones that sing," she would have felt quite lonely. And so she bequeathed me that which was most dear to her heart: the dead batteries she had jealously hoarded throughout her widowhood.

With her, a whole world has disappeared. From time to time, I will buy some new batteries to put on grandmother's tomb.

Grandmother died at the cock's first crowing.

monsieur Soja. Soja, c'est le chef du village, doyen et sorcier à la fois, celui à qui incombe le lourd devoir de trouver une femme à tout étranger qui passe la nuit au village. Grand-mère a chargé Soja, le moment venu, de mettre sa petite radio dans sa tombe. Comme cela, elle pourrait écouter de la musique.

Ainsi, toute la richesse de grand-mère irait à mon frère, monsieur Rakoto. Sa maison en falafa, deux ou trois hectares de terrain, une vingtaine de têtes de bétail, une cinquantaine de volailles, les ustensiles de cuisine. . . Mais elle ne m'avait pas oublié. Elle a dit à tout le monde qu'elle me réservait la meilleure part de l'héritage. Que ce serait une très grande surprise pour moi, son petit-fils préféré.

La grande surprise se trouvait dans une énorme caisse de presque un mètre cube. Je ne pourrais en prendre possession qu'après l'enterrement.

Après, je suivis donc monsieur Soja pour ouvrir la lourde caisse. Dans la boîte, il y avait toutes les piles usagées que grand-mère avait utilisées pour sa radio.

Grand-mère n'aimait pas la solitude. C'est pourquoi elle vendait des pistaches au marché. C'est pourquoi elle allait au lavoir du quartier pour faire sa lessive. La nuit, c'était la radio qui lui tenait compagnie. Sans piles, "ces pierres magiques et bavardes qui chantent", elle se serait trouvée seule. Aussi me léguait-elle ce qui lui tenait le plus à coeur: les piles usées et jalousement collectionnées durant son veuvage.

Avec elle, c'est un monde qui a disparu. De temps en temps, j'achèterai des piles neuves que je porterai sur la tombe de grand-mère.

Grand-mère est morte au premier cocorico.

Serge Henri Rodin

Born in 1949, Serge Henri Rodin teaches literature at the University of Antananarivo. An author-composer of songs in both Malagasy and French, he has also written two short stories: Chien de soleil *(Wretched sun), published in* Recherches et Cultures *5, 1990, and whose translation is reproduced below, as well as* La rédemption de l'hérésiarque *(The heresiarch's redemption, yet unpublished). Serge Rodin is director of the Madagascar branch of* Grand Océan, *the most important francophone literary journal in the Indian Ocean.*

Wretched Sun

In a hostile and real universe,
very real and quite authentic, the last
plunderers, an episode of the chaotic
life of a City defector,
integrated into a horde.

When purple gladioli, the only flowers in this place and in this time, were torn to shreds on the robe of *He-who-lowers-not-his-eyes, Father-of-little-boy*[1] and he came rushing down the south side among the rocky outgrowths of the *Hill-with-holes.* The detonations had stopped the implacable course of the sun. *He-who-lowers-not-his-eyes* rose up—ephemeral sacred pheasant—into space only to find himself hunched up back in the shade, inside an excavation that had been awaiting him there for twenty-eight years.

What his companion heard was a laugh that came from the most profound depths of his being, punctuated by rumblings. This laugh commanded *Father-of-little-boy* to flee, far away from the herd that flouted them down below, too far for him and too late, from now on.

Translated from the French by Marjolijn de Jager

Serge Henri Rodin

Né en 1949, Serge Henri Rodin est professeur de littérature à l'Université d'Antananarivo. Auteur-compositeur de chansons en malgache et en français, il a aussi écrit deux nouvelles: La rédemption de l'hérésiarque *(encore inédite) et* Chien de soleil *(parue dans* Recherches et Cultures *5, 1990). Cette dernière nouvelle est reproduite ci-dessous. Serge Rodin est responsable de l'antenne Madagascar de* Grand Océan, *l'importante revue francophone de l'Océan Indien.*

Chien de soleil

> Dans un univers hostile et réel,
> très réel et authentique, les derniers
> prédateurs, un épisode de la vie
> chaotique d'un transfuge de la Ville,
> intégré dans une horde.

Quand, seules fleurs en ces lieux et en ces temps, des glaïeuls pourpres se déchirèrent sur la toge de *Celui-qui-ne-baisse-pas-les-yeux*, *Père-du-petit-garçon* et lui dévalaient le versant sud, parmi les excroissances rocheuses, de la *Colline-trouée*. Les détonations avaient arrêté la course implacable du soleil. *Celui-qui-ne-baisse-pas-les-yeux* s'éleva—éphemère faisan sacré—dans l'espace pour se retrouver, ramassé, à l'ombre, dans une excavation qui l'attendait là depuis vingt-huit ans.

C'était un rire venu du fin fond de l'être que son compagnon entendit, entrecoupé de gargouillis. Ce rire ordonna à *Père-du-petit-garçon* de s'enfuir loin du troupeau qui les narguait en bas, là-bas, trop loin pour lui et trop tard désormais.

Ce fut le grondement de plus en plus proche de brodequins qui libéra *Père-du-petit-garçon* du sortilège de l'agonie et le décida à se faufiler entre les remparts de pierre. Tel un enfant ayant grandi derrière les zébus, il avait acquis un rythme

What delivered *Father-of-little-boy* from the bewitchment of the death throes and made him decide to slither through the ramparts of stone was the rumble of the boots[2] that came closer and closer. Like a child raised to follow zebus, he had acquired an unusual rhythm; the ochre soil, this wretched sun, and especially fear had their part in it. And the herd. Yes, the herd? Life first, life that would be better and better protected as the sun fled; nothing had whistled past his ears and no brightness had burned his eyes.

Bent over in three, his right hand above his eyes, *Old-one-who-knew* was looking for the rising of some dust. His eyes were no more than two slits when he noticed—but how was this possible coming from that impossible side—the frail outline of *Father-of-little-boy*, breaking through the evening grey with his red pagne.[3] Painfully feeling his age, *Old-one-who-knew* stood up to wail his grief.

Very quickly, the villagers gathered on the small hillock that served as a lookout. His eyes averted, *Father-of-little-boy* recounted the loss of the herd. The saliva spat between his leather soles cruelly reminded him of his weakness as an elder of the City; *Blue-eyes*[4] was insulting him and the women—even the one whom he so desired since his inclusion in the group—were hissing the expression of their scorn between their teeth. It was nothing to be proud of—being a survivor without any booty.

The village? but was it really a village? hidden at the bottom of a seasonal waterfall, about ten shelters—nothing that deserved the word hut—as many families, roughly thirty people in all. *He-who-lowers-not-his-eyes* had demarcated its site and the paths of withdrawal. The village would move away, increase or decrease in numbers according to its expeditions and the threats it suffered. Four rifles, from the military rifle to the modified blunderbuss, were theirs, and *Blue-eyes* had the prerogative of guarding and distributing them. But for this last and

inhabituel; la terre ocre, ce chien de soleil et surtout la peur y étaient pour quelque chose. Et le troupeau. Oui le troupeau? La vie d'abord, la vie qui serait de plus en plus préservée avec la fuite du soleil; rien n'avait sifflé à ses oreilles et aucun éclat n'avait brûlé ses yeux.

Plié en trois, la main droite au dessus des yeux, *Vieillard-qui-savait* guettait quelque soulèvement de poussière. Ses yeux ne furent plus que deux traits quand il aperçut—mais du côté impossible—rompant le gris du soir avec son pagne rouge, la frêle silhouette de *Père-du-petit-garçon.* Ressentant durement son âge, *Vieillard-qui-savait* se releva pour crier sa douleur.

Très vite, le village se retrouva sur la petite éminence qui servait de poste de guet. Le regard en fuite, *Père-du-petit-garçon* relata la perte du troupeau. Le crachat placé entre ses semelles de cuir lui rappela cruellement sa faiblesse d'ancien de la Ville; *Yeux-bleus* l'insultait et les femmes—même celle qu'il désirait depuis son intégration—lui sifflaient leur mépris entre leurs dents. Ce n'était pas une fierté d'être un survivant sans butin.

Le village? mais était-ce bien un village? caché au bas d'une cascade saisonnière, une dizaine d'abris—rien qui méritait le nom de case—autant de familles, soit une trentaine de personnes. *Celui-qui-ne-baisse-pas-les-yeux* en avait délimité l'emplacement et les voies de repli. Le village se déplaçait, se peuplait et se dépeuplait en fonction des expéditions et des menaces. Quatre fusils, de l'arme militaire au tromblon amélioré, dont la garde et la distribution étaient les prérogatives de *Yeux-bleus.* Mais pour cette dernière et catastrophique expédition, lances et frondes avaient été jugées suffisantes.

Chien de soleil.

La décision de lever le camp fut très rapide à prendre, la cascade endormie était trop proche de la présence des brodequins et les morts pouvaient parler, ressuscités par quelque sorcellerie citadine.

disastrous expedition, spears and slingshots had been deemed sufficient.

Wretched sun.

The decision to strike camp was made very rapidly, the dormant waterfall was too close to where the boots were present and the dead might speak, resuscitated by some urban witchcraft.

It was a horde caked with red earth, starved and silent, that halted three days later on the heights of *The-hill-of-fools.* Farther below, toward the West, there were a few hamlets and sustenance to be found. But for a while they would first need to be forgotten and assimilate with the peasants of this valley.

Wretched sun.

Three women and *Father-of-little-boy* were delegated to go down and barter: products from earlier looting in exchange for food. *Old-one-who-knew* had advised *Blue-eyes* against offering a rifle. And yet, a single one of those could bring them survival for as long as it would take to be forgotten.

They had never come so close to the rim. Here no one could have heard about them: only *Blue-eyes* and his legend might have challenged such a distance, but *Blue-eyes* and his people would be staying on the heights if the "clan" was to be accepted by the poor folks down below.

The women—moving hastily along—were refusing to talk with *Father-of-little-boy,* even though two of them were captives,[5] peasant women nobody would have thought capable of being integrated into a horde of desperate people. The elder of the City knew that if he were to fail, it would be the last "mission" before his exclusion from the "clan." He also recognized the fact that they tolerated him—despite his inabilities as a warrior—only because *Old-one-who-knew* protected him—something mysterious to all and especially to *Blue-eyes.* Perhaps he enjoyed the long evenings, once the sun was gone, spent in discussion with *Father-of-little-boy?* And then, of

Ce fut une horde rougie de terre, affamée et silencieuse, qui s'arrêta, trois jours après, sur les hauteurs de *La-colline-de-fous.* Plus bas vers l'Ouest, il y avait quelques hameaux et de quoi se sustenter. Mais il fallait se faire oublier un temps et composer avec les paysans de cette vallée.

Chien de soleil.

Trois femmes et *Père-du-petit-garçon* furent délégués pour aller y faire du troc: produits de pillages antérieurs contre de la nourriture. *Vieillard-qui-savait* avait déconseillé à *Yeux-bleus* de proposer un fusil. Pourtant l'échange d'un seul pouvait les faire survivre le temps nécessaire pour être oubliés.

Ils n'étaient jamais venus si près des rebords, ici personne ne pouvait avoir entendu parler d'eux: seuls *Yeux-bleus* et sa légende pouvaient défier autant d'espace, mais *Yeux-bleus* et les siens resteraient sur les hauteurs si le "clan" était accepté par les gueux d'en bas.

Les femmes—dans leur pas hâtif—refusaient de converser avec *Père-du-petit-garçon,* pourtant deux d'entre elles étaient des captives, des paysanes que personne n'aurait cru capables de s'intégrer à une horde de désespérés. L'ancien de la Ville savait que pour lui, ce serait la dernière "mission" avant l'exclusion du "clan", s'il échouait. Il reconnaissait aussi qu'il n'était encore toléré—malgré ses inaptitudes à être un vrai guerrier—qu'à cause de la protection—inexplicable pour tous et surtout pour *Yeux-bleus*—de *Vieillard-qui-savait.* Ce dernier appréciait-il, une fois le soleil disparu, les longues veillées que tous les deux passaient à discourir? Bien sûr, il y avait aussi le fait qu'ils étaient les seuls sans famille.

Chien de soleil.

Le groupe ne s'était pas aperçu que depuis qu'il avait atteint la vallée et s'était avancé vers le *Hameau-à-canne-à-sucre,* des enfants, cachés par les hautes herbes, l'avaient repéré puis précédé. L'alerte fut donnée et les hommes—des quatre hameaux

course, there was also the fact that they were the only ones without a family.

Wretched sun.

The group had not noticed that since they had reached the valley and moved toward the *Sugar-cane-hamlet*, they had been spotted by some children hidden by the high grass and these had gone ahead of them. The alert was given and the men—from the four neighboring settlements bringing together about fifty inhabitants—hurriedly came back from the fields.

These people, too, had come from other places and had settled here about thirty years before. Nothing had predisposed them to become resolute and unsociable peasants, but their almost-isolated comfort had transformed them. The children were raised to report on any intrusion and the adults had learned to defend themselves. Still, they weren't rich farmers and did not need to fear the famous bands of pillagers. Nevertheless, they knew that sooner or later these social outcasts, hunted as they were, would be pushed toward the lost valleys of the West and they had prepared themselves for this.

Wretched sun.

Three elders came forward toward the new arrivals and were able to conclude immediately, by their posture and the expression on the women's faces especially, that these were plunderers. *Father-of-little-boy* greeted them and decided that it was useless to get bogged down in niceties: these peasants knew what they were dealing with.

Father-of-little-boy spoke at length—mostly to reassure them—despite the men's faces that grew more and more closed. This speech went on longer than it should have; the elders spoke only to ask questions and finally to raise the bidding:[6] appalled, *Father-of-little-boy* understood that they wanted a rifle and ammunition in exchange for rice, corn, sugar, and a few chickens. He couldn't decide.

voisins qui rassemblaient une cinquantaine d'habitants—revinrent à la hâte des champs.

C'étaient aussi des gens venus d'ailleurs qui s'étaient installés là, il y avait de cela une trentaine d'années. Rien ne les avait prédisposés à devenir des paysans déterminés et farouches, mais leur prospérité quasi-isolée les avait transformés. Les enfants étaient éduqués à rendre compte de toute intrusion et les adultes avaient appris à se défendre. Toutefois ils n'étaient pas de gros éleveurs et n'avaient pas à craindre les celèbres bandes de rapineurs. Néanmoins, ils savaient que tôt ou tard, ces asociaux, traqués, seraient repoussés vers les vallées perdues de l'Ouest, et ils s'étaient préparés à cela.

Chien de soleil.

Trois anciens vinrent au devant des arrivants et tout de suite ils purent déduire, de l'allure et de la mine des femmes surtout, leur état de prédateurs. *Père-du-petit-garçon* salua et décida que c'était inutile de se perdre en circonlocutions: ces paysans savaient ce qu'ils étaient.

Père-du-petit-garçon parla longuement—pour rassurer surtout—malgré les visages de plus en plus fermés de ces hommes. Ces palabres durèrent plus qu'elles ne devaient durer; les vieux ne parlaient que pour poser des questions et finalement faire monter les enchères: *Père-du-petit-garçon,* atterré, sut qu'ils voulaient un fusil et des munitions contre du riz, du maïs, du sucre et quelques poulets. Il ne pouvait décider.

Une des femmes, celle qui était d'origine noble, commença à élever la voix. Pour elle, ces vieillards sans honneur, incapables de satisfaire une femme, avaient exagérément gonflé leur prétention rien que pour connaître l'état de leur "clan" et le nombre de leurs fusils. Elle fit taire *Père-du-petit-garçon* avec un rappel voilé de sa situation et menaça: le troc initial ou le pillage de nuit suivi de la destruction des maisons. Les trois paysans se

One of the women, the only one who came from noble stock, began to raise her voice. For her, these old men lacking in honor, unable to satisfy any woman, had grossly exaggerated their claims in order to find out what their "clan's" state really was and how many rifles they possessed. With a veiled reminder of his position, she silenced *Father-of-little-boy* and threatened them: it was to be the initial bargain or else they would come looting during the night to be followed by the destruction of the homes. The three peasants rose and advised the group to go and inquire among more sensible people.

Wretched sun.

With rage in his heart and an immense weariness in his legs, *Father-of-little-boy* took the path back, followed by the women, their lips twisted in rebuke. The climb seemed interminable to them and when they arrived on the heights of *The-hill-of-fools,* a make-shift camp had been set up close to a spring, or rather some re-emerging water, reduced to a thin thread found in a subsidence. The exchange suggested by the peasants was rejected with general disdain, but *Old-one-who-knew* advised moderation; the "clan" was in a pitiful state and the village of *Where-numerous-plantations-extend* was only a half day's walking away. *Blue-eyes* designated those warriors who were to carry the rifles and specified the strategy: the riflemen would go around the hamlets by the North and attack from the West; spearmen and those with the slingshots would fan out in the East. Some did not agree and a discussion ensued.

Wretched sun.

The first to die was *Old-one-who-knew.* His eyes strangely lost in space, he had hoisted himself out over the edge: the spear had pierced his right side but his warrior's cry had been heard one last time.

They had been surrounded. The ruthless peasants had split up around the rim and, from the overhang above the camp, they

levèrent et conseillèrent au groupe d'aller s'enquérir auprès de plus avisés.

Chien de soleil.

C'était avec la rage au coeur et une immense lassitude aux jambes que *Père-du-petit-garçon* reprit, suivi des femmes aux lèvres tordues d'imprécation, le chemin du retour. L'escalade leur parut interminable et quand ils arrivèrent sur les hauteurs de la *Colline-de-fous*, un camp de fortune avait été installé près d'une source, une resurgence plutôt, réduite à un mince filet, trouvée dans un affaissement. L'échange proposé par les paysans fut rejeté dans le mépris général, mais *Vieillard-qui-savait* conseilla la modération, le "clan" était en piteux état et le village de *Là-où-s'étendaient-de-nombreuses-plantations* n'était qu'à une demi-journée de marche. *Yeux-bleus* désigna les guerriers qui porteraient des fusils et précisa la stratégie: les fusiliers contourneraient les hameaux par le Nord et attaqueraient par l'Ouest; lanciers et frondeurs se déploieraient à l'Est. Mais certains n'étaient pas de cet avis et ils discutèrent.

Chien de soleil.

Le premier à mourir fut *Vieillard-qui-savait.* Les yeux étrangement perdus, il s'était hissé en dehors de l'affaissement: la lance lui avait transpercé le flanc droit mais son cri de guerrier s'était fait entendre une ultime fois.

Ils étaient cernés. Les paysans dénaturés s'étaient répartis autour de l'affaissement et, surplombant le camp, avaient attaqué sans sommation, sans fusil mais en nombre. La "délégation" avait été suivie et le retranchement repéré. La sécurité traditionnelle des hauteurs, le fait d'avoir affaire à des agriculteurs et l'épuisement avaient endormi la horde. Déjà trois hommes étaient à terre et les porteurs de fusil n'avaient pas encore pu riposter; le guerrier chargé de l'arme militaire, une pierre en plein visage, s'effondra sur le ruisselet. *Yeux-bleus* criait des ordres et

had attacked without any warning, without any rifles, but in large numbers. The "delegation" had been followed and their position spotted. The traditional safety of heights, the fact they were dealing with farmers, and their exhaustion had lessened the vigilance of the horde. Three men had already been slain and the riflemen had not yet been able to shoot back; the warrior with the military rifle collapsed into the rivulet, a stone right in the middle of his face. *Blue-eyes* was screaming orders and counterorders in the confusion and amidst the shrieking of the women and children.

Wretched sun.

What had to be attempted was to focus on a point easy to climb and to escape from there, abandoning everything that might slow down a rapid flight. *Blue-eyes* began the ascent, a spear in his hand: behind him a warrior was firing to give him cover. The assailants, bewildered by the truth of the rumors they had heard about *Blue-eyes,* the warrior come from elsewhere, retreated from this living legend and allowed him to make his get-away. The rest of the horde followed. *Father-of-little-boy* brought up the rear, rifle in hand; but he had not used it, not knowing how.

Wretched sun.

There were no more than twenty of them now, of whom only two were real warriors besides *Blue-eyes.* They pulled themselves up through craggy paths toward the *Great-bushy-hills,* higher up in the East. But the children were slowing down the flight, the women could no longer carry them since they had insisted on carrying the maximum in things, despite orders to the contrary. The others, those swamp slaves, had apparently not pursued them any further, but considering what those bastards were capable of, they would have to remain on guard without any let-up. They decided upon a resting point in a place from which they had a good view.

contrordres dans la confusion et les cris des femmes et des enfants.

Chien de soleil.

Il fallait tenter de se concentrer sur un point facile à remonter et de s'enfuir par là en abandonnant tout ce qui pourrait gêner une fuite rapide. *Yeux-bleus* ouvrit l'escalade, une lance à la main: derrière lui un guerrier tirait pour le couvrir. Les assaillants, stupéfaits par la véracité des ouï-dire sur *Yeux-bleus,* le guerrier venu d'ailleurs, reculèrent devant cette légende vivante et lui permirent de prendre pied. Le reste de la horde suivit. *Père-du-petit-garçon* fermait la file, l'arme militaire aux mains; mais il n'en avait pas usé, ne le sachant pas.

Chien de soleil.

Ils n'étaient plus qu'une vingtaine, dont seulement deux vrais guerriers en plus de *Yeux-bleus.* Ils se hissèrent, par des sentiers escarpés, vers les *Grandes-collines-aux-arbustes,* plus haut à l'Est. Mais les enfants retardaient la fuite, les femmes ne pouvaient plus s'en charger, ayant tenu à transporter le maximum d'objets malgré les ordres. Les autres, ces esclaves de marais, ne les avaient apparemment pas pourchassés, mais après ce dont ces excréments de chien étaient capables, il fallait être constamment sur le qui-vive. Une halte fut décidée en un lieu d'où le guet était aisé.

Chien de soleil.

Ils n'étaient plus rien. Des squelettes mangeurs de racines. Leurs enfants iraient-ils mendier dans les cités? La mort dans l'âme et la honte au visage, *Yeux-bleus* se résolut à appeler *Père-du-petit-garçon:* celui-ci n'avait-il pas l'habitude de converser avec *Vieillard-qui-savait?* Ils firent ensemble l'inventaire des possibilités de direction et d'action. *Père-du-petit-garçon* conclut qu'il ne leur restait que le Sud et, une fois franchie la *Rivière-noire,* l'Ouest. Ils chercheraient une petite vallée où s'établir, ils ne pouvaient plus survivre de rapines. *Yeux-bleus*

Wretched sun.

There was nothing left of them anymore. Skeletal eaters of roots. Would their children be begging in the cities? Death in his heart and shame on his face, *Blue-eyes* made up his mind to call *Father-of-little-boy.* Was he not accustomed to have conversations with *Old-one-who-knew?* Together they reviewed the possibilities of direction and of action. *Father-of-little-boy* came to the conclusion that the only places open to them now were the South and, once the *Black-river* was crossed, the West. They would look for a small valley in which to settle; they could no longer survive off looting. Curiously, *Blue-eyes* agreed; but one last expedition was called for—and to a rather important place—to take materials, food supplies, and seed.

Father-of-little-boy considered this a suicidal undertaking now that they had been spotted: boots and peasants teaming up would be merciless. They called the two warriors and the women to make a decision.

A hostile silence followed *Blue-eyes'* words. Settling down and working the soil, becoming submissive peasants, was unimaginable; perhaps the captive women and children would go South, but not the warriors, men and adolescents who had to keep their heads high. Two women declared themselves prepared to accompany the men.

Blue-eyes was about to be forced to prove himself as Father-of-the-clan when an adolescent came to warn them that the boots and peasants had joined together and were already on the plateau down below.

Wretched sun.

The images of the death of *He-who-lowers-not-his-eyes* paraded before *Father-of-little-boy*'s tear-filled eyes. If the officials were showing themselves in this manner, it meant that others were posted in ambush on the other side.

They all knew this was to be their last involvement as a

paradoxalement, en convint; mais une dernière expédition s'imposait—et sur un centre assez important—pour y prendre du matériel, des vivres et des semences.

Père-du-petit-garçon jugea cette entreprise suicidaire, ils étaient repérés maintenant: brodequins et paysans organisés seraient impitoyables. Ils appelèrent les deux guerriers et les femmes pour décider.

Un silence hostile succéda aux paroles de *Yeux-bleus;* s'établir et travailler la terre, devenir des paysans soumis étaient inconcevables: femmes captives et enfants iraient peut-être vers le Sud mais pas les guerriers—hommes et adolescents—eux devaient garder la tête haute; deux femmes se déclaraient prêtes à accompagner les hommes.

Yeux-bleus allait devoir éprouver sa qualité de Père-du-clan quand un adolescent vint les prévenir que les brodequins et les paysans s'étaient rejoints et qu'ils étaient déjà sur le plateau, en contrebas.

Chien de soleil.

Les images de la mort de *Celui-qui-ne-baisse-pas-les-yeux* défilèrent devant les yeux brouillés de larmes de *Père-du-petit-garçon.* Si les légalistes se montraient ainsi, c'était que d'autres s'étaient alors postés en embuscade de l'autre côté.

Tous savaient que ce serait leur dernier engagement comme "clan" car il fallait se disperser: c'était leur seule issue de survie. *Yeux-bleus*—étant le plus recherché—irait avec les siens vers l'Est, droit sur le piège, et entraînerait sûrement beaucoup de poursuivants derrière son groupe; chaque vrai guerrier accompagné des âgés choisirait une sortie Nord ou Ouest; et *Père-du-petit-garçon* descendrait vers le Sud avec les plus jeunes de la horde. Aucun ne se faisait d'illusion, seuls les moins maudits du groupe du Sud avaient une petite chance.

Tout cela se passa dans la *Région-des-callosités-blanches* par ce qu'il eût été possible de prendre pour une belle journée de saison

"clan," for they would have to disperse: it was their only way out for survival. *Blue-eyes*—being the most wanted one—would go with his people toward the East, straight to the trap, and his group was sure to be pursued by a large number; each true warrior, accompanied by the older ones, would choose an exit North or West; and *Father-of-little-boy* would descend toward the South with the youngest ones of the horde. No one had any illusions—only the least cursed of the southern group had the tiniest chance.

All this happened in the *Region-of-white-calluses* on what might have been taken for a lovely day in the dry season, so lovely that the sun made itself more brilliant, more deadly, even stopping the wind, had there not been these lightning flashes, reflected by the echo, that scattered fleeting purple gladioli on the children of the night. The Earth received them in her breast.

Much, much later, in a place unknown to those of the heights and those of the valleys, more deserted than the *Region-of-cut-rocks,* a small man with strange ways, who now had taken the name *Oldest-one-who-knew,* was patiently answering the questions of an adolescent: no, he would have to wait to be quite hardened before he could leave again; yes, true warriors ought not to be weak, they would live off booty; yes, they would not become old for senility was the punishment for those who settled down; no, for them God had died a long time ago, but he had left this wretched sun; for the others, too, besides.

(Madagascar: Recherches et Cultures
5, "Poésie et Nouvelle," 1990)

sèche, si belle que le soleil se fit plus brillant, plus mortel, arrêtant même le vent, s'il n'y avait eu ces fulgurations, répercutées par l'écho, qui semèrent d'éphémères glaïeuls pourpres sur les enfants de la nuit. La Terre les reçut en son sein.

Longtemps après et dans un lieu ignoré à la fois de ceux des hauteurs et de ceux des vallées, plus désert que la *Région-des-rochers-coupés,* un petit homme aux étranges manières, qui avait pris désormais le nom de *Aîné-qui-savait,* répondait sans impatience aux questions d'un adolescent: non, il fallait attendre d'être bien aguerri pour repartir; oui, les vrais guerriers ne devaient pas s'aveulir, ils vivaient de butin; oui, ils ne restaient pas vieux car la sénilité était la punition de ceux qui s'établissaient; non, pour eux, Dieu était mort depuis longtemps, mais il avait laissé ce chien de soleil; pour les autres aussi d'ailleurs.

(Madagascar: Recherches et Cultures *n° spécial "Poésie et Nouvelle" n° 5, 1990)*

Bao Ralambo

Bao Ralambo is the pseudonym of Stangeline Ralambomanana. Born in 1951, Ralambo is a professor of Spanish at the University of Antananarivo. She is the author of yet unpublished religious hymns and poetry in Malagasy and French. Her main production is in the short story genre: Un rêve éveillé *(Dreaming wide awake),* Une fleur pourpre *(Purple flower),* Blastomycose *(Blastomycosis), and* Le miroir du président *(The president's mirror), whose translation is reproduced below. She has also written a series of autobiographical stories.*

The President's Mirror

Even within the compound of his residence, Monsieur le Président never moved about without his retinue. His entourage was broken up into endless daily upheavals required by his slightest motions: an inspection of his domain, his passing from one wing of the palace to the other, or an ordinary walk. Under any circumstances, it was impossible to see Monsieur le Président, enclosed as he was in the center of the moving cage with its thick bars of flesh and blood. Official trips were most often made by air, or by road when it was truly impossible to travel otherwise. In this case, the security service would deploy the personal security guard and the regular security guard, and would make sure to cordon off each one of Monsieur le Président's triple itineraries; the one he would actually use as well as two others, created merely as a diversion. Depending upon his mood and his premonitions, Monsieur le Président would choose the route to be used at the last minute, more often than not when he was already under way.

One day, something unusual occurred. Monsieur le Président asked to be replaced in the interminably long and armored

---

Translated from the French by Marjolijn de Jager

Bao Ralambo

Bao Ralambo est le nom de plume de Stangeline Ralambomanana. Née en 1951, Bao Ralambo est professeur d'espagnol à l'Université d'Antananarivo. Elle est l'auteur d'hymnes religieux en malgache et en français, et de poèmes encore inédits. Sa production littéraire principale est la nouvelle: Un rêve éveillé, Une fleur pourpre, Blastomycose, *et* Le miroir du président, *qui est reproduite ci-dessous. Enfin, elle a écrit une série de récits autobiographiques.*

Le miroir du président

Même dans l'enceinte de sa résidence, Monsieur le Président ne se déplaçait jamais sans escorte. Son entourage était rompu aux remue-ménage multiquotidiens qu'exigeait le moindre mouvement, inspection du domaine, passage d'une aile du palais à l'autre, ou banale promenade. Il était en toute circonstance impossible d'apercevoir Monsieur le Président, enclos au centre d'une cage mouvante aux épais barreaux de chair et de sang. Les déplacements officiels se faisaient le plus souvent par la voie des airs et, quand il ne pouvait vraiment pas en être autrement, par route. Dans ce dernier cas, le service de sécurité déployait la garde rapprochée, la semi-rapprochée et veillait à boucler le triple itinéraire de Monsieur le Président, celui qu'il prendrait et les autres, pour faire diversion. Selon son humeur et ses pressentiments, Monsieur le Président choisissait au dernier moment, le plus souvent en cours de route, le trajet qu'il emprunterait.

Un jour, quelque chose d'insolite arriva. Monsieur le Président demanda à être remplacé par le chef de sa sécurité personnelle dans l'interminable limousine blindée et choisit d'enfourcher l'une des grosses machines censées le précéder. Le chef de la garde lui énuméra tous les dangers encourus; l'intendant du palais tenta de le retenir; la vieille nourrice, au comble de

limousine by the chief of his personal security guard while he chose to mount one of the huge motorcycles intended to precede him. The security chief enumerated all the dangers he would run; the palace steward tried to stop him; the old nurse, in a state of complete panic, called him "my little pet;" but in vain. Monsieur le Président had already slipped into one of the uniforms of his motorcycle escort. The convoy moved off and made a flawless round in the courtyard of honor before it ventured out at a rather undignified speed under the prompting of the lead motorcyclist. Those people who stopped automatically at the sound of the siren responded perfunctorily and with some surprise to the unusual handwaving of Monsieur le Président. More often than not, they noticed movements of a fat cigar with its glowing tip that reminded them of their children now dead for many years and of the only way in which they could protect those they still had. Another day, Monsieur le Président got it into his head to follow his own vehicle while perched on an armored car behind the submachine gun meant to thwart attempts from all sides. Yet another time, two caravans left the presidential palace at the same time and no one knew where Monsieur le Président was. He had, in fact, decided to stay at home to sit back and laugh at all his puppets as he suckled his eternal cigar. He was pleasantly remembering the long evenings of hide-and-seek and cops-and-robbers that gave life to his childhood village.

One sleepless night when he felt adrift, Monsieur le Président summoned a few members of his cabinet to play as many games of cards as it would take until sleep would tear him away from the all-too-familiar tedium of his responsibilities. Upon his arrival, one of these coerced guests recounted that he had just met a poor wretch walking in the street who had become transfixed by the headlights of his car. He had stopped, thinking it was another one of Monsieur le Président's practical jokes.

l'affolement, l'appela "mon petit loup", mais en vain. Monsieur le Président avait déjà enfilé un uniforme des motards de son escorte. Le convoi s'ébranla et fit un tour impeccable dans la cour d'honneur avant de se lancer à une allure bien peu imposante, sous l'impulsion du motard de tête. Les gens qui s'arrêtaient par réflexe au son de la sirène répondaient, machinalement et quelque peu étonnés, aux inhabituelles salutations de la main de Monsieur le Président. Le plus souvent, ils apercevaient les signaux d'un gros cigare à la pointe incandescente qui leur rappelait leurs enfants morts voilà bien des années et le seul moyen de garder ceux qui leur restaient. Un autre jour, Monsieur le Président se mit en tête de suivre sa propre voiture, perché sur un blindé léger et derrière la mitraillette censée dissuader les tentations de tous bords. Un autre, encore, deux caravanes quittèrent simultanément la résidence et personne ne sut où était Monsieur le Président. En fait, il avait choisi de rester chez lui à se gausser de toutes ses marionnettes tout en tétant son éternel cigare. Il se rappelait agréablement les longues soirées de cache-cache et de "police-voleurs" qui peuplaient le village de son enfance.

Par une nuit d'insomnie et de dérive, Monsieur le Président convoqua quelques membres de son cabinet pour autant de parties de cartes qu'il faudrait jusqu'à ce que le sommeil vînt l'arracher au familier ennui de sa charge. L'un de ces invités forcés raconta en arrivant qu'il venait de croiser sur la route un pauvre hère à pied que les phares de sa voiture avaient hébété. Il s'était arrêté, croyant en une dernière facétie de Monsieur le Président. Seul le regard clair et calme du gueux l'assura qu'il se trompait. Le Président joua mal, de plus en plus mal, et ses partenaires ne surent plus comment tricher pour perdre! A l'aube, le Président lança les cartes qu'il avait en mains, renversa la table et cria qu'il voulait cet homme devant lui avant le lever du jour. Un commando armé de torches et d'armes blanches écuma sur le champ les villages environnants ainsi que la route qui

Only the clear and calm stare of the beggar assured him that he was wrong. The President played badly, worse and worse as the evening wore on, and his partners ran out of ways to cheat so they would lose! Toward dawn, the President threw down his cards, turned the table upside down and screamed that he wanted that man brought to him before sunrise. Commandos armed with torches and bladed weapons immediately began scouring the surrounding villages as well as the road that led to the capital. They entered every hut, shoved women and children aside, and with their torches they blinded the terrified faces of the men who were transferred from one nightmare into the other. By five o'clock they had returned and rushed to get back underneath their khaki covers until the sound of the bugle at half past.

The man said nothing, didn't even try to justify himself, which would have been the normal reaction of a normal citizen. All he did was wrap himself more tightly in the filthy cover, the color of misery, he used as a *lamba.*[1] He didn't seem to notice the bad and ostentatious taste in which the dead halls he crossed were drowning. He was equally impervious to the excess of light flooding the mass of plastered concrete. Nor did he feel the thick Persian carpets on which his feet left never-ending marks of the red earth which could no longer nourish him.[2] Standing before Monsieur le Président, he showed no emotion whatsoever, no surprise. His gaze remained clear and calm as if he had been waiting for this moment since the beginning of time. After having encircled the wretch with a long, uncertain look, Monsieur le Président patted his forehead and temples with a small immaculate handkerchief before he sat down heavily in his easy chair, distraught . . .

"Who are you?"

"The Rambler. I have seen you somewhere before . . ."

"Of course! . . . Where do you come from?"

menait à la capitale. Ils réveillèrent toutes les chaumières, bousculant femmes et enfants, aveuglant de leurs torches les visages effrayés des hommes qui passaient d'un cauchemar à un autre. A cinq heures, ils furent de retour et s'empressèrent de rejoindre leurs couvertures kaki jusqu'au clairon de la demie.

L'homme ne dit rien, ne chercha même pas à se justifier, ce qui aurait été la réaction normale d'un citoyen normal. Il s'enroula juste un peu plus dans l'immonde couverture couleur de misère qui lui servait de lamba. Il ne semblait pas s'apercevoir du mauvais goût tapageur qui noyait l'horrible suite de salles mortes qu'il traversait. Il était tout aussi hermétique à l'excès de lumière qui inondait tout cet amas de béton plâtré. Il ne sentait pas non plus les moelleux tapis persans sur lesquels ses pieds appliquaient jusqu'à n'en plus pouvoir le sceau de la terre rouge qui ne le nourrissait plus. Arrivé en face de Monsieur le Président, il ne montra aucune émotion, aucune surprise. Son regard restait clair et calme, comme s'il attendait ce moment depuis l'éternité des temps. Après avoir enveloppé le misérable d'un long regard incertain, Monsieur le Président se tamponna le front et les tempes avec un petit mouchoir immaculé avant de prendre place pesamment dans son fauteuil, effondré. . .

— Qui es-tu?

— Le Filandreux. Je t'ai déjà vu quelque part. . .

— Bien sûr!. . . D'où viens-tu?

— Du village du mépris. Je t'ai déjà vu mais je n'arrive pas à me souvenir où. . .

— Dans les journaux, à la télévision, sur une affiche. . . As-tu une famille?

— Non. . . Non, je ne crois pas. Je ne sais pas lire et la ville n'est pas mon domaine. Mais où. . .

— Pourquoi ton village a-t-il un nom si abject?

— Ce n'est pas son nom, mais de là viennent tous ceux qui sont appelés à être honnis. Je te connais. . .

"From the village of contempt. I have seen you before but I can't recall where . . ."

"In the papers, on television, on a poster . . . Do you have a family?"

"No. . . . No, I don't think so. I don't know how to read and the city isn't my area. But where . . ."

"Why does your village have such a despicable name?"

"That's not what it's called,[3] but all those called upon to be execrated come from there. I know you . . ."

"Of course! . . . So then what is the real name of your village?"

"Nobody has even tried to remember that, it's also the village of forgetfulness. . . . But you, your face looks familiar to me . . ."

"Of course! . . . Where did they stop you?"

"On the road. Why do you constantly repeat 'of course,' 'of course'?"

"You know me because I am the President. What were you doing on the road at such an ungodly hour?"

"What's that mean 'ungodly'? . . . The President of what? Of the village assembly? You're a big liar, that isn't you, that's my neighbor's brother-in-law. And yet, I do know you . . ."

"Of course! I'm telling you, because I am the President. Not only of your village's assembly, but of all the assemblies in the country. What do you have to say to that?"

"That's impossible since there is one for every community. That I do know, at least. . . . You're lying again, and that's also why you say 'of course' so well!"

"I don't see the connection, but I can assure you that I am the President, Monsieur le Président!"

"Monsieur le . . ."

"Yes!"

"The one who . . ."

"Yes!"

— Bien sûr!. . . Alors, quel est le vrai nom de ton village?

— Personne n'a cherché à se le rappeler, c'est aussi le village de l'oubli. . . Mais toi, ton visage m'est familier. . .

— Bien sûr!. . . Où t'a-t-on arrêté?

— Sur la route. Pourquoi répètes sans cesse "bien sûr", "bien sûr"?

— Tu me connais parce que je suis le Président. Que faisais-tu sur la route à une heure aussi indue?

— C'est quoi "indue"?. . . Le Président de quoi? De l'assemblée villageoise? T'es un gros menteur, ce n'est pas toi, c'est le beau-frère de ma voisine. Je te connais pourtant. . .

— Bien sûr! Puisque je te dis que je suis le Président. Pas de l'assemblée de ton village seulement, mais de toutes les assemblées du pays. Qu'est-ce que tu dis de ça?

— C'est impossible puisqu'il y en a un par communauté. Ça au moins, je le sais. . . Tu mens encore, et c'est d'ailleurs pour ça que tu sais si bien dire "bien sûr"!

— Je ne vois pas le rapport, mais je puis t'assurer que je suis le Président, Monsieur le Président!

— Monsieur le. . .

— Oui!

— Celui qui. . .

— Oui!

— Le. . .

— Oui!

— Ah!

Un long silence s'établit. Monsieur le Président récupéra un peu de son aplomb et réussit même à sourire dans la contemplation du visage stupide et bouche bée qui lui faisait face. De satisfait, le sourire devint machiavélique. . .

— Tu es sûr. . .

— Mais oui!

— Et ici alors, c'est. . .

"The . . ."

"Yes!"

"Ah!"

A long silence followed. Monsieur le Président regained some of his poise and even managed a smile as he contemplated the stupid and open-mouthed face in front of him. The smile went from a satisfied one to a Machiavellian one . . .

"Are you sure . . ."

"Yes, naturally!"

"And this then is . . ."

"Yes!"

"But I thought you didn't exist!"

"How so, not exist? Ever since you've been here, you haven't stopped telling me that you know me, that you've seen me before, and now suddenly I shouldn't exist?"

"You do, sure . . . but Monsieur le Président . . . I thought that was an invention of all those who suck us dry, who empty us of anything of substance just to keep passing the buck and . . . anyway, I thought that you were nothing but an illusion, a hoax, just like the State itself. . . ."

"But the State exists and so do I!"

Monsieur le Président slapped himself on the chest with zeal.

"But can you show me the State? They forbid us to occupy land under the pretext that it belongs to the State. As far as I know, the State has never come to clear the undergrowth, to work the soil, to sow, to hoe, to water, in short to claim its rights by killing itself on the land for the rest of its life! So, since they talk about you in the same way that they talk about the State, how do you want me to believe in your existence?"

"You see me right here! You can even touch me! I exist and I am what I told you I am!"

"That's fine with me . . . but I have to say, I never would have believed it! . . . and . . . what am I doing here?"

— Oui!

— Mais je croyais que tu n'existais pas!

— Comment ça je n'existe pas? Depuis que tu es là, tu n'arrêtes pas de me dire que tu me connais, que tu m'as déjà vu, et maintenant je n'existerais pas?

— Toi si. . . mais Monsieur le Président. . . je croyais que c'était une invention de tous ces suceurs de moelle qui nous vident de toute substance pour se renvoyer la balle et. . . Ben, je croyais que, tout comme l'Etat, tu n'étais qu'un leurre, une imposture. . .

— Mais l'Etat existe, et j'existe aussi, moi!

Monsieur le Président se frappait la poitrine avec véhémence.

— Mais l'Etat, tu peux me le montrer? On nous interdit d'occuper des terres sous prétexte qu'elles appartiennent à l'Etat. L'Etat n'est jamais venu débroussailler, labourer, semer, sarcler, arroser, bref, faire valoir ses droits en s'éreintant sur la terre toute une vie que je sache!. . . Alors, comme on parle de toi comme on parle de l'Etat, comment veux-tu que je croie en ton existence?

— Moi, tu me vois, moi! Tu peux même me toucher! J'existe et je suis ce que je t'ai dit!

— Je veux bien. . . mais enfin, je ne l'aurais jamais cru!. . . et. . . qu'est-ce que je fais ici?

— Je t'ai fait venir.

— Donc, tu me connais aussi! J'avais raison. . .

— Si tu veux.

— Et c'était où?

— Peu importe. L'essentiel, c'est ce que nous allons faire ensemble.

— Parce que. . .

— Oui!

— Toi et. . .

"I had you brought here."

"So you know me too! I was right . . ."

"If you want."

"And where was that?"

"Doesn't matter. What matters is what we are going to be doing together."

"Because . . ."

"Yes!"

"You and . . ."

"Yes!"

"Well, I must be really dreaming this!"

The Rambler moved the palm of his right hand across his face with short taps, as one might sprinkle water over oneself to wake up. Slowly, he moved forward toward Monsieur le Président, reached out one hand to touch him and pulled it right back as if from a burning fire.

Monsieur le Président dismissed his people. After a short moment of hesitation, he made the same sign to the four bodyguards who watched over him constantly when he was outside of his private quarters.

"What was your name again?"

"The Rambler. What do you want from me?"

"Well now, Rambler, I am going to let you in on a secret that will ensure your happiness."

"Happiness doesn't exist and I sure don't want any part of a secret!"

"But I am telling you that this secret will ensure your happiness . . . that's pretty clear, isn't it? Do I look like I'm lying?"

"Look like, look like . . . what do I know?"

"Trust me and you will be the happiest of men!"

"I see, another trap! That's how they talk, all those bloodsuckers! 'Trust us and you'll be happy!' Words . . . yes, words that match nothing other than our bottomless wretchedness

— Oui!

— Ben je crois que je nage en plein rêve, moi!

Le Filandreux se passa la paume de la main droite à petits coups rapides sur le visage, comme on s'aspergerait à l'eau pour se réveiller. Lentement, il s'avança vers Monsieur le Président, tendit une main pour le toucher et la retira aussitôt, comme d'un feu brûlant.

Monsieur le Président congédia ses gens. Après une brève hésitation, il fit le même signe aux quatre gardes du corps qui veillaient constamment sur sa personne au-delà de ses appartements privés.

— Quel est ton nom déjà?

— Le Filandreux. Qu'est-ce que tu me veux?

— Eh bien, le Filandreux, je vais te révéler un secret qui fera ton bonheur.

— Le bonheur, ça n'existe pas et je ne veux surtout pas d'un secret!

— Mais puisque je te dis que ce secret fera ton bonheur. . . c'est clair, non? Ai-je l'air de mentir?

— L'air, l'air. . . Qu'en sais-je, moi?

— Fais-moi confiance et tu seras le plus heureux des hommes!

— Je vois, c'est un piège encore! C'est comme ça qu'ils parlent, les suceurs de moelle! "Faites-nous confiance et vous serez heureux"! Des mots. . . oui, des mots qui ne correspondent qu'à notre misère sans fond et à leur enflure sans borne! Et pourquoi tu me rendrais heureux? Pourquoi, hein?

— Mais parce que toi aussi, tu m'apporteras quelque chose en échange!

— Ah, je vois. . . intéressé, hein?. . . Remarque, je préfère ce langage. Alors, qu'est-ce que tu veux?

— Voilà! Je vais te dire pourquoi tu te creuses la cervelle pour savoir où l'on s'est vu. . . En fait, on ne se connaît pas, mais tu es mon sosie.

and their own infinite boastfulness! And why would you make me happy? Tell me that, eh, why?"

"Because you, too, you'll bring me something in return!"

"Ah, I see . . . self-interest, eh? . . . Mind you, I certainly like that language better. So, what do you want?"

"There! I'm going to tell you why you're racking your brain trying to figure out where we have seen each other. . . . In fact, we don't know each other, but you are my double."

"What exactly is that, a 'double'"? Besides, either we know each other or we don't know each other, but it cannot be both at the same time!"

"Calm down! A double is a person who looks exactly like another one. And so, you look like me: you have the same features as I do and the same contour, too, which won't hurt matters any!"

"What is all this? I look like you, I look like you, we aren't brothers as far as I know!"

"No, of course not! These are whims of nature: two people who don't know each other at all but who resemble each other more than two brothers do, what am I saying, more than twins do! Do you realize what we can do with that?"

"No, and I don't want to know! And besides, why is it that I look like you and not you who look like me? That makes no sense!"

"Of course it does, of course it does . . . I am Monsieur le Président. People look like me; I don't look like people, not me!"

"Ah!"

"Of course, that's the way things are, and people too . . ."

"And who exactly arranges it like that, 'the way things and people' are?"

"Life . . . destiny . . . and I do, don't forget that!"

"I don't understand anything of what you're saying. . . . You talk and you talk, but none of this tells me what it is you want from me!"

— C'est quoi "un sosie"? Et puis ou l'on se connaît, ou l'on ne se connaît pas, mais ça ne peut pas être les deux à la fois!

— Calme-toi! Un sosie, c'est une personne qui ressemble à une autre. Ainsi, toi, tu me ressembles: tu as les mêmes traits que moi et la même silhouette aussi, ce qui n'est pas pour gâter les choses!

— Qu'est-ce que c'est que cette histoire? Je te ressemble, je te ressemble, on n'est pas frères que je sache!

— Mais non, bien sûr! Ce sont des farces de la nature: deux personnes qui s'ignorent complètement se ressemblent plus que deux frères, que dis-je, que des jumeaux! Tu te rends compte de tout ce qu'on peut faire avec ça?

— Non, et je ne veux pas le savoir! Et puis, pourquoi c'est moi qui te ressemblerais et non toi qui me ressemblerais? Il n'y a pas de raison!

— Mais si, mais si. . . Moi, je suis Monsieur le Président. "On" me ressemble; "je" ne ressemble pas, moi!

— Ah!

— Eh oui, c'est l'ordre des choses et des êtres. . .

— Et qui arrange "l'ordre des choses et des êtres" comme ça?

— C'est la vie. . . le destin. . . et moi, n'oublie pas!

— Je ne comprends rien à rien. . . Tu parles, tu parles, mais tout ça ne me dit pas ce que tu veux de moi!

— J'y arrive, le Filandreux, j'y arrive! A partir de ce jour, tu vivras au Palais avec moi. Fini le vagabondage, finie la misère, fini le ventre creux, finies les loques, fini tout cela! Tu vas avoir l'existence d'un roi! Tu auras juste à prendre ma place quand il m'en viendra l'envie. Avoue que c'est le Pérou que je te propose là!

— C'est quoi le Pérou? C'est que tu m'inquiètes, toi! Tu dis des mots incompréhensibles, tu me bouscules et puis tu veux que je te remplace je ne sais où. Mais je ne veux remplacer personne, moi! Jamais!

"I'm getting to that, Rambler, I'm getting to that! From this day onward, you will live in the Palace with me. Your wandering days are over, your suffering is over, your hollow stomach is over, your tattered rags, it's all over with! You're going to live like a king! All you'll have to do is take my place when I feel like it. You have to admit I'm proposing an Eldorado to you here!"

"What's that, Eldorado? You really worry me! You speak incomprehensible words, you push me around, and then you want me to replace you I don't even know where. But me, I don't want to replace anybody! Never!"

"Of course you do, of course you do. . . . In any case, you don't have the choice any longer. Either you accept or I'll have you eliminated."

"Eliminated how?"

"I'll have you killed, you prize idiot!"

The look in the Rambler's eyes lost its clarity and a wave of panic began to take over.

"But I haven't done anything wrong! I was on the road, they almost ran me over like a dog. I'm almost home and they nab me like an ordinary thief and now you want to take my life!"

"Not if you accept my proposal."

"That's not true! I'll lose my life in either case."

"Don't be so dumb! Every now and then you'll take my place and I'm offering you life in a palace, how can you refuse? Ungrateful, ungrateful, I deal only with ungrateful wretches!"

"But I'll never learn how to take your place . . . I am the Rambler, not Monsieur le Président!"

"You'll learn, you'll learn . . . I'll show you . . . We'll start with what's easiest and then you'll see what a good time we're going to have together! I'm already shivering with delight . . ."

"You what? . . ."

"I know what I mean. So, it's a deal?"

"Well . . ."

— Mais si, mais si. . . De toute façon, tu n'as plus le choix. Ou tu acceptes, ou je te fais supprimer.

— Supprimer comment?

— Je te fais tuer, triple idiot!

Le regard du Filandreux perdit son eau claire et une vague de panique commença à l'envahir.

— Mais je n'ai rien fait, moi! J'étais sur la route, on manque de m'écraser comme un chien. J'arrive presque chez moi, on me harponne comme un vulgaire bandit et maintenant, tu veux prendre ma vie!

— Pas si tu acceptes ma proposition.

— Ce n'est pas vrai! Dans tous les cas, je perds ma vie.

— Ne sois pas si bête! Tu me remplaceras de temps en temps et je t'offre une vie de château, comment peux-tu refuser? Ingrat, ingrat, je n'ai affaire qu'à des ingrats! . . .

— . . . Mais je ne saurai jamais te remplacer. . . Je suis le Filandreux, pas Monsieur le Président!

— Mais si, tu sauras. . . Je te montrerai. . . On commencera par le plus facile, et puis tu verras comme on va vite s'amuser tous les deux! J'en frémis déjà de délices. . .

— Tu quoi? . . .

— Je me comprends. Alors, c'est d'accord?

— Ben. . .

— Ne me fais pas de la peine!

— . . . On peut toujours . . . essayer?. . .

— C'est ça, c'est ça, essayons!

L'homme en hardes qui franchit ce matin-là les grilles du palais ne ressortit plus. On fit boire à tous ceux qui l'avaient vu une de ces potions de l'oubli qui viennent du fin fond des âges. Ils ne furent plus que deux à se souvenir, si l'on excepte la vieille nourrice, fidèle jusqu'à la mort, qui s'occupait seule des appartements privés de Monsieur le Président. Une fois de plus, l'ancienne qui avait reçu dans ses bras le nouveau-né qui

"Don't give me a hard time!"

" . . . We can always . . . give it a try? . . ."

"There we go, there we go, let's give it a try!"

The man in rags who had passed through the palace gates that morning did not leave again. Everyone who had seen him was forced to drink one of those age-old potions that causes forgetfulness. Now only the two of them and the old nurse remembered. Faithful unto death, she was the only one who took care of the private quarters of Monsieur le Président. The old woman who had held in her arms the newborn who was to become Monsieur le Président congratulated herself once again on having remained unmarried. That way she was free from any attachment, any pressure, and any influence, since her parents had joined the ancestors fifteen suns before. This baby, for whose sake she had been torn away from the flesh of her flesh, from her family, and from her land, was now the only thing she had not lost,[4] the one thing that mattered. And in her celibacy she had found the answer to her feelings of maternal love, conjugal love, and the love of a daughter and a sister. Little by little, she had learned to live through him, in him, to end up by melting all her own desires and ambitions inside his. Her old woman's heart would beat to the rhythm of his joys and his pain and all that was not him quite simply did not exist.

She helped her little pet to realize his newest whim. Without anyone noticing it, the Rambler was set up in the room next to the nurse's room. His old clothes were burned and he learned to be Monsieur le Président, or rather to seem like him. After some time, he was able to take his place in short appearances without any speeches. Soon thereafter, he took on the President's voice, his gestures, postures, and even his thoughts. Both of them were having a good time with this continuous hide-and-seek between the object and the image and were glad to complicate the game by including the old nurse among their

allait devenir Monsieur le Président se félicita de son célibat. Il était ainsi libre de toute attache, de toute pression et de toute emprise, ses parents ayant rejoint les ancêtres depuis quinze soleils. Ce bébé pour lequel on l'arracha à la chair de sa chair, à sa famille et à sa terre était maintenant tout ce qu'elle n'avait pas perdu, l'essentiel. Et elle avait trouvé dans son célibat la réponse à son amour de mère, d'épouse, de fille, de soeur. Elle avait peu à peu appris à vivre à travers lui, en lui pour finir par fondre tous ses désirs et ses ambitions dans les siens. Son vieux coeur de femme battait au rythme de ses joies et de ses douleurs et tout ce qui n'était pas lui n'était pas, tout simplement.

Elle aida son petit loup à réaliser son nouveau caprice. Sans que personne s'en rendît compte, le Filandreux fut installé dans la chambre contiguë à celle de la nourrice. Ses nippes furent brûlées et il apprit à être Monsieur le Président, ou plutôt à le paraître. Au bout de quelque temps, il put le remplacer dans les brèves apparitions sans discours. Bien vite par la suite, il s'appropria sa voix, ses gestes, attitudes et jusques à ses pensées. L'un et l'autre s'amusèrent de ce cache-cache continu entre l'objet et l'image et compliquèrent volontairement le jeu en incluant entre leurs victimes la vieille nourrice. Celle-ci reconnaissait le Filandreux au regard. Mais la luxure, le cynisme et l'exercice du pouvoir aidant, ses yeux se voilèrent de débauche et perdirent à jamais leur eau claire, plongeant la vieille femme dans des doutes infinis. Elle pressentit un jour qu'ils échangeaient leurs chambres et eut de plus en plus peur de ces deux insensés qui tentaient les dieux au-delà des limites. En outre, elle sentait bien que la tacite complicité qui croissait entre le petit et son image la reléguait de plus en plus au rang de spectatrice, en tous les cas impuissante, aux poings liés. Elle essaya bien de les raisonner un soir tranquille où elle les servait à table mais leurs rires fusèrent et s'enflèrent jusqu'à faire trembler les couverts, les meubles, la pièce et la soupière entre

victims. She would recognize the Rambler by the look in his eyes. But aided by lust, cynicism, and the exercise of power, his eyes became veiled with corruption and lost their clear look forever, submerging the old woman in never-ending doubts. One day she had a feeling that they were exchanging rooms and she became more and more afraid of these two madmen who were tempting the gods beyond any limits. Besides, she had the intense sensation that the tacit complicity growing between her little pet and his image relegated her more and more to the rank of a spectator, helpless in any event, and with her hands tied. One quiet evening, when she was serving them dinner, she tried to reason with them, but their laughter rang out and swelled until the utensils, the furniture, the room, and the soup tureen in her hands were shaking. She fled, terrorized, pursued by the interminable explosion of their delirium.

"Did you see the old one? I think she just had the biggest scare of her whole life!"

"Don't call her 'the old one'! She's the only thing I care about."

"Well now, getting sentimental? That's a new one! I thought you were well above having any feelings."

"Of course I am, but I can't bear to have anyone make fun of her. She's given me everything."

"And grateful, too! It's getting better all the time!"

"Be quiet, you don't understand anything, you don't respect anything, you'll never be anything but a pathetic puppet!"

"Eh, take it easy! First of all, I've had good training, you're the one who knows that best, and all we have to do is look around to assure ourselves of that! So, if you think I'm a failure, then that's because you're one yourself!"

"Now you're insulting me! You're insulting me! Careful, you, I am Monsieur le Président."

"I'll have you know that I, too, am Monsieur le Président."

ses mains. Elle s'enfuit, terrorisée, poursuivie par l'interminable explosion de délire.

— Tu as vu la vieille? Je crois qu'elle vient d'avoir la plus belle frousse de sa vie!

— Ne l'appelle pas "la vieille"! Elle est tout ce à quoi je tiens.

— Tiens, sentimental? C'est nouveau ça! Je te croyais largement au-dessus de tout état d'âme.

— Bien sûr que si, mais je ne supporte pas qu'on se moque d'elle. Elle m'a tout donné.

— Reconnaissant! De mieux en mieux!

— Tais-toi, tu ne comprends rien, tu ne respectes rien, tu ne seras jamais qu'un pauvre guignol!

— Eh, doucement! D'abord, j'ai été à bonne école, tu es bien placé pour le savoir et il n'y a qu'à regarder autour de nous pour s'en assurer! Maintenant, si tu me trouves raté, c'est que tu l'es toi-même!

— Mais tu m'insultes! Tu m'insultes! Fais attention à toi, je suis Monsieur le Président.

— Je te fais remarquer que moi aussi, je suis Monsieur le Président.

— Tu n'es qu'un imposteur, pire, une imposture!

— Imposture toi-même! Je suis toi et tu es moi, que tu le veuilles ou non!

— Oui, oui. . . de loin, tu peux abuser mais il suffit de gratter un peu pour que le vernis s'écaille!

— Je trouve que personne ne s'en est jamais apparemment aperçu et tu t'en portes plutôt bien! Arrête de me jeter la pierre, nous sommes dans la même galère ou la même barque, comme tu veux, et tu y es pour beaucoup, non?

— Arrête de me chercher querelle alors!

— Ce n'est tout de même pas ma faute si tu piques la mouche pour moins que rien!

— Mammy n'est pas rien! Elle seule m'a parfois adouci. . .

"You, you're nothing but an impostor, even worse, a fraud!"

"Fraud yourself! I am you and you are me, whether you like it or not!"

"Sure, of course . . . from a distance you can fool anyone, but all you need to do is scratch a little to have the glaze come off in flakes!"

"It's my observation that no one has ever seemed to notice and that you seem to be faring quite well with it all! Stop throwing stones at me, we're stuck in the same mess, or the same boat if you will, and you have a lot to do with that, don't you?"

"Then stop picking a fight with me!"

"Well, it isn't my fault if you get all upset about less than nothing!"

"Mammy is not nothing! She's the only one who could sometimes soften me . . ."

"You? Soften? I've never met anyone more cynical than you. You ought to see how you treat everyone around you, from the gardeners to the ministers of state. . . . Even women don't find any favor in your eyes, well, with the exception of grandma. . . . You make light of everyone and then you get all hot and bothered about an old . . . grandmother who, in the final analysis, is nothing to you. . . . I really don't understand this. . . ."

"Where Mammy is concerned, you can't understand. You'll never understand. . . . And it really doesn't matter very much at all, provided that you leave her alone. . . . As to the rest, I refuse to take individual destinies into consideration. The only thing of interest to me is the people as a whole, and the nation within the international community. . . ."

"Let's talk about that, then, your people: a tide of starving folk, oppressed enough to give up the ghost, held down by a handful of potbellied, insatiable pigs without scruples or morality! And as far as your nation goes, can that even be seriously discussed when more than two-thirds of them are aware of nothing but

— Adouci, toi? Plus cynique que toi, je n'en ai jamais rencontré. Il faut voir comment tu traites tous ceux qui t'entourent, depuis les jardiniers jusqu'aux ministres... Les femmes elles-mêmes ne trouvent aucune grâce à tes yeux, enfin, sauf la grand-mère... Tu te joues de tous et de chacun et tu fais toute une histoire pour une vi... grand-mère qui ne t'est rien en fin de compte... Je ne comprends vraiment pas...

— Pour Mammy, tu ne peux pas comprendre. Tu ne le pourras jamais... Et peu importe d'ailleurs pourvu que tu la laisses tranquille... Pour le reste, je refuse de prendre en considération les destins individuels. Seul le peuple dans sa globalité m'intéresse, et la nation au sein de la communauté internationale...

— Parlons-en de ton peuple: une marée de crève-la-faim opprimée jusqu'à rendre l'âme par une poignée de porcs pansus, inassouvis, sans scrupules ni morale! Et ta nation, peut-on seulement en parler sérieusement quand plus des deux tiers de ses composantes n'ont conscience que de leurs mains vides, leur ventre désespérément creux et leurs enfants partis en eaux?

— Tu es vraiment ignoble!

— Non, non, réaliste seulement.

— Mais tu as bien vu tout ce que j'ai fait pour eux depuis que tu es là! Seulement, ils ne me croient pas, ils ne m'obéissent pas, ils s'opposent même à moi qui ne veux que leur bien! Ils n'ont qu'à s'en prendre à eux-mêmes, s'ils sont ce qu'ils sont!

— Que tu le veuilles ou non, ils sont pourtant le reflet fidèle de ce que tu es. En fin de compte, ton... comment dis-tu déjà?... ton... sosie, c'est ça! ton sosie, c'est eux et non pas moi.

— Ne sois pas cruel!

— Ce n'est pas moi qui suis cruel mais la vérité, et nul ne peut la changer. Tu peux la maquiller, la contrefaire, la cacher, elle continue d'être quelque part, pure et cruelle, et elle te transpercera un jour, avec ou sans ton consentement.

their empty hands, their desperately hollow bellies, and their children dissolved in tears?"

"You really are vile!"

"No, no, I'm just a realist."

"But you've clearly seen everything that I've done for them since you've been here! Only, they don't believe me, they don't obey me, they even go against me, me who wants nothing but what's good for them! They can just go ahead and blame themselves, if that's all they are!"

"Whether you like it or not, they are nevertheless the faithful reflection of what you are. In the final analysis, your . . . what did you call it again? . . . your . . . double, that's it! your double, it's them, not me."

"Don't be cruel!"

"I'm not the one who's cruel—truth is, and no one can change that. You can put makeup on it, disguise it, hide it, it persists in being somewhere, pure and cruel, and one day it will go right through you, with or without your permission."

"Stop it, stop it . . . and don't make me regret having pulled you out of the mire!"

"How did you help me out? We made a contract and each of us is fulfilling his commitment. I owe you nothing and besides, I've had enough of it, I'm going back where I came from. . . . Perhaps there I'll find the dawn of my soul back again. . . ."

"You're forgetting who I am!"

"I am no longer your husk."

"You cannot leave without my permission!"

"I'm leaving anyway. . . ."

"I'll chain you down, I'll imprison you as long as it'll take you to forget your own existence!"

"You won't keep me here. . . ."

Purposefully, the Rambler went over to the heavy door that separated the private quarters of Monsieur le Président from

— Arrête, arrête. . . et ne me fais pas regretter de t'avoir tiré de la fange!

— En quoi m'as-tu aidé? Nous avons passé un contrat et chacun remplit ses engagements. Je ne te dois rien et d'ailleurs, j'en ai assez, je retourne chez moi. . . J'y retrouverai peut-être l'aurore de mon âme. . .

— Tu oublies qui je suis!

— Je ne suis plus ton écorce. . .

— Tu ne pourras pas partir sans ma permission!

— Je partirai quand même. . .

— Je t'enchaînerai, je t'enfermerai jusqu'à ce que tu oublies ta propre existence!

— Tu ne me retiendras pas. . .

Le Filandreux alla résolument vers la lourde porte qui séparait les appartements privés de Monsieur le Président du reste du Palais. Monsieur le Président se jeta sur lui. Les deux hommes se battirent au corps à corps, roulèrent sur le sol, se soulevèrent, tombèrent à nouveau et se perdirent dans une lutte sauvage et démente où chacun ne savait plus s'il s'en prenait à l'autre ou à lui-même. . . Un des deux hommes réussit à prendre le dessus, étrangla l'autre dans l'étau de ses mains et ressentit, désespéré, la même suffocation qu'il lisait sur le visage qui reflétait le sien.

Lorsque la vieille nourrice, alarmée par les bruits sourds, parvint au seuil de la pièce, elle découvrit un homme effondré sur un autre. L'un gisait, inerte, et l'autre était sur lui, secoué de longs sanglots convulsifs. . . Son petit loup?. . . Le Filandreux?. . . Monsieur le Président?. . . Son sosie?. . . Mais qui pouvait le savoir avec certitude? . . . Les dieux avaient frappé.

the rest of the Palace. Monsieur le Président threw himself on him. The two men struggled hand-to-hand, rolled over the floor, rose, fell back down, and fought a savage and demented battle in which neither any longer knew whether he was taking it out on the other or on himself. . . . One of them managed to get the upper hand, strangled the other one in the vise of his hands and felt within himself, desperately, the same suffocation that he read on the face which was the mirror of his own.

When the old nurse, alarmed by the muffled noises, reached the threshold, she discovered one man collapsed upon the other. One lay there inert, and the other was on top of him, shaking with long, convulsive sobs. . . . Her little pet? . . . The Rambler? . . . Monsieur le Président? . . . His double? . . . Who could know this with any certainty? . . . The gods had struck.

Jean-Claude Fota

Born in 1958, Jean-Claude Fota has written a volume of poetry, Cris d'îles *(Island cries), yet unpublished. He has also written several short stories, one of which, "L'escale" (Stopover), was awarded first prize in 1991 in that genre by Radio France International. Among his other short stories, most of them unpublished, are:* L'épingle de sûreté *(The safety pin),* Radevil ou la damnation *(Radevil or damnation),* La corde *(The rope),* L'enclave *(The enclave), and* Marche et chôme *(Walk no work), whose translation is reproduced below.*

Walk No Work

1

"It bolted," the diviner[1] said.
Yes, destiny bolted like a crazed horse!
It dashed off right as it arrived at the crossroads.
And now no one knows what direction it will take.
No one knows.
But I am here and all is well.
The one I attend to has nothing to fear.
Destiny does not kill.
The one I attend to will be fine.
Here is Tafara, son of Biankosy,
The one who steps over lianas in our forests.
And here is Job, his son, who is going far away to sit astride the benches.[2]

Change yourself around, destiny, for what he is undertaking is good.
Change yourself around, for I, the diviner, remove ill fortunes.

Translated from the French by Marjolijn de Jager

Jean-Claude Fota

Né en 1958, Jean-Claude Fota est l'auteur d'un volume de poésie, Cris d'îles, *encore inédit. Il a aussi écrit plusieurs nouvelles, dont l'une a remporté le prix Radio France International en 1991. Parmi ses nouvelles, inédites pour la plupart, on compte:* L'épingle de sûreté, Radevil ou la damnation, La corde, L'enclave L'escale *(primée en 1991 par Radio France International), et* Marche et chôme, *qui est reproduite ci-dessous.*

Marche et chôme

1

"Il s'est emballé", dit le devin.
Oui, le destin s'est emballé comme un cheval fou!
Il s'est rué juste en arrivant au carrefour.
Et nul ne sait, maintenant, quelle direction il va prendre.
Nul le sait.
Mais je suis là et tout va bien.
Celui que je soigne n'a rien à craindre.
Le destin ne tue pas.
Celui que je soigne ira bien.
Voici Tafara, fils de Biankosy,
Celui qui, dans nos forêts enjambe les lianes.
Et voici Job, son fils qui va partir loin, chevaucher les bancs.

Change-toi, destin, car ce qu'il entreprend est bon.
Change-toi car moi, le devin, j'enlève les mauvais sorts.

En descendant les escaliers de l'hachélème, Job se souvint du visage crispé de l'Ombiasa. Cela remontait pourtant très loin dans le passé, mais il ne pouvait l'oublier. Ou plutôt ce qui était en train de lui arriver lui faisait se souvenir.

— Il s'est emballé de nouveau, dit-il en regardant les marches

Going down the stairs of the *hachélème*,[3] Job remembered the Ombiasa's[4] strained face. Yes, that was a long way back, but he could not forget him. Or rather, what was in the process of happening to him made him remember.

"It bolted again," he said, looking at the steps of the stairs spattered with the seepage from the cracked buckets of the garbage collectors. As he was passing through, the mosquitoes took off from the red brick walls by the thousands and permeated the stairwell. A real Egyptian plague, he said to himself, clearing a bit of space in front of his nose with the back of his hand, as if to try to breathe normally. Below, a little boy with a filthy bucket on his head was watching him come down and cried:

"Rotten rice! Rotten rice for pigs!"

"It bolted again," Job told him in a broken voice. With a look of interest, the little boy stopped.

"D'ya have 'rotten rice for pigs,' sir?"

"It's more a rotten destiny," Job answered, looking at the crumbly ditch he would have to step over before he could reach the more or less dry central alley. Now he was walking along a trench, covered with stone slabs in some places, his eyes still riveted on the ground. Then further on, before he reached the sidewalk, he passed a woman with a baby on her back, an old soubique[5] on her head, who was crying out in a loud voice: BOTTLES AND RAGS, WE BUY BOTTLES AND RAGS!

2

What had just occurred was going to turn Job's life upside down.

He was far from suspecting that such a disaster could befall him, happen to him who believed that he was part of the inheritors: *"those who had the best chance of pulling through and who had never become demoralized throughout all those black years of the decade of the eighties."*[6]

Recently graduated after a flawless period at the university,

de l'escalier éclaboussées par le suintement des seaux fêlés des ramasseurs d'ordures. Sur son passage, les moustiques se décollèrent par milliers des parois en briques rouges et remplissaient la cage d'escalier. Une véritable plaie d'Egypte, se dit-il, en dégageant du revers de la main un peu d'espace devant le nez, comme pour pouvoir respirer normalement. En bas, un petit garçon, un seau crasseux sur la tête, le regardait venir en criant:

— Riz pourri! Riz pourri pour porc!

— Il s'est emballé de nouveau, lui dit Job, la voix cassée. Le petit garçon, l'air intéressé s'est arrêté.

— Z'avez du "riz pourri pour porc", m'sié?

— Un destin pourri plutôt, répondit Job en regardant la petite rigole vétuste qu'il devait enjamber avant d'atteindre l'allée centrale à peu près sèche. Il marchait maintenant le long d'une tranchée recouverte par endroit de dalles, les yeux toujours rivés au sol. Puis plus loin, avant d'atteindre le trottoir, il croisa une femme portant un bébé dans le dos, une vieille soubique sur la tête et criant à voix forte: BOUTEILLES ET CHIFFONS, NOUS ACHETONS! BOUTEILLES ET CHIFFONS. . .

2

Ce qui venait de se produire allait bouleverser la vie de Job.

Il était loin de se douter qu'une telle catastrophe pouvait lui tomber dessus, lui qui croyait faire partie des héritiers: *"ceux qui avaient le plus de chance de s'en sortir et qui étaient restés indémoralisables pendant toute ces années noires de la décennie 80".*

Fraîchement diplômé après un parcours sans faute à l'université, Job croyait que dans ce ciel noir et profond de la décennie 80, une petite étoile brillait pour *lui.* "Il n'y a aucune raison de ne pas y arriver", se plaisait-il à dire lorsqu'entre amis ils parlaient de "cette vie qui ne fait pas de cadeau". Certains d'entre eux y voyaient, de sa part, une sorte d'arrogance et d'irrespect vis-à-vis

Job believed that in that dark and deep sky of the eighties a small star was shining just for *him.* "There is no reason at all not to make it," he would happily state when they were talking among friends about "this life that gives nothing away for free." Some of them saw in him a certain arrogance and lack of respect where destiny was concerned. But they were quite familiar with Job's good-boy optimism. With his irony as well. His naive adolescent's safeguarded dream. His unaffected lust for life. Job's freshness as they would say.

That was the Job of before.

That was he until the day when he had the abominable idea of underlining in one sitting every letter he had received. That day, to be cursed a thousand times, when he had the misfortune of making a game of underlining with a red marker the characters of the mail he had just received. That way having revealed the holy secret of the shapes that lay in ambush. Having awakened them. Job should be pitied for underlining them one by one this way, suspecting nothing, telling himself to underline! Underline some more and play. Cross the words. Cross the letters. Underline and kill the time here and now. Underline and go all the way. It was as if he were whipping a crazed horse!

Yet, the situation, completely unremarkable in the beginning, foreshadowed nothing out of the ordinary. Job had just received two letters. One came from a local company that announced "it is with regret that we cannot accept your application," as usual. Job was a little moved but not surprised. No, not at all. He was ready to begin all over again and right away. To write letters again, for hours on end, in his most decorative handwriting, and to tell them "it is my great pleasure." That is how each one of his innumerable letters was composed with the greatest of care. Dotting the i, placing the commas, slanting the letters, their size, the care of the layout, not one of these tiny details had been left to chance. He had made the most of

du destin. Mais ils connaissaient bien l'optimisme bon enfant de Job. Son ironie aussi. Son rêve préservé d'adolescent naïf. Sa joie de vivre inentamée. La fraîcheur de Job comme ils disaient.

C'était le Job d'avant.

C'était lui jusqu'au jour où il eut l'abominable idée de souligner d'un trait toutes les lettres reçues. Ce jour mille fois maudit où il eut le malheur de jouer à souligner au feutre rouge les caractères du courrier qu'il venait de recevoir. D'avoir ainsi révélé le sacré secret des figures embusquées. De les avoir réveillées. Il faut plaindre Job qui jouait à les souligner ainsi une à une sans se douter de rien, en se disant souligne! Souligne encore et joue. Croise les mots. Croise les lettres. Souligne et tue le temps ici-même. Souligne et va jusqu'au bout. C'était comme s'il fouettait le cheval fou!

La situation, toute banale au début, ne présageait pourtant rien d'extraordinaire. Job venait de recevoir deux lettres. L'une lui venait d'une entreprise de la place qui lui annonçait qu'elle était "au regret de ne pas pouvoir donner satisfaction à sa demande", comme d'habitude. Job était un peu ému mais pas surpris. Non pas du tout. Il était prêt à recommencer tout de suite. A calligraphier à nouveau des lettres, des heures durant, pour leur dire "j'ai l'honneur". C'était ainsi que chacun de ses nombreux courriers furent rédigés avec le plus grand soin. Les points sur les i, l'emplacement des virgules, l'inclinaison des lettres, leur dimension, la précision des tracés, aucun de ces menus détails n'avaient été laissés au hasard. Les précieux conseils du vieux calligraphe-tatoueur Ibonimaboroko, son ami et maître, avaient été mis à profit.

—Que tu noircisses le papier, que tu tatoues la peau, quoi que tu fasses, lui disait-il, fais-le bien. Ne te contente pas de ton seul talent. Travaille et applique-toi jusqu'à ce que ton oeuvre soit satisfaite d'elle-même. *"Jusqu'à ce que ton oeuvre soit satisfaite d'elle-même."* C'était ainsi que ces lettres furent longtemps

the invaluable advice of the old calligrapher-tattoo artist, Ibonimaboroko, his friend and master.

"Whether you blacken paper, whether you tattoo skin, whatever you do," he told him, "do it well. Don't be content with your talent alone. Work and apply yourself until your creation is pleased with itself." *Until your creation is pleased with itself.* That is how his letters were refined at length in the secrecy of his room, before he folded them in four as he did himself, out of respect for those who would receive them.

The other letter was from his father who was sick, dying perhaps, and who was asking him in essence to come back home. The letter was reminding him that he was of "the age to be of help." It was telling him that the news from home was all bad. That his cousin Antoue had gone mad. Fit to be tied because she had lost her man and her first-born son. Wretched and mad and only twenty years old. That Job's uncle had asked Job's mother: what is he actually doing over there, *the kid*, without any work? That his mother had answered: *the kid* needs our help, so sell one of our cows. And that the uncle had said: never!

Then the letter had told him of the death of Ibonimaboroko, that genius of a tattoo artist who had taught him to write so beautifully. Job felt as if the letter had announced his own father's death. But he shouldn't weep. Sure, he was of the age to be of help, but he ought not to think about that. The news was bad but what could he do about it, even if he went back home? He, too, had his own problems and who was bothering with them? No, he shouldn't weep over his fate.

"Even if it gets on the nerves of the morons," he said, "I won't let it get me down. I will not leave here."

Then he dropped his father's letter, written by a literate cousin on school notebook paper, and picked up the typewritten one. The paper was good and that made you like the written word. Job spent an inordinate amount of time turning it over and over

peaufinées dans le secret de la chambre, avant d'être pliées en quatre comme lui, dans le respect de ceux qui allaient les recevoir.

L'autre courrier venait de son père, malade, peut-être mourant, qui lui demandait en substance de rentrer au pays. La lettre lui rappelait qu'il avait "l'âge d'aider." Elle lui disait que les nouvelles là-bas étaient toutes mauvaises. Que sa cousine Antoue était devenue folle. Folle à lier d'avoir perdu son homme et son fils premier-né. Misérable et folle déjà à vingt ans. Que l'oncle de Job aurait demandé à sa mère: mais qu'est-ce qu'il fait là-bas, *le petit,* sans travail? Que sa mère lui aurait répondu: *le petit* a besoin qu'on l'aide, vends donc une de nos vaches. Et l'oncle qui aurait dit: jamais!

Puis la lettre lui apprit la mort d'Ibonimaboroko, le tatoueur de génie qui lui avait appris la calligraphie. Job avait l'impression que la lettre lui annonçât la mort de son père à lui. Mais il ne fallait pas qu'il pleure. Il avait l'âge d'aider, d'accord, mais ne devait pas y penser. Les nouvelles sont mauvaises mais que pouvait-il y faire, même s'il rentrait au pays. Il avait aussi ses problèmes à lui et qui s'en occupe? Non, il ne fallait pas qu'il pleure sur son sort.

— Même si cela énerve les imbéciles, dit-il, je tiendrai le coup. Je ne bougerai pas d'ici.

Il laissa alors tomber la lettre de son père, écrite par un cousin lettré sur un cahier d'écolier, puis il prit celle écrite à la machine. Le papier était bon et cela faisait aimer l'écrit. Job passa un temps fou à le retourner de long en large. A le palper de ses doigts tremblants. A sentir la moindre odeur qui l'imprégnait. Le parfum délicat des secrétaires. La sueur des entreprises. L'odeur de leur labeur envié. Puis, dans sa rage de vouloir prendre sa place dans tout cela, il manqua de s'effondrer.

C'était alors qu'il eut l'abominable idée de souligner les lettres. De les souligner une à une comme ça, histoire de passer le

in his hands. Rubbing it with trembling fingers. Smelling every little whiff with which it was impregnated. The delicate perfume of secretaries. The sweat of companies. The smell of their envied hard work. Then, in his furious desire to take his place among all these, he almost broke down.

That is when the abominable idea of underlining letters came to him. Underlining them one by one like that, a question of passing the time, of suppressing the voice that was speaking to him, realizing it had been underlined! Underline and play. Don't let guilt take the upper hand. Underline and kill the voice. Now even kill time. Cross the words. Cross the letters. Underline and go all the way!

Underline!

Then the underlined letters appeared one by one as if activated by the underlining. Job was having fun giving them a nickname as they appeared.

Here was **w** that wicked death, **a** the little slut, **l** but why this tall banana, **k** kaput destroyed defeated, **n** nullified, **o** for the oaf who'd live an entire life his temples drenched in filthy water . . .

Job studied the work and laughed.

Then he mixed the letters up, a question of changing their order. He wanted to see if they were capable of sorting things out![7] He started over again several times, trying to make some sense out of what he was doing. For example, he could play out the story here of his entrance into the world, why not. Then he made "wicked death" **w** come back twice, the tall banana **l** but why, the **k** kaput destroyed defeated, the **r** three times as if recoiling before the foreshadowing of Job's failure. An unexpected message then appeared:

WALK NO WORK!

This new combination threw him for a loop. He could have confined himself to laughing at it, then going on his way. But it was his misfortune to take it seriously. He examined the other

temps, d'étouffer la voix qui lui parlait, en se disant souligné! Souligne et joue. Ne laisse pas la culpabilité prendre le dessus. Souligne et tue la voix. Tue le temps maintenant même. Croise les mots. Croise les lettres. Souligne et va jusqu'au bout!

Souligne!

Les lettres soulignées apparurent alors une à une comme activées par le soulignement. Cela amusait Job de leur donner un sobriquet au fur et à mesure qu'elles apparurent.

Voici ***m*** la méchante mort, ***a*** la petite garce, ***r*** des reins brisés de la République, ***c*** des cornes des cocus, ***h*** banane tiens pourquoi ça, ***œ*** les fausses jumelles et enfin ***t*** de toute la vie à vivre la tempe trempée d'eau sale. . .

Job contempla le travail et rit.

Ensuite il mélangea les lettres, histoire de leur faire changer d'ordre. Il voulait voir si elles étaient capables de modifier l'ordre des choses! Il recommença plusieurs fois en essayant de donner un sens à ce qu'il faisait. Il pouvait par exemple y jouer l'histoire de sa venue au monde, pourquoi pas. Il fit alors revenir deux fois "la menace de mort" ***m***, "la corne du con" ***c***, "la banane" ***h***, tiens pourquoi ça! Puis ***e*** la jumelle d'***o*** revint trois fois en allant à vau-l'eau comme pour préfigurer à l'échec de Job. Un message inattendu apparut alors:

MARCHE ET CHOME!

Cette nouvelle combinaison le bouleversa. Il aurait pu se contenter d'en rire puis, passer son chemin. Mais il eut le malheur de le prendre au sérieux. Il examina les autres courriers et entreprit de les souligner un à un: marche et chôme, marche et chôme partout. Embusqués en des endroits inimaginables. Sous le vernis des formules peaufinées. Dans toutes les lettres reçues comme une terrible injonction:

MARCHE ET CHOME! MARCHE ET CHOME!

Et voilà que deux mots furent suffisants pour déstabiliser sa tête hyper-entraînée à réfléchir. Son cerveau fraîchement formé

mail and began to underline them one by one: walk no work, walk no work everywhere. Lying in ambush in unimaginable places. Underneath the polish of refined formulas. In every letter he had received like a dreadful injunction:

WALK NO WORK! WALK NO WORK!

And suddenly here were three words enough to destabilize his head, highly-coached to be thoughtful. His brain, freshly trained to have a clear view into the fog of the decade of the eighties, had become an immense field in which three words danced around like a crazed horse:

WALK NO WORK! WALK NO WORK! WALK NO WORK!

3

The outside air made you sigh with relief!

Job had many contradictory desires. Desire to be alone. To walk amidst the crowd. To watch people. To pass unnoticed. To walk in the shade, quietly . . .

Workers were leaving the center of town.

They were all heading in the same direction. Only Job was walking the opposite way. They were clustering together at the grade crossing. A train would soon be coming through. They were waiting, impatiently wanting to dive across the track. Then, when old Micheline[8] had passed, they threw themselves across in one solid wave. Like a disaster brought down upon the city.

"Faces juxtaposed to make a crowd," Job said to himself.

The human tide, he was seeing it come. He saw it face on, storming straight ahead, like a starved beast, tearing everything down as it passed. He was jolted from every side. Blows were raining down on his ribs. On his shoulders. Job was like a wisp of straw carried off by the current. He despised this nauseating mass of workers drowning him. He had the feeling he no longer existed except for this tiny thought jamming his head.

pour voir clair dans les brumes de la décennie 80, devenu un immense champ où deux mots dansèrent comme un cheval fou:

MARCHE ET CHOME! MARCHE ET CHOME! MARCHE ET CHOME!

3

L'air du dehors faisait dire ouf!

Job avait plein d'envies contradictoires. Envie d'être seul. De marcher dans la foule. De regarder les gens. De passer inaperçu. De marcher à l'ombre, tranquillement. . .

Les travailleurs quittaient le centre ville.

Ils allaient tous dans la même direction. Il n'y avait que Job qui marchait dans le sens inverse. Ils s'agglutinaient à l'entrée du passage à niveau. Un train allait passer. Ils attendaient impatients de s'engouffrer dans la voie. Puis, lorsque la vieille Micheline fut passée, ils se précipitèrent en une seule vague. Comme une catastrophe abattue sur la ville.

— Des faciès juxtaposés pour que ça fasse du monde, se dit Job.

La marée humaine, il la voyait venir. Il la voyait de face fonçant tout droit, comme une bête affamée, raclant tout sur son passage. Il se fit bousculer de partout. Il pleuvait des coups aux côtés. Aux épaules. Job était comme un fétu de paille emporté par le courant. Il détestait cette masse nauséabonde de travailleurs qui le noyait. Il avait l'impression de ne plus exister que par cette petite pensée qui grouillait par-devers sa tête. De ne rester présent que par ce fil ténu. . . Il essayait de remonter le courant en se disant ça va, je suis là. Mais à travers les rumeurs de la rue, les bruits de conversations, il crut soudain entendre: MARCHE ET CHOME!

4

Un groupe de soldats sortait du stade en rang serré. Ils venaient sans doute de répéter pour le défilé de la fête nationale.

To remain present by only this thread. . . . He tried to go against the current, telling himself, it's alright, I am here. But through the noises of the street, the sounds of conversations, he suddenly thought he heard: WALK NO WORK!

4

A group of soldiers in tight formation was coming out of the stadium. Undoubtedly they had just been rehearsing for the parade of the national holiday. With a twinge of sadness, Job remembered that independence day would be in just a few days and that he and the independence were the same age. Independence without a penny—what a waste!

Standing on the sidewalk, below the weeping jacaranda trees, he was watching the soldiers pass by. Their heavy hobnailed boots were crushing the grains of sand, and their heels were hammering the dry asphalt in unison, resounding like the stretched skin of drums: walk no work! walk no work! walk no work!

5

Job didn't know where to go.

He contented himself with being outside to get away from the confined space of his room. He followed his own footsteps haphazardly along the stadium to watch the pigeons. Yet he despised pigeons. He despised their "arrogant angelicism" as he said. Their way of making fun of you by narrowly missing your head at great speed, always in a hurry. Their way of being beautiful as if to please the angels. Yet just think about what they carry around in filth, these wall splatterers.

But what fascinated him about them was their intelligence. Had they taken possession of the city, it would not have surprised him. Job didn't like pigeons but he did respect them. He respected their extraordinary abilities. They, who had nothing but one pair of wings and a few grams of brain!

Job se souvint avec un pincement au coeur: la fête de l'indépendance était dans quelques jours et qu'il avait le même âge qu'elle, l'indépendance. L'indépendance sans le sou, quel gâchis!

Debout sur le trottoir, sous les jacarandas en pleurs, il regardait passer les soldats. Leurs lourds brodequins ferrés écrasaient les grains de sable, et leurs talons en martelant à l'unisson l'asphalte sec résonnaient comme la peau tendue des tambours: marche et chôme! marche et chôme! marche et chôme!

5

Job ne savait pas où aller.

Il se contentait d'être dehors pour fuir l'espace confiné de sa chambre. Il allait au hasard de ses pas le long du stade à regarder les pigeons. Il détestait pourtant les pigeons. Il détestait leur "angélisme arrogant" comme il disait. Leur manière de se moquer de vous en vous frôlant la tête à toute vitesse, toujours pressés. Leur manière d'être beau comme pour plaire aux anges. Allez pourtant savoir ce qu'ils transportent comme saloperies ces maculeurs de murs.

Mais ce qui le fascinait chez eux c'était leur intelligence. Ils allaient prendre possession de la ville que cela ne l'aurait pas étonné. Job n'aimait pas les pigeons mais il les respectait. Il respectait leurs extraordinaires facultés. Eux qui n'avaient qu'une paire d'ailes et quelques grammes de cervelle!

—C'est curieux, se disait-il tout à coup, pensif. On peut donc faire tout ce qu'un pigeon sait faire, rien qu'avec une toute petite quantité de cervelle?

Il regardait le pigeon qui était là, devant lui, sur le trottoir en train de se dandiner, picorant quelque chose au milieu des bouts de papiers et de feuilles, déployant tout à coup les deux ailes, s'élevant dans les airs au-dessus de lui, sans le frôler, se posant plus loin derrière puis, trempant son bec dans une flaque d'eau

"It's odd," he suddenly said to himself, thoughtfully. "So we can do anything a pigeon knows how to do, even though it has only a tiny bit of brain?"

He was watching the pigeon right in front of him, on the sidewalk, busily preening, picking at something in the middle of bits of paper and leaves, suddenly spreading its two wings, rising into the air above him, without brushing against him, then coming down farther away behind him, dipping its beak into a puddle of water that might well have been some drunken man's piss, and all the while looking at him maliciously.

"Nothing but a tiny bit of brain," Job said to himself.

He then raised his hand to his head to appraise its capacity and realized for the first time that he had a rather sizeable skull . . .

He was now passing a bookstore with a window full of books, magazines, and newspapers. Looking at the headlines without really stopping he thought he read RECIT where he should have read ECRIT.[9] Then suddenly, they were there again, hidden away but recognizable through the interlaced lines. Job became aware that he had become able to identify them immediately. They were there, as if underlined, accentuated, arranging themselves with diabolical speed: walk no work! walk no work everywhere. On the signs of stores, on banners, on posters, on everything that was written, Job would find the secret message again, meant for him personally:

WALK NO WORK!

6

Heloïse was about his age.

She worked as secretary in an advisory company. She had a small apartment in the insurance personnel housing. Job was Heloïse's friend. He was Heloïse's out-of-work lover, but that remained a secret. Their secret. They would never speak of this point. Of what Job did for a living. No never. They had forgotten

qui pouvait bien être une pisse d'ivrogne, tout en le regardant d'un air malicieux.

— Rien qu'une toute petite quantité de cervelle, se dit Job.

Il porta alors la main à la tête pour en apprécier la capacité et réalisa pour la première fois qu'il avait le crâne plutôt volumineux. . .

Il passait à présent devant une librairie dont la vitrine était garnie de livres, de magazines et de journaux. En regardant les gros titres sans vraiment s'y attarder il crut lire RECIT là où il convenait de lire ECRIT. Puis soudain, elles étaient à nouveau là, planquées mais reconnaissables à travers les signes entrelacés. Job s'aperçut qu'il était devenu capable de les identifier promptement. Elles étaient là, comme soulignées, mises en relief, s'ordonnant à une vitesse diaboliquement rapide: marche et chôme! marche et chôme partout. Sur les enseignes des magasins, sur les banderoles, sur les affiches, sur tout ce qui était écrit, Job retrouvait ce message clandestin qui lui était personnellement destiné:

MARCHE ET CHOME!

6

Héloïse avait à peu près son âge.

Elle travaillait comme secrétaire dans une société de Conseil. Elle avait un petit appartement à la cité des Assureurs. Job était l'ami d'Héloïse. Il était l'amant sans travail d'Héloïse mais cela restait secret. Leur secret. Ils ne parlaient jamais de cet aspect. De ce que Job faisait pour vivre. Non jamais. Ils avaient oublié cela. Ils avaient joué à l'oublier. A être égaux et heureux tous les deux.

Job était l'amant sans travail d'Héloïse mais ce détail n'avait pas d'importance. Elle disait l'aimer tel qu'il était, vaille que vaille. Tel qu'il était.

— Souffres-tu d'être mon amie, Héloïse?

about that. They had played at forgetting it. At being equals and happy together.

Job was Heloïse's out-of-work lover but this was a detail of no importance. She used to say that for better or worse she loved him as he was. As he was.

"Do you suffer from being my friend, Heloïse?"

"Of course not, what an idea, since I love you."

Then one day they couldn't take it anymore. It had exploded right in the middle of the month. A simple question of dough. A ridiculous little story of money to buy noodles. Heloïse was saying that she'd had it up to her ears with this deal. She was saying that she'd had enough of a guy "like that." That she'd been living with it long enough. That she couldn't put up with him the rest of her life. . . .

She, Heloïse, had been truthful during that scene. She had not pronounced the word exactly, but for Job everything had been spelled out: walk no work, my love. Walk no work, for real. WALK NO WORK!

7

Job was taking stock.

There had been his studies, which he finished. But that had not been enough. Not for finding a job.

There had been Heloïse who had slammed the door in his face.

Then there had been loneliness.

Now Job had left the *hachélèmes.* And in his new neighborhood in the "Housing of the Morons," the used water was stagnating on the surface of decayed, mosquito-infested ditches. And the mosquitoes infiltrated the worm-eaten boards that divided Job's lodging.

There was a multitude of things he was trying to do. But he couldn't manage to make them stick. To make them take shape. To make them into a project. He was living every moment by watching over himself. By being careful not to tip over.

— Mais non, quelle idée puisque je t'aime.

Puis un jour ils n'avaient plus tenu le coup. Cela a explosé au bon milieu du mois. Une simple histoire de sou. Une ridicule petite histoire de sou pour s'acheter des nouilles. Héloïse disait en avoir par-dessus la tête de cette histoire-là. Elle disait qu'elle en avait marre d'un type "comme ça". Que ce qui a été vécu était suffisant. Qu'elle ne pouvait plus le supporter toute la vie. . .

Elle a été vraie dans cette scène-là, Héloïse. Elle n'avait pas directement prononcé le mot, mais pour Job tout avait été dit: marche et chôme, mon amour. Marche et chôme pour de vrai. MARCHE ET CHOME!

7

Job faisait le point.

Il y avait eu les études accomplies. Mais cela n'avait pas été suffisant. Pas pour trouver un job.

Il y avait Héloïse qui lui avait claqué la porte au nez.

Puis, il y avait la solitude.

Job avait maintenant quitté les hachélèmes. Et dans son nouveau quartier à la "Cité des Imbéciles" les eaux usées stagnaient en surface dans des rigoles vétustes, infestées de moustiques. Et les moustiques s'infiltraient entre les planches vermoulues qui cloisonnaient le logis de Job. . .

Il y avait une myriade de choses qu'il essayait de faire. Mais il n'arrivait pas à les faire tenir. A les faire prendre corps. A en faire un projet. Il vivait chaque instant à veiller sur lui-même. A faire attention de ne pas basculer.

— C'est plutôt cela, la pauvreté, disait Job. Pas tant le manque d'argent, mais surtout cette incapacité à faire prendre corps ce qui nous tient à coeur.

Job se demandait si ce n'était pas une prétention de sa part que de vouloir garder toutes ces illusions. Créer un emploi au lieu d'en chercher. Job y avait songé. Ce serait possible disait-il,

"That is what poverty really is," Job would say. "Not so much the lack of money, but especially this inability to make that which matters to us take shape."

Job wondered if it wasn't a conceit on his part to want to safeguard all these illusions. To create employment rather than go looking for one. Job had thought of it. It would be possible, he told himself, when rats have credit at the bank. When chickens have a guarantor.[10]

There was a multitude of things.

First, though, Job would have had to be able to tear himself away from the present moment. To plan ahead without spreading himself too thinly. But time itself had become dislocated. And all his hopes with it.

There was a multitude of things. His 250 letters of application sent out for nothing. The 250 stamps glued on with his saliva so they would stick. Sure, they didn't even stick very well! And then that smell of rotten glue that stuck to your tongue and made you want to throw up. Phew! Not surprising that people spat in the post office.

There was also the infernal whispering of mosquitoes in his place of wooden boards in the "Housing of Morons." Myriads and myriads of insects armed with their hideous proboscis to pump out your blood.

There was his cousin Antoue who had become mad from losing her son.

There was his father awaiting his return. His beloved mother, whom he had traded for a life without love, in a spot without work, in a city without soul, she whom he loved above all else in the world . . .

There was Job looking in vain for a job, dropped into existence as if he were looking for himself without finding himself.

There was his destiny that was too tough, that had bolted

lorsque les rats auront des crédits à la banque. Lorsque les poules auront du répondant.

Il y avait une myriade de choses.

Il fallait d'abord que Job eût été capable de s'arracher à l'instant. De se projeter plus loin sans se disperser. Mais le temps lui-même s'était disloqué. Et avec lui, toutes ses espérances.

Il y avait une myriade de choses. Ses 250 lettres de candidature expédiées pour rien. Les 250 timbres collés à la salive pour que ça tienne. Tu parles, ça ne collait même pas bien! Et puis cette odeur de gomme pourrie qui vous collait à la langue et qui vous donnait envie de vomir. Pouah! Quoi d'étonnant si les gens crachaient dans les locaux des PTT.

Il y avait aussi la susurration infernale des moustiques dans la maison en planches de la "Cité des Imbéciles." Des myriades et des myriades de bestioles armées de trompes infectes pour vous pomper le sang.

Il y avait sa cousine Antoue devenue folle d'avoir perdu son fils.

Il y avait son père qui attendait son retour. Sa mère bien-aimée qu'il avait troquée contre une existence sans amour, dans un coin sans travail, dans une ville sans âme, elle qu'il aimait par-dessus tout au monde. . .

Il y avait Job qui cherchait un job en vain, lâché dans l'existence, comme s'il se cherchait sans se trouver.

Il y avait son destin trop fort qui s'était à nouveau emballé *comme un cheval fou* sans que quiconque n'y pût quelque chose désormais!

8

Héloïse allait être oubliée.

C'était d'une autre maintenant que Job disait du bien. Une jeune fille. Une petite. Elle était venue le voir. C'était la veille de la fête nationale. Elle avait deux lampions multicolores pour ses

again *like a crazed horse* and nobody could do anything about it anymore!

8

Heloïse would be forgotten.

Now there was another of whom Job had good things to say. A young girl. A little one. She had come to see him. It was the evening before the national holiday. She had two multicolored paper lanterns for her little brothers. She wanted a sun for herself. A beautiful sun on her left shoulder. She had come to have a sun tattooed on her shoulder. She said she didn't have much with which to pay for it. But Job did it with pleasure. He thought it was beautiful that he could give her a sun for the celebration. Her skin was nice to touch, soft and sensual . . . but covered with mosquito bites.

A few days after the celebration she suffered her attack. The bearer of the sun died of malaria. Job heard it through a friend of hers who wanted the same tattoo as something to remember her by. So he was never to see her again . . .

"The mosquitoes will end up by getting us all," Job said.

There was life to be lived all by himself, his temples drenched in filthy water. . . .

9

Another letter arrived in the course of the winter. But Job was no longer waiting for it. He read it without surprise. Without enthusiasm. Yet it was an invitation for an interview. The first one in three years. Job didn't immediately tear it up. Instead, he took a pencil telling himself to underline. Underline the letters. Cross the words. Underline and go all the way. Then he underlined the letters. Crossed the words. Underlined and went all the way. He underlined!

They were all there. The wicked little death. The little slut of

petits frères. Elle voulait un soleil pour elle. Un beau soleil sur son épaule gauche. Elle était venue pour se faire tatouer un soleil sur son épaule. Elle disait ne pas avoir grand chose pour payer. Mais Job le fit avec plaisir. Il trouvait cela beau de pouvoir offrir un soleil pour la fête. La peau était agréable au toucher, lisse et sensuelle. . . mais criblée de piqûres de moustiques.

Quelques jours après la fête elle eut sa crise. La porteuse de soleil est morte impaludée. Job l'avait appris par une amie à elle qui voulait d'un même tatouage en souvenir d'elle. Il ne la reverra donc jamais plus. . .

— Les moustiques finiront par nous avoir tous, dit Job.

Il y avait la vie à vivre tout seul, les tempes trempées d'eau sale. . .

9

Une autre lettre arriva au cours de l'hiver. Mais Job ne l'attendait plus. Il l'avait lue sans surprise. Sans enthousiasme. C'était pourtant une convocation pour un entretien. La première en trois ans. Job ne la déchira pas tout de suite. Au lieu de cela il prit un crayon en se disant: souligne. Souligne les lettres. Croise les mots. Souligne et va jusqu'au bout. Puis il souligna les lettres. Croisa les mots. Souligna et alla jusqu'au bout. Il souligna!

Elles étaient toutes là. La méchante petite mort. La petite garce d'***a***. Et puis ***e*** la jumelle d'***o***. Et puis toute la vie à vivre les tempes trempées d'eau sale! Job souriait. Il sentit qu'un changement s'était accompli en lui. Elles étaient toutes là, belles et ostensibles comme des filles à marier. Mais cela n'avait plus aucun pouvoir sur lui. Comme si leur charme s'estompait tout à coup. Job riait déjà de sa naïveté retrouvée. Son optimisme bon enfant. La fraîcheur de Job, comme disaient ses amis d'antan. Il se moquait bien du travail que les gens prétendaient lui offrir à présent.

an **a**. And then the **k** kaput destroyed, defeated. And then all of life to be lived with temples drenched in filthy water! Job was smiling. He sensed that a change had occurred in him. They were all there, lovely and conspicuous like young girls to be married. But none of this had any power over him any more. As if their charm had suddenly faded. Job was already laughing at having found his naïveté again. His good-boy optimism. Job's freshness, as his friends of earlier days used to say. He really couldn't care less about the work that people were claiming to give him now.

"I will begin right here and in my *own* way," he said, "and I will rise as high as the pigeons."

Then he tore up the paper. Now he had more of a reason to stay than ever before. That of not saying those who had left were right. Those who had failed the tests. Those who had abandoned the promises made to his generation for good. Or those who had remained demotivated throughout the black years of the decade of the eighties.

He then decided not to listen anymore to that voice jamming inside his head and claiming to rule over him. Not to talk about the world anymore that, in any event, had never belonged to him. About the word itself, which he was no longer afraid of losing. About laughter that had become dull, saddened. About love that no longer knew how to handle itself. About dignity that had fled. For now, he wanted to get rid of his pretentiousness in fighting all of that. In fighting against loneliness and vacant lots. Against mosquitoes and the mud in the ditches. Instead of being preoccupied with all that, Job had made the decision to get up early and to go around the humid alleyways of the *hachélèmes* once again, fruitfully.

Like the *tanrec*[11] hibernating in the red laterite, Job was now merely one with the desolate landscape of the "Housing of Morons." He had to camouflage himself this way, so that destiny would not go back on its track again. Would not recognize him.

— Je commencerai ici-même et à *ma* façon, dit-il, et je m'élèverai aussi haut que les pigeons.

Puis il déchira le papier. Il avait maintenant une raison de vouloir rester plus que jamais. Celle de ne pas donner raison à ceux qui étaient partis. A ceux qui avaient échoué aux épreuves. A ceux qui avaient renoncé à tout jamais aux promesses faites à sa génération. Ou encore à ceux qui étaient restés démobilisés durant les années noires de la décennie 80.

Il décida alors de ne plus écouter cette voix qui grouillait dans sa tête et qui prétendait le gouverner. De ne plus parler du monde qui, de toute façon, ne lui avait jamais appartenu. De la parole elle-même, qu'il ne craignait plus de perdre. Du rire qui s'était affadi, attristé. De l'amour qui ne savait plus s'y prendre. De la dignité qui avait foutu le camp. Il voulait provisoirement se débarrasser de sa prétention de lutter contre tout cela. Contre la solitude et les terrains vagues. Contre les moustiques et la boue des caniveaux. Au lieu de s'occuper de cela, Job avait pris la décision de se lever de bonne heure et de parcourir à nouveau, utilement, les allées humides des hachélèmes.

Comme le "tanrec hibernant dans la latérite rouge", Job ne faisait qu'un à présent avec le paysage désolant de la "Cité des Imbéciles". Il lui fallait se camoufler ainsi, pour pas que le destin repère ses traces. Pour pas qu'il le reconnaisse. En enjambant les égouts à ciel ouvert où couvaient tranquillement les larves de moustique, avec la ferme intention d'y aller, sans passion excessive certes, mais résolument, il s'aperçut qu'il était en plein dedans, dans *"cette vie qui ne faisait pas de cadeau"*.

"Nul ne sait quelle direction il va prendre", disait l'Ombiasa à propos de son "terrible destin". Mais Job croyait avoir une chance car pour lui, la vie elle-même était chance.

— Le soleil brille aussi sur le cul des chiens, dit-il.

Le simple fait *d'être là* était une incommensurable virtualité. Cela l'aidait à se convaincre qu'il pouvait encore aboutir à quelque

Striding across the open sewers in which mosquito larvae were breeding quietly, firmly intending to go there, without any inordinate passion certainly, but resolutely, he noticed that he was right in the middle of it, of "this life that gives nothing away for free."

"No one knows which direction it will take," the *ombiasa* used to say regarding his "terrible destiny." But Job thought he had a chance because for him life itself was chance.

"The sun shines on the rear end of dogs as well," he said.

The simple fact of *being there* was an unequaled potentiality. This helped him to convince himself that he could still amount to something acceptable. That he could still regain his dignity, build himself a future, and thus know the true strength of his will, his ability to be there without disappearing, all those things that from here on would be essential for his survival: cunning, laughter, intelligence, patience, love for his own people, his generosity as he said.

He firmly intended to do his best from now on and noticed that he was already running short of time. Thinking of this destiny that was too awful, too pretentious to rule over him, to govern his life, he said:

"I'll let you have the rest of this whole day, but the future will be entirely mine and I'll have the last word over you."

Then in the humid alleyways of the *hachélèmes*, he walked in the morning steam, seething with rage. It seemed very strange to him, but rather calming, to hear his own voice cry out in turn, but just for now, as he had sworn to himself:

"BOTTLES AND RAGS! WE BUY BOTTLES AND RAGS! WE BUY BOTTLES AND RAGS . . ."

chose d'acceptable. Qu'il pouvait encore reconquérir sa dignité, se construire un avenir, connaître ainsi la force réelle de sa volonté, son aptitude à être là, sans disparaître, toutes ces choses désormais essentielles pour sa survie: la ruse, le rire, l'intelligence, la patience, l'amour pour les siens, sa générosité comme il disait.

Il avait la ferme intention de faire de son mieux désormais et s'aperçut que le temps déjà lui faisait défaut. En pensant à ce destin trop moche, trop prétentieux de régner sur lui, de régenter sa vie, il dit:

— Je te laisse l'entièreté de ce jour, mais l'avenir sera à moi tout à fait et j'aurai le dernier mot sur toi.

Puis, dans les allées humides des hachélèmes, il marchait dans la vapeur du matin, la rage au coeur. Cela lui faisait tout drôle, mais plus rassérénant, d'entendre sa propre voix crier à son tour, mais provisoirement, comme il se l'était juré:

— BOUTEILLES ET CHIFFONS! NOUS ACHETONS! BOUTEILLES ET CHIFFONS! NOUS ACHETONS! BOUTEILLES ET CHIFFONS. . .

Lila Ratsifandriamanana

Born in 1959, Lila Ratsifandriamanana is a teacher of natural sciences in Antananarivo. She has published novels, plays, and poetry in Malagasy and, under the pen name of Lila, has written poetry and short stories in French. One of the latter, Dieu descendra sur la terre demain! *(God will come down to earth tomorrow!), is reproduced below.*

God Will Come Down to Earth Tomorrow!

Here is the very latest scoop! It's gone around the world with the speed of light . . .

Finally, a decision worthy of the wisdom of the Divine. It's about time that he came down: to see with human eyes what is really going on down here. From up high, everything is illusion, an impression. . . . Things are scaled down both in time and in space. His field of vision is too vast! He can embrace half of humanity with a single glance. But then humanity appears in a different proportion, that of a microscopic world! The immense magnifying glass of the heavens does not allow for an inspection of every little nook, of every minute detail. And then, too, divine time was not conceived of in the same dimension as the human calendar. To have an idea of how things move when accelerated by gravity, he must have another look at the images in slow motion. That way he might have noticed a few signs of the suffering and wretchedness that lay at the root of his doubts . . .

Yes, be quick. . . . Time rushes headlong into the abyss of the past. . . . The deplorable state of those he amasses daily in his kingdom has convinced him. Let's imagine the spectacle: thirty percent are individuals keratinized by old age, thirty percent are young people under stress or mutilated through hideous accidents. Twenty percent are scrawny children wasted by

---

Translated from the French by Marjolijn de Jager

Lila Ratsifandriamanana

Née en 1959, Lila Ratsifandriamanana est professeur de sciences naturelles à Antananarivo. Elle a publié des romans, des pièces de théâtre, et de la poésie en malgache. Sous le nom de plume de Lila, elle a aussi écrit de la poésie et des nouvelles en français, dont l'une d'elles est reproduite ci-dessous: Dieu descendra sur la terre demain!

Dieu descendra sur la terre demain!

C'est le tout dernier scoop! Il a fait le tour des continents avec la célérité de la lumière. . .

Enfin, une décision digne de la sagesse divine. Il est temps qu'il descende: Voir ce qui se passe ici-bas avec les yeux des hommes. De là-haut, tout est fiction, impression. . . Les choses sont réduites aussi bien dans le temps que dans l'espace. Trop vaste, son champ de vision! Il peut embrasser la moitié de l'humanité d'un seul coup d'oeil. Mais alors, celle-ci apparaît sous une autre proportion: un monde microscopique! L'immense loupe de la voûte céleste ne permet pas d'inspecter les moindres recoins, les menus détails. Et puis, le temps divin n'est pas conçu avec la même dimension que le calendrier humain. Pour avoir une idée des mouvements suivant l'accélération gravitationnelle, il doit repasser les images au ralenti. Il a pu détecter ainsi quelques indices de souffrance et de misère qui furent à l'origine de ses doutes. . .

Oui, se dépêcher. . . Le temps se précipite dans le gouffre du passé. . . L'état lamentable de ceux qu'il recueille journalièrement dans son royaume l'a convaincu. Imaginons le spectacle: trente pour cent d'individus kératinisés par la vieillesse, trente pour cent de jeunes stressés ou mutilés par d'effroyables accidents. Vingt pour cent d'enfants squelettiques rongés par la malnutrition. . . Les remettre en état, leur redonner leur visage d'anges, Dieu ne connaît plus le répit. A chaque fois, il doit user

malnutrition. . . . Getting them back into shape, giving them back their angel faces—God no longer knows rest. Every time, he must use his prodigious artistic talent. And to say that he created the world for these little innocents! A world too cruel to understand divine tenderness . . .

God did not make it to the end of his work: the rest?

Lovely creatures, seemingly vigorous! But for whom he must save what is most important: the soul! The task is difficult. . . . In the heavenly atmosphere a perpetual friction reigns between divine wisdom and satanic treachery! A thousand evil spells dangle inexorably from the devil's tail. It is a relentless struggle: storm on earth, thunder somewhere in heaven. . . . But, Supreme Being of all time and all place, God has never known the other side of victory. . . . This time it's been decided. Better to prevent than to cure. He will come directly down and bring the most powerful of his remedies: reason, wisdom, and love.

He could have sent a messenger. Only past experience had not been very convincing. The ultimate wisdom? To come down himself. Too many tears, too many lamentations, too many prayers had reached his ears. His natural amplifier, made up of a complicated tangle of Hertzian waves, spared him nothing!

God meditates a moment and becomes lost in a pool of nostalgia. As an unparalleled painter, the earth had been his masterpiece. The harmony of meticulously chosen colors enhanced the grace and beauty of the shapes. Deftly he weaves the various nuances of the rainbow into his canvas. The blue of the ocean is filled with purity! The white of the snow expresses grandeur. . . . The emerald green of vegetation revives hope. . . . The red of the flame tree reveals love and strength! And then, all over the place, a tender touch of pink to soften the total picture. He has never grown tired of contemplating this miracle. But one day . . . a deep despondency . . . loneliness. . . .

de son talent prodigieux d'artiste. Et dire qu'il a édifié le monde pour ces petits innocents! Un monde trop cruel pour comprendre la tendresse divine. . .

Dieu n'est pas arrivé au bout de son compte: le reste?

De belles créatures apparemment solides! Mais pour lesquelles il doit sauver le plus important: l'âme! La tâche est difficile. . . Dans l'atmosphère céleste règne une friction perpétuelle entre la sagesse divine et la perfidie satanique! Mille maléfices pendent inexorablement à la queue diabolique. La lutte est acharnée: orage sur la terre, tonnerre quelque part dans le ciel. . . Mais, Suprême Etre de toujours et de partout, Dieu n'a jamais connu les revers de la victoire. . . Cette fois c'est décidé. Mieux vaut prévenir que guérir. Il descendra sur place, apportera le plus puissant de ses remèdes: la raison, la sagesse et l'amour.

Il avait pu envoyer un messager. Seulement, les expériences vécues jusqu'alors étaient peu convaincantes. L'ultime sagesse? Se déplacer soi-même. Trop de larmes, trop de lamentations, trop de prières sont parvenues à son oreille. Son amplificateur naturel composé d'un enchevêtrement complexe d'ondes hertziennes ne lui a rien épargné!

Dieu médite un moment et se noie dans une mare de nostalgie. En tant que peintre incomparable, la terre avait été son chef-d'oeuvre. L'harmonie des couleurs minutieusement choisies rehaussait la grâce et la beauté des silhouettes. En un tour de main, il a gravé sur sa toile les diverses nuances de l'arcenciel. Le bleu de l'océan est plein de pureté! Le blanc de neige exprime la majesté. . . L'émeraude des verdures ravive l'espoir. . . Le rouge des flamboyants révèle l'amour et la force! Et puis, un peu partout, une tendre touche de rose pour adoucir l'ensemble. Il ne s'est jamais lassé de contempler cette merveille. Mais un jour. . . Profonde mélancolie. . . solitude. . . Et il succomba à l'idée d'insuffler la vie et le mouvement à sa toile. Depuis, moins d'ennui, mais plus de soucis et il oublia son repos.

And he gave in to the idea of breathing life and movement into his canvas. Since then, less boredom, but greater worries, and he forgot about resting.

Today, he is contemplating from up high in his heaven. Grey, grey, grey everywhere! Impressive. . . . He adjusts his best nanoscope: a long gold-tinged band wraps itself around the little ball of earth and continues from one end to the other with the monotony of the desert and desolation. Where has the green of the prairies gone? He searches and his lens reflects a horrible brick red.[1] A gritty red of shame. . . . A deep wound! Further on, much further on, a reflection of thick ash,[2] oily with grief, masks the limpidness of the oceans. This disparate mixture of colors looks very much like modern surrealist painting. God is accepting: Picasso is a painter of genius who has fascinated humanity. When God welcomed him into his kingdom, the latter encouraged him to change his style. But God has inflexible loyalty. He wouldn't let himself be influenced. More than ever, his principle is the same: give earth back its original unaffectedness.

Still, he has certain fears: without his being aware of it, man has become very powerful. He didn't hesitate to pillage the earth and to extract from its entrails the treasures it was hiding. And man constructed infernal machines: cars, robots, spaceships, and weapons of all kinds.

God has unlimited forbearance! He even entertains himself as he peers at those devices flying desperately back and forth across space. Probably looking for the face of the Divine in the infinity of the universe. . . .

He reassures himself:

His face is not yet within the range of human distance. On the other hand, his heart is so very close by. His heart that is breaking because of so many absurdities. Is man not able to maintain a life with nature and not above her? God thought he

Aujourd'hui, il contemple du haut de sa voûte. Du gris, du gris, du gris partout! Impressionnant. . . Il ajuste son meilleur nanoscope: une longue bande mordorée enlace la petite boule terrestre et persiste d'un bout à l'autre avec la monotonie du désert et de la désolation. Où est-il donc le vert des prairies? Il cherche et son objectif reflète un rouge brique horrible. Un rouge terreux de honte. . . Profonde blessure! Plus loin, encore plus loin, un reflet de cendre épais, huileux de détresse, voile la limpidité des océans. Ce mélange disparate de couleurs ressemble bien à la peinture surréaliste moderne. Dieu accepte: Picasso est un peintre génial qui a captivé l'humanité. Quand il l'avait recueilli dans son royaume, celui-ci l'avait incité à changer de style. Mais Dieu est d'une fidélité rigoureuse. Il ne se laissa pas influencer. Plus que jamais, son principe est le même: redonner à la terre son naturel d'origine.

Il a toutefois des craintes: à son insu, l'homme est devenu très puissant. Il n'a pas hésité à piller la terre, et à sortir de ses entrailles les trésors qu'elle recelait. Et l'homme a construit ces machines infernales: voitures, robots, vaisseaux spatiaux, armes de toutes sortes.

Dieu est d'une indulgence sans limite! Il s'amuse même à contempler ces engins qui sillonnent désespérément l'espace. Vraisemblablement à la recherche du visage divin dans l'infinité de l'univers. . .

Il se rassure:

Son visage n'est pas encore à portée d'une distance humaine. Son coeur par ailleurs est si proche. Son coeur qui se brise à cause de tant d'absurdités. L'homme ne peut-il pas s'obstiner à vivre avec la nature et non au-dessus de celle-ci? Dieu a cru avoir suffisamment enseigné de sa sagesse et de son honnêteté. Aujourd'hui, il reconnaît avoir tort. . .

La plus récente de ses inquiétudes? C'est le trou que ces petits diables d'hommes viennent de percer au sommet de son

had taught enough of his wisdom and honesty. Today, he recognizes that he has been wrong. . . .

The most recent of his worries? It is the hole those little devils of men have just pierced in the top of his geodesic dome. They really are incorrigible! God ventures a glance across the hideous wound. A pitiful spectacle! The tuft of ice with which he had so tenderly capped his Masterpiece is in the process of melting into the grey of the ocean. In vain, he makes an attempt at turning away a ray of sunlight that is too sharp. Clearly the ultraviolet no longer obeys him! This waveband needs to be revised. And to say that any little nothing would suffice to block this gaping hole! If only man would not waste his time getting lost in the amassing of chemical formulas. If only man had not given in to the spell of temptation. He favored pride and vanity over modesty. The result? Vile competition, cheating, carnage, and the world torn apart on every side. . . .

Yes, God will have much to do to reestablish order on earth.

On earth?

While awaiting God's arrival, there is a general mobilization! Let's be reassured! It isn't yet the third world war. Just practice. Actually, how did we catch wind of this enormous piece of news?

It's a classic story: one evening, a humble believer, still cognizant of divine activities, entrusts this to his beloved spouse. The wife, as all of Eve's descendants (there, too, God must have made a serious error when he created her with the face of an angel) . . . the wife, of course, could not keep the secret and in less than no time all of humanity was brought up to date! The news is official! Abnormal sounds picked up by the best satellites confirm it. The media being what they are today, the happy event was on page one of every daily paper two days after the secret was out.

Immediately, evil and worries are pushed back into oblivion.

géoïde. Ils sont vraiment incorrigibles! Dieu risque un coup d'oeil à travers la plaie horrible. Spectacle pitoyable! La touffe de glace avec laquelle il a tendrement coiffé son Chef-d'oeuvre est en train de fondre dans le gris de l'océan. Il tente vainement de détourner un rayon trop perçant du soleil. Décidément l'ultraviolet ne lui obéit plus! Cette bande de fréquence est à réviser. Et dire qu'un rien suffirait à obturer ce trou béant! Si seulement l'homme ne perdait pas son temps à se noyer dans cet amoncellement de formules chimiques. Si seulement l'homme n'avait pas cédé au charme de la tentation. Il a préféré l'orgueil, la vanité à la modestie. Le résultat? Vile concurrence, tromperie, carnage et le monde est déchiré de toutes parts. . .

Oui, Dieu aura beaucoup à faire pour rétablir l'ordre sur la terre.

Sur la terre?

En attendant l'arrivée de Dieu, c'est la mobilisation générale! Rassurons-nous! Ce n'est pas encore la troisième guerre mondiale. Juste un entraînement. Au fait, comment a-t-on eu vent de la prodigieuse nouvelle?

L'histoire est classique: un soir, un humble fidèle qui a encore la perception des activités divines, en fit la confidence à sa chère épouse. La femme, comme toutes descendantes d'Eve (Là encore, Dieu avait dû faire une grave erreur en la créant avec un visage d'ange). . . La femme, bien entendu, ne tint pas le secret et en moins de rien, l'humanité entière fut mise au courant! La nouvelle est formelle! Les bruits anormaux captés par les meilleurs satellites la confirment. Les médias étant actuellement ce qu'ils sont, le surlendemain de la confidence, l'heureux évènement est à la une de tous les quotidiens.

Aussitôt, maux et soucis sont refoulés dans les oubliettes. Dieu vient avant tout! Il vient avant le problème de la faim au Sahel, le surpeuplement de la Chine, les ravages de la drogue en Amérique Latine! (Les trafiquants respirent un moment au

God comes before everything! He comes before the problem of hunger in the Sahel, of overpopulation in China, of the ravages of drugs in Latin America! (The dealers breathe their cocaine breath a moment. . . .) God comes before the debt of the Third World, the threat of AIDS, the Israeli-Lebanese conflict, racism in South-Africa. . . . The list could easily become very long! But we shall see later on, yes, later! The chaos in the East? Come now! That's not serious. . . . The whims of the stock market? Childishness! Finally, the destruction of the environment, the natural disasters . . . cyclones in Jamaica, floods in Bangladesh, earthquakes in Armenia . . . we turn back to God! After all, he has a share in the responsibility, too. And, at this point, he will be the only one able to remove the imminence of the collapse!

Yes, God comes before everything, he will be the cure for the thousand human evils.

"D-day" is approaching. The churches are filled with new followers. From New York to Tokyo, passing through London, Paris, Moscow, and Beijing, extraordinary summits are held, one after the other, by the great leaders of nations. Finally! for once in human history, a common ground. The Vatican, from its end, is humming and feverishly preparing the festivities. It's not every day that God comes down to earth.

Here, between parentheses, a crucial point is to be made:

Who will be the first to welcome the Supreme Being? To which blessed nation will this right be granted? Each one attempts to demonstrate its superiority as compared to the others. Nobody wants to give up his or her place. It's a very delicate question! A conflict might explode at the last moment. . . . Present-day economic classification is not a sufficient criterion. So? How can fervor of faith, sanctity, and servitude be measured? Surely the problem is a difficult one and the software able to resolve it has not yet been perfected. Fortunately, the Pope is there with his wisdom and his impartiality. He had

souffle de la cocaïne. . .). Dieu vient avant la dette du Tiers-monde, la menace du SIDA, le conflit israélo-libanais, le racisme en Afrique du Sud. . . La liste risque d'être assez longue! Mais on verra plus tard, oui plus tard! Le remue-ménage de l'Est? Allons donc! Ce n'est pas sérieux. . . Les caprices de la bourse? Enfantillage! Enfin, la dégradation de l'environnement, les fléaux naturels. . . Cyclones sur la Jamaïque, inondation au Bangladesh, séïsme en Arménie. . . On s'en remet à Dieu! Après tout, il a aussi sa part de responsabilité. Et, au point où on en est, il sera le seul à pouvoir éloigner l'imminence de la débâcle!

Oui, Dieu vient avant tout, il sera le remède aux mille maux humains.

Le jour "D" approche. Les églises se comblent de nouveaux adeptes. De New-York à Tokyo, en passant par Londres, Paris, Moscou et Pékin, se succèdent les sommets extraordinaires des grands chefs d'état. Enfin! un terrain d'entente pour une fois, dans l'histoire de l'humanité. Le Vatican de son côté bourdonne et prépare fébrilement les festivités. Ce n'est pas tous les jours que Dieu descend sur la Terre.

Ici, une parenthèse est ouverte, concernant un point crucial:

Qui va donner en premier l'hospitalité à l'Etre Suprême? A quel bienheureux pays ce droit va-t-il être octroyé? Chacun tente de démontrer sa supériorité vis-à-vis des autres. Personne ne veut céder la place. La question est très délicate! Un conflit risque d'éclater au dernier moment. . . Le classement économique actuel n'est pas un critère suffisant. Alors? Comment mesurer l'intensité de la foi, la sainteté et la servitude? Le problème est certes difficile et le logiciel capable de le résoudre n'est pas encore mis au point. Heureusement, le Pape est là avec sa sagesse et son équité. On a failli l'oublier au cours de ces brûlantes discussions, mais il a su révéler de sa présence au bon moment. . .

almost been forgotten in the course of these burning discussions, but he managed to make his presence known at the right moment. . . .

Up high, resting on cushions of thick clouds, God is dreaming. . . . He already sees himself on earth! He has landed right in the middle of New York! He is dizzy. He is not at ease. His height as a man reduces him in the sight of these tall skyscrapers that clutter up the horizon. Yet, he doesn't really expect to find his Garden of Eden back here! It's a paleography buried from now on in the haziness of oblivion.

God has trouble breathing. The air is sodden, without any doubt because of the lack of respect for the atmospheric norm. He finds it equally difficult to become accustomed to the blinking of the bright neon lights, the frenzy of the innumerable machines that clog Manhattan's arteries. The sidewalks are swarming with rushing, worried automatons, their gestures agitated. He finds it really difficult to adjust! Sometimes it is hard to accept the evidence. . . . He feels the earth give way beneath his feet, at a rate he has not known until now. See here! He quickly recalculates: the rotational speed is almost unchanging! Inexplicable, this acceleration that suddenly appears as his calculations progress. . . .

So the earth is no longer what it had been. God recognizes that man must have worked at a great pace and with considerable effort. Capitalizing heavily on his intelligence, he has done his best to attain absolute truth on the verge of intricacy. Does not this thirst for perfection express the intensity of his love for life? God has no reason at all to reproach him. . . . One thing is certain: man does not have the same sense of possession as he does. The entire universe vibrates in his hands. Nothingness as well as time beyond any existence belongs to him. He is able to be in the past as well as in the present and the future. As for man, space and time are missing.

Là-haut, reposant sur des coussins de nuages moelleux, Dieu rêve. . . Il se voit déjà sur la terre! Il a atterri en plein dans New York! Il a le vertige. Il n'est pas dans sa peau. Sa taille d'homme l'amenuise au regard de ces hauts gratte-ciel qui inondent l'horizon. Il ne s'attend tout de même pas à retrouver son paradis d'Eden! C'est une paléogéographie désormais enfouie dans la nébulosité de l'oubli.

Dieu a du mal à respirer. L'air est saturé, sans aucun doute par non-respect de la norme atmosphérique. Il a autant de mal à s'accommoder aux clignotements des néons lumineux, à la frénésie des innombrables machines qui défoncent les artères de Manhattan. Les trottoirs pullulent d'automates pressés, inquiets, aux gestes convulsifs. Il a vraiment du mal à s'adapter! Difficile parfois d'accepter l'évidence. . . Il sent la terre se dérober dangereusement sous ses pieds, à une allure qu'il a méconnue jusqu'alors. Voyons! Il refait rapidement ses calculs: la vitesse de rotation est quasi uniforme! Inexplicable, cette accélération qui apparaît soudain au fur et à mesure de ses opérations. . .

Ainsi, la terre n'est plus ce qu'elle avait été. Dieu reconnait: l'homme a dû travailler au rythme d'un effort considérable. Exploitant à fond son intelligence, il s'est évertué à atteindre la vérité absolue à la limite de la complexité. Cette soif de plénitude n'exprime-t-elle pas l'intensité de son amour pour la vie? Dieu n'a aucune raison de le blâmer. . . Une chose est certaine: l'homme n'a pas la même notion de possession que lui. L'univers entier tressaille entre ses mains. Le néant ainsi que le temps au-delà de toute existence lui appartient. Il peut aussi bien être dans le passé, le présent et l'avenir. Quant à l'homme, l'espace et le temps font défaut.

Il ne pouvait plus se contenter de sa modeste part de vie! L'un a voulu accaparer celle de l'autre. . . Personne n'est satisfait de ce qu'il possède. . . Tout le monde se dépêche de vivre. . .

He could no longer be content with his modest bit of life! Each one wanted to grasp what was the other's. . . . Nobody is satisfied with what he has. . . . Everybody is in a rush to live. . . . The brevity of existence makes it even more thrilling and everyone forgets the appeal of simple and natural happiness. . . .

Caught up in the turmoil of an endless dream God continues on his way. Suddenly he finds himself in a narrow alleyway of Bujumbura. Crouched in the shade of barrels scattered inside a miserable shed, a young boy sits crying. It is hot, terribly hot. God feels the sweat forming beads on his brow. He goes up to the child who doesn't see him. He is blind. . . .

God wakes up with a start. With difficulty, he rubs his eyes. Clearly, he has slept badly. But in his thoughts, images are becoming sharper. Now he knows whom he will visit, how to penetrate a billion human hearts, how to appease a few billion torments. . . . Tomorrow! He will be among men and he will simply say: "The unique, the best one among all the roses on earth, will always be the one you plant in your own garden. . . ." Even if real roses have disappeared today, along with the desire to plant them at home!

But let's get back to earth: everything is in good order. Everything has been beautifully organized to welcome the Supreme Being. Thousands of audio-visual monstrosities are turned toward the sky. In the observatory in London no one sleeps anymore. There is a thousand times more work to do there than when Halley's Comet passed.

In a forgotten corner of Bujumbura, a young blind boy is crying bitter tears. He knows about the news, he has heard the talk in the town. He has felt the excitement around him in the rushed comings and goings of people, in the unusual racket, in the resolute rhythm of the drums. His buddies in the street feverishly comment on the event. But he, poor blind child, is not like everybody else. He will not see the face of God. That will be the one

La brièveté de l'existence la rend encore plus exaltante, et chacun oublie l'attrait d'un bonheur simple et naturel. . .

Dieu poursuit son chemin dans les remous d'un rêve infini. Il se retrouve soudain dans une ruelle étroite de Bujumbura. Tapi à l'ombre de tonneaux éparpillés dans un misérable hangar, un jeune garçon est en train de pleurer. Il fait chaud, terriblement chaud. Dieu sent la sueur lui perler au front. Il s'approche de l'enfant mais celui-ci ne le voit pas. Il est aveugle. . .

Dieu se réveille en sursaut. Il se frotte péniblement les yeux. Visiblement, il a mal dormi. Mais des images se précisent dans sa pensée. Il sait désormais à qui rendre visite, comment pénétrer dans un milliard de coeurs humains, comment apaiser quelques milliards de tourments. . . Demain! Il sera parmi les hommes et dira simplement: "L'unique, la meilleure parmi toutes les roses sur la terre, sera toujours celle que l'on plante dans son propre jardin. . ." Même si aujourd'hui les véritables roses ont disparu avec l'envie de les planter chez soi!

Mais revenons sur terre: tout est en ordre. Tout est parfaitement organisé pour l'accueil de l'Etre Suprême. Des milliers de monstres audio-visuels sont braqués sur le ciel. A l'observatoire de Londres, on ne dort plus. Il y a là mille fois plus de travail que lors du passage de la comète de Halley.

Dans un coin perdu de Bujumbura, un jeune garçon aveugle est en train de pleurer à chaudes larmes. Il est au courant de la nouvelle, d'après les rumeurs de la ville. Il a senti l'excitation alentour aux allées et venues pressantes des gens, au tapage inhabituel, au rythme décidé des tam-tams. Ses camarades de rue commentent fébrilement l'évènement. Mais lui, le pauvre aveugle, il n'est pas comme tout le monde. Il ne verra pas le visage de Dieu. Ce serait l'unique et véritable regret de sa triste existence. Dieu, pourtant, n'a pas été tout à fait tendre à son égard en lui offrant la cécité à la naissance. Mais il s'y est habitué depuis. Il a même une perception accentuée des choses. A

and only true regret of his sad existence. God, however, was not altogether merciful to him when he presented him with blindness at birth. But he has become used to it since then. He even has a heightened perception of things. Through the thick veil of his eyes, he has been able to discover the beauty and tenderness of his mother, the brightness and warmth of the sun. He has been able to appreciate the purity of the Tanganyika where he would often go to quench his thirst. But he has also seen a reflection of darkness on his ebony skin. He has seen the wretchedness that has led him to beg in the streets of the city there. He has read the lack of understanding on the face of those who have rebuked his existence. He has seen the hostile expressions of contempt in the sound of his buddies' laughter. He has seen other things. He has seen more of them than those who have the gift of sight.

But tomorrow, no matter what he does, he will not see the face of God. And the child weeps in his bitterness and despair.

In the labyrinth of his sobs, he notices the sounds of footsteps dragging over the arid soil. It is his mother. She comes closer. He senses her. He recognizes her easily by her heavy tread. A familiar smell emerges from her sweating body. His mother? A presence, a comfort, a perfume in his loneliness, a semblance of color in his extinguished world—she had made a habit of sitting by his side at the end of her interminable days of laundering. She would talk to him, describe things to him in minute detail, the humans who populate his restricted world. And she did her best to give a better impression of the monotony of her daily existence. Her warm breath, her voice quivering with tenderness reassured the child. But that hoarse voice would betray a weariness. This evening, however, an unusual elation came across her words . . . in her words. . . .

"Tomorrow, son, is going to be a wonderful day. God has heard our prayers at last. He will come to us and surely he will hold out his hand to us."

travers le voile épais de ses yeux, il a pu distinguer la beauté et la tendresse maternelle, la clarté et la chaleur du soleil. Il a pu apprécier la pureté du Tanganyika, où il apaisait souvent sa soif. Mais il a vu aussi un reflet de ténèbres sur sa peau ébène. Il y a vu la misère qui l'a poussé à mendier dans les rues de la ville. Il a lu l'incompréhension sur le visage de ceux qui condamnent son existence. Il a vu les traits hostiles du mépris au son du rire de ses camarades. Il en a vu d'autres. Il en a vu plus que celui qui possédait la vue.

Mais demain, quoi qu'il fasse, il ne verra pas le visage de Dieu. Et l'enfant pleure son amertume et son désespoir.

Dans les dédales de ses sanglots, il perçoit des bruits de pas traînant sur le sol aride. C'est sa mère. Elle s'approche. Il la sent. Il la reconnaît facilement à sa démarche lourde. Une odeur familière émane de son corps en sueur. Sa mère? Une présence, un réconfort, un parfum dans sa solitude, un semblant de couleur dans son monde éteint. . . elle prenait l'habitude de s'asseoir à ses côtés au bout de ses journées d'interminable lessive. Elle lui parlait, lui décrivait avec minutie les choses, les êtres qui peuplent son monde étriqué. Et elle s'efforçait de donner une meilleure impression à la monotonie du quotidien. Son haleine chaude, sa voix vibrante de tendresse rassurait l'enfant. Mais cette voix rauque trahissait la lassitude. Ce soir, pourtant, une exaltation inhabituelle transparaît à travers ses paroles. . .

— Demain, mon fils, sera un jour merveilleux. Dieu a enfin entendu nos prières. Il viendra vers nous et nous tendra sûrement la main.

L'enfant se tait. Il ne partage pas son enthousiasme. Dieu apportera-t-il le mil qui manque à la case? Dieu saura-t-il atténuer la chaleur torride consumant sa chair et sa volonté? Dieu saura-t-il vêtir son corps dénudé par la misère? Saura-t-il alléger l'éternelle fatigue de sa mère? Saura-t-il alors lui donner la vue qui lui manque tant. . . La vue et le goût de vivre? Et enfin,

The child remains silent. He does not share her enthusiasm. Will God bring the millet they do not have in their hut? Will God know how to lessen the sweltering heat that is eating his flesh and his willpower? Will God know how to clothe his body naked in its wretchedness? Will he know how to soothe his mother's everlasting fatigue? Will he also know how to give him sight which he misses so much . . . sight and the zest for life? And lastly, will he at least see this God they talk about so much? He is convinced the opposite will be true. He no longer hopes for answers to his questions. Questions he'll be hauling along throughout an interminable life.

"Me, I won't see him," he mumbles very quietly.

His mother turns to him and looks deep into his lightless eyes, brimming with tears. She remains silent. She runs her hands through the tight tuft of charred hair. Only she could understand this helpless grief. But deep inside herself profound beliefs lie anchored. Her son will see God like everyone else. Better than everyone else! He will look at him with his heart. And then God will come to meet him. . . .

And so everyone on earth is waiting. A waiting unique in the world. A waiting woven from feelings that are as old as the earth. Such as the impatience of a child on Christmas Eve, such as the anxiousness of the lover before an uncertain rendezvous, such as the agitation of woman torn apart by the pains of childbirth, such as the agony of the dying. . . . A waiting made of doubts and hope!

Up high, God is very calm. He has decided to come down. He will come. He will come with the face of serenity, loyalty, modesty, love, and courage. He who honestly wants to see him will see him. . . .

Let us remember, though: God's time is not measured on human scale! Will he come down to earth TOMORROW?

le verra-t-il au moins, ce Dieu dont on parle tant? Il est persuadé du contraire. Il n'espère plus de réponses à ses questions. Des questions qu'il traînera encore durant une vie interminable.

— Moi, je ne le verrai pas, murmure-t-il tout bas.

Sa mère se tourne vers lui et plonge son regard dans les yeux éteints et bouillants de larmes. Elle reste silencieuse. Elle passe les mains dans la touffe serrée de cheveux calcinés. Elle seule pouvait comprendre cette détresse impuissante. Mais en son for intérieur sont ancrées de profondes convictions. Son fils verra Dieu comme tout le monde. Mieux que tout le monde! Il le regardera avec le coeur. Et Dieu viendra alors à sa rencontre. . .

Ainsi, chacun sur la terre attend. Une attente unique au monde. Une attente tressée de sentiments vieux comme la terre. Telle l'impatience de l'enfant à la veille de Noël, telle l'anxiété de l'amant au rendez-vous incertain, tel l'émoi de la femme déchirée par les douleurs de l'accouchement, tel le tourment de l'agonisant. . . Une attente faite de doutes et d'espoir!

Là-haut, Dieu est très calme. Il a décidé de venir. Il viendra. Il viendra avec le visage de la sérénité, la loyauté, la modestie, l'amour et le courage. Celui qui veut sincèrement le voir le verra. . .

Rappelons-nous toutefois: le temps pour Dieu n'est pas conçu à l'échelle humaine! Descendra-t-il sur la terre DEMAIN?

Alice Ravoson

Born in 1956, Alice Ravoson is a geography teacher. She has written several short stories, so far unpublished, among which are Eau la vie, eau la mort *(Water life, water death) and* Aux cimes des aloalo *(In the top of the* aloalo[1]*), whose translation is reproduced below.*

In the Top of the Aloalo

The telephone rang.

"Madame, the number you requested!"

I nodded my head in thanks to the receptionist of the Capricorn Hotel where we were staying.

"Is that you, Anne? Hello! This is Marielle. We just arrived in Tulear,[2] a gorgeous trip. You have no idea how fantastic the south of Madagascar is; the baobab trees, the desert-like plateau, the sandstone massifs of Isalo shaped like ruins . . . I feel as if I'm dreaming. We've taken lots of pictures. I'll show them to you. I'm very happy. And how's everything in Tananarive, OK?"

"Hi, Marielle. I'm so pleased for you. . . . But, actually . . ." As she hesitated, I was gripped by a dark premonition. My throat tightened. My insides as well.

"Anne, don't tell me that . . .?"

"Yes, Marielle. I am so terribly sorry."

I put the receiver down. My eyes were staring into space.

A small room in the cancer ward, back there, six hundred kilometers away. A tiny figure drowning in the white sheets. And all those things: tubes with serum, catheters, drains, bottles, oxygen mask. Bony hands clutching at the pillow. Eyes darting in a face haggard with suffering, whose call for help was so piercing. And moaning, more moaning. Months of moaning. In vain . . .

Translated from the French by Marjolijn de Jager

Alice Ravoson

Née en 1956, Alice Ravoson est professeur de géographie. Elle est l'auteur de plusieurs nouvelles, encore inédites, parmi lesquelles: Eau la vie, eau la mort *et* Aux cimes des aloalo, *présentée ci-dessous.*

Aux cimes des aloalo

Une sonnerie de téléphone.

— Madame, le numéro que vous avez demandé!

De la tête, je fis un signe de remerciement au réceptionniste de l'Hôtel Capricorne, où nous étions descendus.

— C'est toi, Anne? Bonjour! Ici Marielle. Nous venons juste d'arriver à Tuléar, un voyage superbe. Tu peux pas imaginer à quel point le sud de Madagascar est fantastique; les baobabs, le plateau désertique, les massifs de grès ruiniformes de l'Isalo. . . J'ai l'impression de rêver. On a fait plein de photos. Je vous en passerai. Je suis très heureuse. Et à Tananarive, ça va?

— Bonjour Marielle. Je suis contente pour toi. . . Mais, au fait. . . A son hésitation, un sombre pressentiment me saisit. Ma gorge se noua. Mes entrailles aussi.

— Anne, ne me dis pas que. . . ?

— Si Marielle. Je suis désolée.

Je reposais le combiné. Mes yeux se perdirent dans le vague.

Une petite chambre, du service de cancérologie, là-bas à six cent kilomètres d'ici. Une petite forme, noyée dans les draps blancs. Et tout ce tas de choses: tubulures de sérum, sondes, drains, flacons, masque à oxygène. Des mains osseuses qui se crispent sur l'oreiller. Des yeux qui remuent au milieu d'un visage défait par la souffrance, et dont l'appel au secours était si pénétrant. Et des gémissements, encore des gémissements. Des mois de gémissements. En vain. . .

La voix de Marc, mon collègue et copain, qui me secondait

It was the voice of Marc, my colleague and friend who was assisting me with the tourists we were guiding, that pulled me out of my distracted state. The dreadful news that needed no explanation plunged the entire group into great consternation.

"Marielle, we don't know what to say . . ."

In the distance, the sound of the waves crashing onto the beach kept repeating itself, indefinitely. Indifferently.

"We feel so guilty," Michel, one of our tourists, confessed quite sincerely. "If only we hadn't insisted so much on your coming. From now on that will cause some real problems with your in-laws, won't it?"

"If it were just my in-laws! The whole society will never forgive me for not having been at my mother-in-law's bedside as the end came near. Just as it will condemn me mercilessly for having allowed myself to take this trip, this vacation in fact, when my place was next to her and my duty was to be caring for her."

"In any case," Suzy, Michel's wife, responded, "the damage has been done. The only thing left to do now is repair what can be repaired. We'll pay your plane ticket back."

"With the cyclone, the flight for tomorrow, which is Sunday, has been canceled," the receptionist interrupted. "The next flight is Thursday."

"What about the bush-taxis?"[3]

Usually so nervous, I was surprised at my own calm. "Listen," I told them, "traditionally the Malagasy people do not have burials on Mondays or Tuesdays, those days are taboo for interment. So it won't happen until Wednesday.[4] If I take the Sunday bush-taxi tomorrow, I'll have less chance of arriving there earlier than if I leave in your all-terrain vehicle on Monday as planned. So"—my voice composed and authoritarian—"since I cannot be there either way before midday on Wednesday, that is to say only for the burial, this is what I suggest: you've invested a lot of money in this trip. You've prepared for it for months. You were ready to

auprès des touristes que nous guidions, m'arracha de mon égarement. La redoutable nouvelle se passait de mots, et plongea tout le groupe dans l'atterrement.

— Marielle, nous ne savons quoi te dire. . .

Au loin, le bruit des vagues, s'écrasant sur la plage, se répétait indéfiniment. Indifféremment.

— Nous nous sentons coupables, avoua sans hypocrisie Michel, l'un de nos touristes. Si nous n'avions pas tant insisté pour que tu viennes. Ça risque désormais de poser des problèmes auprès de ta belle-famille, n'est-ce pas?

— S'il n'y avait que ma belle famille! Toute la société ne me pardonnera jamais de n'avoir pas été au chevet de ma belle-mère lors de sa fin. Tout comme elle me condamnera impitoyablement de m'être permis ce voyage, voire ces vacances, alors que ma place était auprès d'elle, et mon devoir de la soigner.

— De toute manière, rétorqua Suzy, la femme de Michel, le mal est fait. Il ne reste qu'à réparer les dégats. On te paie les frais d'avion de retour.

— Avec le cyclone, le vol de demain dimanche est annulé, coupa le réceptionniste. Le suivant sera pour jeudi.

— Et le taxi-brousse?

D'habitude si nerveuse, je m'étonnais moi-même de mon calme. "Ecoutez, leur dis-je, par tradition, les Malgaches n'enterrent ni le lundi, ni le mardi, jours tabous pour cela. Ce sera donc pour mercredi. Si je prends le taxi-brousse demain dimanche, j'aurais moins de chance d'y arriver plus tôt, qu'en repartant avec vous lundi comme prévu avec votre tout-terrain. Alors—ma voix se fit posée et autoritaire—comme d'une façon ou d'une autre je ne pourrais y être avant mercredi au milieu de la journée, soit juste pour l'enterrement, voici ce que je vous propose:

— Vous avez beaucoup investi financièrement dans ce voyage. Sa préparation vous a pris des mois. Vous étiez prêts à

brave the approaching cyclone as well as the insecurity of roads threatened by the *dahalo.*[5] Now that we're so close to our goal, I think it's unfair that everything should be ruined by this most regrettable event, whose consequences you should not have to shoulder. We are going to erase this fatal phone call from today's experiences. I shall acquit myself of my task as planned and as stated in my contract with you. And there must be no further question of any mourning before we arrive in Tananarive. For me, my mother-in-law will be alive for another four days."

"Marielle! we can't possibly be that heartless," Michel shrieked as he jumped up from his chair.

He couldn't go on, and sat back down in great confusion when he understood by the look I gave him that I would neither tolerate any commentary nor any continuation of this discussion. In any case, I was already turning my back on them and returning to my room. I had barely fifteen minutes left in which to get ready for the rest of the program: visiting the city.

Established during colonial times, Tulear presented a variety of districts of rather classical architecture. What surprised my foreign friends was the absence of that flagrant dualism that existed in the capital city, Tananarive, where residential areas with luxurious homes stood in bitter contrast with seedy districts, crossroads of misery, filth, and delinquency.

"It seems as if the social divide is less clear-cut here, Marielle?"

"That's not surprising! That dualism always exists in proportion to demographic pressure. Tulear has a fifth of the population of Tananarive." Like an automaton, I gave my speech on the historical sites, the social institutions and other original aspects of that part of the island. Nearby, the tombs of the Mahafaly, a regional ethnicity, held the group's attention. I was trailing behind at a fair distance, flustered by the idea of having to grapple with the theme of death. It had just marked a turning point in a chapter of my life.

braver ce cyclone qui s'approche, cette insécurité de certains passages menacés par les *dahalo*. Si près du but, je trouve injuste que tout soit gâché par un incident, regrettable, je le conçois, mais dont vous n'avez pas à assumer les retombées. Par conséquent, nous allons effacer de notre vécu d'aujourd'hui ce coup de téléphone fatal. Je m'acquitterai de ma tâche tel qu'il fut prévu dans mon contrat auprès de vous. Et pas une seconde avant l'arrivée à Tananarive, il ne devra plus être question de ce deuil. Pour moi, belle-maman vivra quatre jours de plus.

— Marielle! nous ne pouvons manquer d'humanité à ce point, hurla Michel, en bondissant de son fauteuil.

Il ne put continuer, et se rassit confusément, ayant compris, au regard que je levais sur lui, que je n'admettais, ni de commentaires, ni aucune suite à la discussion. D'ailleurs je leur tournais déjà le dos, et rejoignais ma chambre. Je ne disposais que d'à peine un quart d'heure pour me préparer à la suite du programme: la visite de la ville.

De fondation coloniale, Tuléar affichait divers quartiers d'architecure plutôt classique. Ce qui étonnait mes amis étrangers, c'était, par rapport à Tananarive, la capitale, l'absence de ce dualisme flagrant, opposant unités résidentielles aux villas luxueuses, avec des bas-quartiers, carrefours de misère, de saleté et de délinquance.

— Il semble qu'ici, les clivages sociaux soient moins tranchés, Marielle?

— Forcément! ce dualisme est toujours à la dimension de la pression démographique. Tuléar a cinq fois moins d'habitants que Tananarive. Comme une automate, je débitais mon speech sur les sites historiques, les institutions sociales et autres originalités relatives à cette partie de l'île. Dans la périphérie, l'attention du groupe fut retenue par les tombeaux Mahafaly, un groupe ethnique de la région. Moi, je m'attardais assez loin derrière, désemparée à l'idée d'aborder le thème de la mort.

"What are these flat shafts of sculpted wood the tombs are studded with everywhere?"

"Look at them carefully," Marc, my colleague said. "These shafts, called *aloalo* show figurines set one on top of the other. They symbolize the ideals to which people aspire throughout their lifetime. At the top of the *aloalo* the most important element is found."

"In other words, the person's ambition or dream."

"Exactly."

Claudia and Joseph, a subdued married couple, remarked: "On the top of this *aloalo,* you can see a man and a woman in the act of copulation. One wouldn't have thought that the sexual aspect could occupy a vital place in a society that is essentially rather traditional."

"Not in the sense of the physical pleasure it brings," Marc interrupted. "But through fertility, which the act represents. Fertility, the source of human reproduction, is the basis of the socio-economic continuation of those groups that have not yet been touched by the impact of technology."

"Here, on the other hand, there's a zebu at the top!"

"Quite common in a world with a rural culture. Other than prestige, the volume of livestock represents a resource that can be turned into monetary gain in the case of difficulties."

"Come here, quickly," Suzy called out. "Here's a truck and there even an airplane. I don't understand!"

"That reflects an inevitable mutation of society, Suzy. Following contact with more materialistic cultures, ideals are becoming laden with less abstract connotations that are more realistic in the 'contemporary' world, so to speak."

"Marielle, are you alright?" Michel worried. "You're so quiet, your look is so distant?"

"I'm alright," I assured him. "But it's time to go back. Remember that dinner is waiting for us at eight o'clock at "La

Elle venait de marquer un tournant dans un chapitre de ma vie.

— Qu'est-ce donc que ces tiges plates en bois sculpté, et piquées partout sur les tombeaux?

— Regardez bien, nota Marc, mon collègue. Ces tiges, appelées "aloalo", montrent des figurines montées les unes sur les autres. Elles symbolisent les idéaux auxquels aspirent les gens au cours de leur vie. Aux cimes des aloalo se trouve l'élément qui a le plus d'importance.

— L'ambition ou le rêve en somme.

— Exactement.

Claudia et Joseph, des époux discrets, remarquèrent: "Sur le sommet de cet aloalo, on voit un homme et une femme en train de s'accoupler. On n'aurait pas cru que l'aspect sexuel pouvait occuper une place primordiale dans une société à caractère plutôt traditionnel".

— Pas dans le sens du plaisir physique en soi qu'il procure, intervint Marc. Mais à travers la fécondité que cet acte représente. Fécondité source de reproduction humaine, base de la perpétuation socio-économique de ces groupes non encore touchés par les impacts de la technologie.

— Ici par contre, on a un zébu à la cime!

— Normal, dans un univers à civilisation pastorale. Outre le prestige, le volume du cheptel représente des ressources monétarisables en cas de problèmes.

— Venez vite, cria Suzy. Ici, c'est un camion, et là même un avion. Je ne comprends pas!

— C'est le reflet d'une mutation inévitable de la sotiété, Suzy. Suite aux contacts avec ces cultures plus matérialistes, les idéaux s'imprègnent de connotations moins abstraites, plus "modernement" réalistes, si l'on peut dire.

Marielle, ça ne va pas? s'inquiéta Michel. Ton mutisme, ton regard absent?

Plazza" and that at eleven this evening we're going dancing at the "Zaza Club."

Marc threw me a murderous glance: "You're not going to . . .?" He didn't have time to finish his sentence.

"See you in a bit," I cut him off dryly, "I still have to get to the post office[6] to try and reach my husband by phone. If it works."

It didn't. Which was to be expected. Unpredictable during the dry season, communication became downright impossible as soon as the weather turned the least bit inclement. We came back from the nightclub towards dawn. Marc followed me into my room. Before I could get a word out, he grabbed me roughly by my arm and lashed out at me:

"Marielle, I've never seen you like this! You were dancing like a crazy woman, you wouldn't even get off the dance floor. Is your heart made of stone, or what? Not to speak of simple indecency! And yet I've never known you to be anything but sweet and sensible. And your silence, your staring eyes, it's as if your soul is transfixed! Marielle, I beg of you, come back to yourself!"

Something was clutching at me painfully, I didn't know where, but it hurt so badly. A stone? A heart? And a soul? . . . did I even have one any longer? had I ever had one?

The following day we awakened to abominable weather; the cyclonic depression had come closer to the southern part of the island. The more persistent the rains became, the more staunch the group's determination to reach Ifaty. At about thirty kilometers farther north of Tulear, this site was famous for its idyllic setting, its exotic bungalows, and the excursions it had to offer[7]—Trips in lurching pirogues,[8] the same way in which, ten centuries ago, our ancestors had challenged seven thousand kilometers of hostile ocean, from South-East Asia all the way to the Great Island, not to forget the excursions into the limestone caves of Sarodrano[9] and the always baffling pursuit of the "seven lakes."[10]

— Ça va très bien, affirmai-je. Mais il est temps qu'on rentre. Je vous rappelle que le dîner nous attend à "La Plazza" à vingt heures, et qu'à partir de vingt-trois heures, on descend danser au "Zaza club".

Marc me lança une oeillade assassine : "Tu ne va pas? . . ." Il n'eut pas le temps de finir.

A tout à l'heure, coupai-je sèchement, je dois encore aller à la poste pour essayer de joindre mon mari par téléphone. Si j'y arrive.

Je n'y arrivai pas. C'était d'ailleurs à prévoir. Aléatoire en saison sèche, la communication devenait carrément impossible avec le moindre mauvais temps. Nous rentrâmes du night club au petit matin. Marc me suivit dans ma chambre. Sans que je puisse placer un mot, il me saisit brusquement par le bras et fustigea:

— Marielle, je ne te reconnais pas! Tu dansais comme une forcenée, sans vouloir quitter la piste. Aurais-tu donc une pierre à la place du coeur? Sans parler de l'indécence! Je t'avais toujours connue gentille et sensée pourtant. Et ce mutisme, ces yeux fixes, ton âme est comme envoûtée! Marielle, je t'en supplie, reviens à toi!

Quelque chose m'étreignait douloureusement, je ne savais où, mais ça faisait si mal. Une pierre? Un coeur? Et, une âme? . . . en avais-je encore? en avais-je jamais eu?

Le jour suivant nous réveilla sur un temps abominable, la dépression cyclonique se rapprochant du sud de l'île. Autant les pluies se firent persistantes, autant la détermination du groupe à atteindre Ifaty se fit encore plus farouche. A une trentaine de kilomètres plus au nord de Tuléar, ce site était célèbre pour sa place idyllique, ses bungalows exotiques et les ballades qu'on y offrait. Sur des pirogues à balancier à la façon dont nos ancêtres avaient, il y a plus de dix siècles, défié sept mille kilomètres d'océan hostile depuis l'Asie du Sud-est, jusqu'à la Grande île,

The trip to Ifaty was arduous. The entire stretch of road was nothing but a dreadful quagmire.

"What was your relationship with your in-laws?" Michel inquired. Caught by surprise, I couldn't find anything to say.

"That plant formation you see over there is the bush," I heard myself say mechanically. As opposed to the herbaceous savanna we saw on the high central plains, the species here are perennials, ligneous, and thorny." I let my hand wander over a spiny euphorbia. As I felt the sharp pain, I thought of her. "Still more injections? always more injections? will I get better? tell me quickly that I'll get better? even if it isn't true, tell me anyway." I passed my hand through her white hair and gently pressed her hand. Our eyes met. Then, as she turned toward the nurse, she let her know without saying a word that she was ready. The morphine always had a quick effect. She would sink immediately into a lethargy that would suspend the pain of the metastasis for a while. For how long?

"What are those odd-looking candelabras over there?" Claudia asked. "Are those cacti?"

"No, those are didieraceae,"[11] Michel answered. "It's true that they look rather mournful, don't they?" "No, they're pretty!" Suzy retorted. Mournful? morbid, if you ask me. In any case, I would find the candelabra in question at the foot of the bed of the deceased. Had they dressed her in white? Had they surrounded her with many flowers? One day, as I was changing her, I had said to her: "Off with these, these nun's pajamas, today you're going to be dressed for springtime. Look out the window. Did you see the sun, mother? It's beautiful, right?"

She burst out laughing. "Hand me a mirror," she said, "it's been a while since I've looked at myself with admiration. How many months have we been in this hospital now? But why are you rolling down the blinds, pull them up, it makes it too dark, Marielle!"

sans compter aussi, les excursions dans les grottes calcaires de "Sarodrano" et la recherche, toujours énigmatique, des "sept lacs".

Le déplacement vers Ifaty fut un peu laborieux. Sur toute sa totalité la route ne fut qu'un épouvantable bourbier.

— Quelles étaient tes relations avec ta belle-famille? s'enquit Michel. Prise de court, je ne trouvais rien à balbutier.

— La formation végétale que vous voyez là est le bush, m'entendis-je dire machinalement. A la différence de la savane à herbacées que nous avions vue sur les hautes terres centrales, les espèces sont ici ligneuses, vivaces et épineuses. Je promenais ma main sur un euphorbiacée à piquants. A la douleur vive qui me saisit, j'eus une pensée pour elle. "Encore des piqûres? toujours des piqûres? est-ce que je guérirai? dites-moi vite que je guérirai? même si ce n'est pas vrai, dites-le-moi quand même." Je passais ma main dans ses cheveux blancs, et je lui serrais doucement la main. Nos regards se croisaient. Alors, se tournant vers l'infirmière, elle fit comprendre, sans mot dire, qu'elle était prête. L'effet de la morphine ne se faisait jamais attendre. Elle sombra aussitôt dans une léthargie retenant en sursis les douleurs de la métastase pour un moment. Jusqu'à quand?

— C'est quoi ces drôles de candélabres là-bas? demanda Claudia, c'est des cactées ça?

— Non, c'est des didiéracées, répondit Michel. C'est vrai que ça fait plutôt lugubre, n'est-ce pas? Non, c'est joli! rétorqua Suzy. Lugubre? macabre plutôt, à mon avis. De toute façon, le candélabre en question, je le trouvais au pied du lit de la morte. L'a-t-on habillée de blanc? A-t-on mis beaucoup de fleurs? Un jour en la changeant, je lui avais dit: "Ouste, ces pyjamas de religieuse, aujourd'hui, tu t'habilles comme le printemps. Regarde par la fenêtre. T'as vu le soleil belle-maman, il fait beau, hein?"

— Elle pouffa de rire. Passe-moi une glace, dit-elle, ça fait un temps que je me suis pas admirée. Combien de mois déjà

My hands were trembling as I grabbed the mirror out of my purse. "If only it were magic. It would be enough to tell it: make her pretty, mirror! the prettiest of mothers-in-law!" She didn't have to endure the spectacle of her ghoulish reflection; the doctor came into the room and miraculously changed the conversation.

"What are you two accomplices cooking up now?" he said, teasing us.

"Marielle is my guardian angel," my mother-in-law answered.

"And yet I've been strict with you," she added later, when I was gently cleaning her, running the sponge and soap froth along her body. As if my gestures could regenerate what was no more than skin over bones. A terribly wrinkled skin.

How absurd life could be, really. She who was so radiant in the family photographs. Attentive to every little detail where her children and grandchildren were concerned.

"How can you let her impose herself so much on the relationship with your husband?"

My sister, my brothers couldn't understand it. If my in-laws were so violently opposed to my registering for the entrance examination to the Ecole Normale Supérieure, it wasn't out of gratuitous malice.

"That's pretty self-centered of you," my sisters-in-law would say. "You'll be studying at night while your husband cooks the rice, washes the dishes, or does the laundry?"

In fact, my own father was scandalized by the situation and didn't mince his words: "Doesn't your husband earn enough to keep you alive?" It's true that Jacques was a civil servant. The ideal situation for the generation of my parents. But he was ambitious as well.

"My darling, what a pity it would be and foolish also to trudge along like that in mediocrity," he would say to me. "I know your potential, you'll pass the entrance exam. You'll do

sommes-nous dans cet hôpital? Mais pourquoi mets-tu ces stores, relève-les, ça fait sombre Marielle!

Mes mains tremblaient en saisissant le miroir dans mon sac. "Si au moins il était magique. Il suffirait de lui dire: fais-la jolie, miroir! la plus jolie des belles-mamans!" Elle n'eut pas à endurer le spectacle de son reflet cauchemardesque, l'entrée du médecin ayant miraculeusement détourné la conversation.

— Que mijotent les deux complices, dit-il en nous taquinant.

— Marielle est mon ange gardien, répliqua ma belle-mère.

— Pourtant j'ai été sévère avec toi, ajouta-t-elle plus tard, lorsque je lui fis doucement la toilette, en promenant l'éponge et la mousse sur le corps. Comme si mes gestes pouvaient régénérer ce qui n'était plus que de la peau sur les os. Une peau affreusement ridée.

Ce que la vie pouvait être absurde, tout de même. Elle, si radieuse, sur les photos de famille. Attentive aux moindres détails concernant ses enfants et petits-enfants.

— Comment peux-tu admettre qu'elle s'impose ainsi dans tes relations avec ton mari?

Ma soeur, mes frères ne pouvaient pas comprendre. Si ma belle famille s'opposait de façon aussi ferme à ce que je m'inscrive à ce concours d'entrée à l'Ecole Normale Supérieure, ce n'était pas par méchanceté gratuite.

— Quel égoïsme de ta part, me disaient mes belles-soeurs. Tu apprendrais donc des leçons le soir pendant que ton mari fera cuire le riz, lavera la vaisselle ou fera la lessive?

En fait, mon propre père était scandalisé de la situation et ne me ménageait pas les mots: "Ton mari ne gagne-t-il pas suffisamment pour te faire vivre?" C'est vrai que Jacques était fonctionnaire. La situation idéale pour la génération de mes parents. Mais il était aussi ambitieux.

— Ma chérie, ce serait dommage et bête de piétiner comme ça dans la médiocrité, me disait-il. Je connais tes potentialités,

the five years of training. What are five years? What are five years in our lifetime? A somewhat difficult stage to get through, that's all; think of our children, they'll grow up in better circumstances. And as for yourself, you'll flourish. You'll have a profession that better suits your personality. Instead of stagnating like this teaching middle school." He himself went ahead with the formalities of registration, and went so far as to sign for me. We had just enough time to take a swim in Ifaty and then we were called to lunch.

"What a godsend! rock lobsters grilled with cheese," Joseph called out. The others had a hard time choosing between squid, prawns, or sea cucumber.

"What are you having, Marielle?"

"Shrimp."

"Have some lobster," Michel suggested. "It's our treat. An opportunity to taste something you can't have every day."

"And who says that I eat shrimp every day," I cut him off. "It looks like there's plenty, but since they're meant almost exclusively for export, what little comes to our local market is not really affordable."

"It's your rice that makes you so touchy," he added as he went on teasing me. "Look at us, we'd go anywhere and we'd adapt ourselves to any menu. You, you couldn't be more desperately attached to your plate of rice!"

"I don't have to adapt myself, Michel. I'm in my own country!"

"Still, I imagine that at the top of the *aloalo*s, for young Malagasy intellectuals like yourself, a trip to Europe, what am I saying, an expatriation to our country holds a strong place."

"Much less so than you may think," I affirmed. "The fact that in your developed country the houses are larger and more beautiful, the streets wider, the bars of soap more perfumed and the toothpaste less expensive, does not mean that's a guarantee for happiness."

tu réussiras à ce concours. Tu suivras la formation pendant cinq ans. C'est quoi, cinq ans? C'est quoi cinq dans notre vie? un passage un peu dur à passer, c'est tout, pense à nos enfants, ils auront une condition meilleure. Toi-même, ça t'aidera à mieux t'épanouir. Tu auras une profession plus adaptée à ta personnalité. Au lieu de croupir ainsi dans ton statut d'enseignante de collège. Il procéda lui-même aux formalités de l'inscription, allant jusqu'à signer à ma place. Nous eûmes juste le temps de nous baigner à Ifaty, et déjà on nous fit signe pour le déjeuner.

— Quelle aubaine! ces langoustes grillées au fromage, lança Joseph. Les autres eurent du mal à arrêter leur choix entre calamars, camarons ou concombres de mer.

— Qu'est-ce que tu prends Marielle?

— Des crevettes.

— Prends donc des langoustes, avança Michel. Tu manges à nos frais. C'est l'occasion pour toi de goûter ce dont tu n'as pas les moyens tous les jours.

— Et qui te dit que je mange des crevettes tous les jours, coupai-je. Ça a l'air abondant, mais comme c'est destiné presqu'exclusivement à l'exportation, le peu qui nous arrive sur le marché local n'est pas à la portée de nos bourses.

— C'est ton riz qui te rend susceptible comme ça, ajouta-til en continuant de me taquiner. Regarde-nous, on irait n'importe où, on s'adapterait à tous les menus. Toi, t'es attachée à ton plat de riz de façon on ne peut plus désespérée!

— Je n'ai pas à m'adapter Michel. Je suis dans mon pays!

— Pourtant, j'imagine bien qu'aux cimes des aloalo, pour des jeunes intellectuels malgaches comme toi, un voyage en Europe, que dis-je, un expatriement chez nous figure en bonne place.

— Beaucoup moins que tu ne le crois, affirmai-je. Ce n'est pas parce que dans ton pays développé, les maisons sont plus grandes et plus belles, les rues plus grandes, les savonnettes

"Why then are you so determined to work hard and always harder, to work as a tourist guide so you can have the means to write your thesis, even if it means being away from home, separated from your children, to the point of arguing with your in-laws, if it weren't for wanting to be richer and living in comfort?"

I was looking at the sea before me. An intensely blue sea with gentle, restful waves caused by the coral reef a few kilometers away from the beach.

"Comfort maybe," Marc admitted, "but not disconnected from our roots. Not by having your compatriots reproach us over there that we have come to take away your bread. Besides, we are needed more right here. Without wanting to assume an exaggerated sense of responsibility, when we teach in the schools, when we take care of our patients, when we raise the consciousness of our peasants, we feel nevertheless that we are contributing something. In your country, everyone has everything, so that nobody needs anyone else any longer."

"Not as much as you think, though," Joseph set him straight.

"All the same," Marc interrupted. "We cannot possibly conceive of living like that for oneself and not knowing whom or what to cling to in case of need."

"If it entertains you to support each other like that in your interdependence, then it's no wonder that the solution to your underdevelopment will take an almost infinite amount of time," Michel said ironically.

"Well, are we going to take that pirogue ride or not?"

"You're crazy, Marielle. Can't you see it's raining now?"

"I don't care. That's what we came for, or at least that's what I thought."

The boatman explained to me that it wasn't foolhardy yet if we didn't go out too far. I didn't let him say that twice. I jumped into the boat and sank into a whole slew of memories at the first sliding motions over the water.

plus parfumées et les pâtes dentifrices à meilleur marché que c'en est une garantie de bonheur.

— Et pourquoi donc t'acharnes-tu ainsi alors à travailler encore et toujours plus, à travailler comme guide touristique pour te donner les moyens de financer la mise en forme de ta thèse, quitte à te séparer de ton foyer, de tes enfants. Jusqu'à te disputer avec ta belle-famille, si ce n'est pour être plus riche et pour accéder au confort?

Je regardais la mer en face. Une mer, d'un bleu intense aux vagues douces et reposantes à cause du récif corallien situé à quelques kilomètres de la plage.

— Le confort peut-être, admit Marc, mais pas détaché de nos racines. Sans que vos compatriotes ne viennent nous reprocher là-bas, que nous venons manger votre pain chez vous. D'ailleurs on a plus besoin de nous ici. Sans vouloir nous affubler d'un complexe de responsabilités, nous sentons quand même, lorsque nous enseignons dans les écoles, lorsque nous soignons nos malades, lorsque nous conscientisons nos paysans, que nous apportons quelque chose. Dans ton pays, tout le monde a tout, que personne n'a plus besoin de qui que ce soit.

— Pas autant que vous le croyez quand même, rectifia Joseph.

— N'empêche, intervint Marc. Nous n'arrivons pas à concevoir de vivre comme ça pour soi-même et sans savoir à qui ou à quoi s'accrocher en cas de besoin.

— Si vous vous amusez comme ça à vous soutenir dans votre interdépendance, il n'est pas étonnant que la solution à votre sous-développement se pose à une échelle temps quasi-infinie, ironisa Michel.

— Alors, cette ballade en pirogue, on la fait ou non?

— Tu es folle, Marielle. Tu ne vois pas qu'il pleut maintenant?

— Je m'en fous. On est venu pour ça, du moins je le croyais.

That the bridges had been burned for more than a year now between my in-laws and myself didn't mean that a true argument had taken place between us. I had the distressing habit of locking myself into absolute silence at the first little objection from their end. Not out of disdain or anger, but very simply because I was stuck in some sort of incomprehensible fear. In that family every member of my generation was enjoying high socio-professional status: midwife, merchant, bank employee. As my parents-in-law became prouder of talking about their social circle, they became more frustrated at having to answer the question: "And what about Jacques' wife?"

"Eh . . . she's still studying."

Besides, that was not the only concern I was causing them. For reasons of practical and psychological convenience, my husband and I had decided not to have any children during the first two years of our marriage. How many secret prayers, how many candles lit at the foot of the Virgin Mary! and above all, how many herbal potions and other crazy brews were surreptitiously slipped into my tea, which then became revolting to drink![12] It didn't help any that I was Protestant in this deeply Catholic family.[13] So I won't belabor any longer their astounded expressions of outrage when we were all involved in a family discussion and I wasn't able to keep a personal opinion, one that betrayed a rather "leftist" tendency, to myself. . . . I have to recognize that I had given proof of a particularly sharp gift for providing ample reasons for their dislike of me. It was the awareness of this state of affairs that made me refuse to enter into any fight or give any response when the threat of an argument emerged.

"That's mostly what it is, your obstinacy in not wanting to confront the situation in a mature and conscious fashion that causes you to wreck your nights with nightmares, to ruin your health with tranquilizers and sleeping pills, and to insist on working in such an inhuman way."

Le piroguier m'expliqua que si on n'allait pas trop loin, ce n'était pas encore imprudent. Je ne me le fis pas répéter deux fois. Je sautai dans l'embarcation et sombrai aux premiers glissements sur l'eau, dans une foule de souvenirs.

Que les ponts fussent coupés depuis plus d'un an, entre ma belle-famille et moi, ne signifia jamais qu'une véritable dispute avait eu lieu entre nous. J'avais la fâcheuse habitude de m'enfermer dans un mutisme absolu dès la moindre objection de leur part. Non par mépris ou par colère, mais tout simplement parce que j'étais bloquée dans une sorte de peur incompréhensible. Dans cette famille, tous les membres de ma génération jouissaient d'un statut socio-professionnel bien assis: sage-femme, commerçant, agent de banque. Autant mes beaux-parents étaient fiers d'en parler à leur entourage, autant ils étaient frustrés de répondre à la question: "Et la femme de Jacques?"

— Euh ! elle est encore étudiante.

Ce n'était d'ailleurs pas la seule préoccupation que je leur fournissais. Pour des raisons de commodités pratiques et psychologiques, mon mari et moi avions décidé, pendant les deux premières années de notre mariage, de ne pas encore avoir d'enfant. Que de prières secrètes, que de bougies déposées au pied de la Sainte Vierge! et surtout que de tisanes et autres breuvages saugrenus glissés discrètement dans mon thé devenu alors infect! Que je fusse de religion protestante dans cette famille profondément catholique n'était pas pour arranger les choses. Alors, je n'insisterai plus sur leurs expressions scandalisées, estomaquées, lorsque tous réunis autour d'une discussion familiale, je n'ai pas su taire une opinion personnelle relevant d'une tendance plutôt "gauchiste"... Je dois reconnaître que j'avais fait preuve d'un don particulièrement pointu pour accumuler autour de mon personnage les raisons de leur antipathie. C'est la concience de cet état de choses qui faisait que je me refusais à toute combativité, à toute réplique, lorsque la menace de dispute se profilait.

"No, Jacques, don't take it that way. They are parents. I owe them respect. Besides, since I'm an orphan myself, I don't really know how to behave toward those to whom you owe life. Had my own mother been here, I would perhaps have tolerated it, so why not with yours?"

To my husband I didn't add the fact that since I knew how attached he was to his family, I couldn't have borne to see him faced with a difficult choice were the rupture to come between his mother and me. I, however, knew it all too well, in spite of everything. . . .

The straw that broke the camel's back was that Jacques was appointed to a post rather far from Tananarive. How could I have made anybody understand that it would have been madness for me, with only one more year to go in my training, to follow him? My husband set my last hesitations straight.

"We'll be on top of the situation," he reassured me. "Finish your research and don't worry about us. One year will go by in no time."

Not as quickly as all that, when you live it with misplaced criticisms and never-ending incomprehension. Especially since the situation went from bad to worse. Only a few weeks after Jacques and the children had left, I also left the house of my parents-in-law, without any specific explanation, my head filled with words that came back to me obsessively: ungrateful wife, ignoble mother, selfish woman, without a soul, a stone where her heart should be.

Jacques admitted that he was relieved by my decision to rent a room in town. On the other hand, he kept silent about the reports his family gave him about my alleged "infidelity," my licentious conduct. Even when he was still there, it would happen that I might go to the movies with a friend after an exam, or work late at night with a colleague on the preparation of a tourist itinerary. I might even work on finishing my field reports,

— C'est surtout ça, cette obstination à ne pas affronter la situation de façon mature et consciente qui fait que tu gâches tes nuits en cauchemars, que tu te bousilles la santé en calmants et somnifères, et que tu t'acharnes à travailler de façon aussi inhumaine.

— Non, Jacques, ne prends pas les choses comme ça. C'est des parents. Je leur dois le respect. D'ailleurs, étant moi-même orpheline, je ne sais pas très bien quel comportement adopter envers ceux à qui on doit d'avoir vu le jour. Ma propre mère aurait été là, j'aurais peut-être toléré, alors pourquoi pas avec les tiens?

Je n'ajoutais pas à mon mari, que, sachant l'attachement qui le liait avec les siens, je n'aurais pas supporté de le voir confronté à un choix difficile si la rupture venait à s'imposer entre sa mère et moi. Je le savais de mon côté, envers et contre tout...

La goutte qui fit déborder le vase fut l'affectation de Jacques à un poste éloigné de Tananarive. A qui faire comprendre qu'il aurait été insensé pour moi, à un an de la fin de ma formation de tout abandonner pour le suivre? Mon mari eut raison de mes dernières hésitations.

— Nous serons à la hauteur de la situation, me rassura-t-il. Termine tes recherches sans te faire du souci pour nous. Un an sera vite passé.

Pas si vite que ça, lorsqu'on le vit en reproches déplacés, en incompréhensions éternelles. Surtout aussi que la situation évoluait de mal en pis. Quelques semaines seulement après le départ de Jacques et des enfants, je quittais également la maison de mes beaux-parents, sans explication particulière, la tête pleine de mots qui me revenaient de façon obsessionnelle: épouse ingrate, mère indigne, femme égoïste, sans âme, une pierre à la place du coeur.

Jacques m'avoua être soulagé de ma décision de louer une chambre en ville. Il me tut par contre les rapports que les siens lui

trips that were inseparable from my agronomist training, but scandalous in the eyes of the society from which I had come.

"It will be dangerous to go any farther," the boatman told me.

"Let's go back to the beach," I answered regretfully. "No one had ever told me that the sea, the rain, and nostalgia were one."

He looked at me, stunned, then skillfully maneuvered his sails for the return. An extreme weariness came over me as I went to bed that night and, when I woke up, was astonished to find my pillow wet and my eyes swollen.

"Back to Tananarive," Marc yelled from his room.

Personally, I was not unhappy to come to the end of the illusory life of luxury that I led whenever I went on a tourist trip. Besides, Suzy and her friends were nice enough, but their kindness didn't quite manage to entirely cover their prejudices. Such surprise in their eyes that we were not illiterate. We would discuss Tolven's death, some car race circuit, we would talk about some piece by Clayderman, some film by Roland Loffe or the French elections, and they would be taken by surprise.

"Ah, so, you're up to date?" As if culture were the prerogative of the Western world alone . . . for heaven's sake!

"Will your husband be very upset with you?" Joseph asked me.

"Not at all," I answered honestly. "He's never upset with me. But I shall never be sorry enough not to have been by his side at these difficult moments."

"Oh, you'll make up for it with the next exhumation,"[14] Michel suggested.

"I hate those ceremonies," I confessed. "Not in the sense you think," I corrected myself, "but because that is when I am most aware of my irreparable acculturation. Tradition wants us to live those moments of reunion with joy, but all I find there is grief and revolt. The entire philosophy, the concept my race has where death is concerned, escapes me. I feel shame."

faisaient concernant ma présumée "infidélité", mes comportements dévergondés. Quand bien même il était là, il m'était arrivé d'aller au cinéma avec un copain après un examen, ou de travailler tard dans la nuit avec un collègue sur la préparation d'un circuit touristique; et même sur la finition de mes rapports de terrain, déplacements indissociables de ma formation en agronomie, mais scandaleux dans la conception de la société dont j'étais issue.

— Il serait dangereux d'avancer plus loin, me dit le piroguier.

— Regagnons la plage, répondis-je avec regret. On ne m'avait jamais dit que la mer, la pluie et la nostalgie faisaient un.

— Il me regarda d'un air ahuri, puis manoeuvra avec adresse ses voiles pour le demi-tour. Je fus gagnée d'une extrême lassitude en regagnant mon lit le soir, et m'étonnai en me réveillant, que mon oreiller fut aussi mouillé et mes yeux aussi gonflés.

— Cap sur Tananarive, cria Marc de sa chambre.

Personnellement, je n'étais pas mécontente d'en finir avec cette existence illusoirement luxueuse que je menais, le temps d'un itinéraire touristique. D'ailleurs, Suzy et ses amis étaient sympas, mais leur gentillesse n'arrivait pas totalement à bout de leurs préjugés. Que de surprise dans leurs yeux, que nous ne fussions pas analphabètes. On discuterait de la mort de Tolven, sur tel circuit automobile, on parlerait de tel morceau de Clayderman, de tel film de Roland Loffé ou des législatives françaises, et ils se confondent en étonnement.

— Ah! bon, vous êtes au courant? Comme si la culture était l'apanage du monde occidental uniquement. . . enfin!

— Ton mari, il va t'en vouloir beaucoup? me demanda Joseph.

— Pas du tout, répondis-je sincèrement. Il ne m'en veut jamais. Mais je ne regretterai jamais assez de ne pas être à ses côtés lors de ces moments difficiles.

— Bah! tu te rattraperas lors de la prochaine exhumation, suggéra Michel.

"When did you become aware of that?" Marc was worried.

"I was eleven. My mother, whom I had never known but of whom I had fashioned myself an image as a sweet and pretty woman, was suddenly forced upon me, on my lap, in a dreadful state. All sorts of moist, nauseating, grotesque things.[15] I wanted so much to have the experience of joyfulness, but all I felt was revulsion."

"We'll be there in two hours," said Claudia, who deemed it better to change the conversation.

Immediately images began to speed up at a mad pace inside my head.

"Can I go on this trip, doctor?"

"Yes, Marielle, you need a change of scenery. Writing a thesis in the room of a cancer patient is too much for the little bitty woman that you are. She'll be around for a few more months, that mother-in-law of yours."

. . . A few more months! I was gone just two days and there she was, gone, while I'm looking at the *aloalos,* the *aloalos.* . . . They danced around inside my head. Dance of death, outrageous beat! On their tops, mother-in-law, suitcase in hand, is leaving the hospital looking radiant.[16]

We cross the threshold of the house in heavy silence.

Jacques, in a black shirt, in front of the door. A hand held out, a tender look, a warm voice . . .

"Marielle, it's good you weren't there, you would not have been able to bear it . . ."

And again I lapsed.

— Je déteste ces cérémonies, avouai-je. Non pas dans le sens que tu crois, rectifiai-je, mais parce que c'est là que je suis le plus consciente de mon irrémédiable acculturation. La tradition veut qu'on vive ces moments de retrouvailles avec joie, moi je n'y puise que chagrin et révolte. C'est toute la philosophie, la conception de ma race vis-à-vis de la mort qui m'échappe. J'ai honte.

— Quand as-tu réalisé cela, s'inquiéta Marc?

— J'avais onze ans. Ma mère, que je n'avais jamais connue mais dont je m'étais fait une certaine image de femme douce et jolie m'avait été imposée, sur les genoux dans un état affreux. Des tas de choses moites, nauséabondes, absurdes. J'aurais tant voulu respirer la joie, je n'étais que révoltée.

— Dans deux heures, on y sera, lança Claudia, qui jugea préférable de détourner la conversation.

Aussitôt les images s'accélérèrent à une allure folle dans ma tête.

— Je peux partir pour ce voyage, docteur?

— Oui, Marielle, tu as besoin de te changer les idées. La rédaction d'une thèse dans une chambre d'un malade cancéreux, c'est trop pour le petit bout de femme que tu es. Elle en a encore pour quelques mois, ta belle-maman.

. . . Quelques mois! deux jours que j'étais partie, et la voilà qui trépasse, pendant que je regarde les aloalo, les aloalo. . . Ils dansèrent dans ma tête. Danse macabre, rythme démentiel! Sur leurs cimes, belle-maman, valise en main, sortant, d'un air radieux de l'hôpital.

Nous franchissons le portail de la maison dans un silence lourd.

Devant la porte, Jacques, en chemise noire. Une main tendue, un regard tendre, une voix chaude. . .

— Marielle, heureusement que tu n'étais pas là, tu n'aurais pas supporté. . .

Et, je sombrais de nouveau.

Poetry / Poésie

David Jaomanoro

(See the bio-bibliographical note in the "Short Stories" section.)

Isabelle

At the tunnel[1] entrance
Isabelle
awaits
a client
At the tunnel entrance
a little girl's
tin dish
repels the passersby

The tin dish is the little girl's
the little girl is Isabelle's
Isabelle works the tunnel entrance[2]
indifferently the tunnel
looks at Isabelle

The little girl is Isabelle's
the little girl's tin dish
repels the passersby
honest folk
who indifferently
look at the child

A crook
the client Isabelle
awaits
at the tunnel entrance
notices the child
and into the tin dish
he drops
five francs.[3]

Poems translated from the French by Marjolijn de Jager

David Jaomanoro

(Voir la note bio-bibliographique dans la section "Nouvelles".)

Isabelle

A l'entrée du tunnel
    Isabelle
    attend
    un client
A l'entrée du tunnel
    la gamelle
    d'une gamine
    de trois ans
    écoeure les passants

La gamelle est à la gamine
la gamine est à Isabelle
Isabelle fait l'entrée du tunnel
d'un oeil indifférent le tunnel
    observe Isabelle

La gamine est à Isabelle
la gamelle de la gamine
    écoeure les passants
    des honnêtes gens
    qui d'un oeil indifférent
    observent l'enfant

    Un truand
    le client qu'Isabelle
    attend
à l'entrée du tunnel
    remarque l'enfant
    et dans la gamelle
    laisse tomber
    cinq francs.

You Are Handsome

You are not fat
but you are handsome

You are handsome
with your dangling ears
Jeannot
my rabbit[4]
with your snaggle-toothed mouth
Jeannot
my rascal

You are handsome
when you play hooky
you resemble your father
you are handsome
when you smile
the corners of your eyes
in tiny folds
how fine
those cries of yours
how fine
that nappy hair
your crafty look

How fine
even in your destitution
your shorts with holes in its behind
your suspenders much too tight
you are more handsome still
because you are not fat.

Thrive on It

To these outstretched hands
I say work
get callused

Tu es beau

Tu n'es pas gros
mais tu es beau

Tu es beau
avec tes oreilles qui pendent
Jeannot
mon lapin
avec ta bouche pleine de chicots
Jeannot
mon galopin

Tu es beau
quand tu fais l'école buissonnière
tu ressembles à ton père
tu es beau
quand tu souris
au coin de tes yeux
en petits plis
c'est beau
tes cris
c'est beau
tes cheveux frisés
ton oeil rusé

C'est beau
même ta misère
ta culotte trouée par derrière
tes bretelles trop tendues
tu es encore plus beau
car tu n'es pas gros.

Profitez

A ces mains tendues
je dis travaillez
prenez des cals

to these closed eyes
I say stay up late
rise early

to these cracked feet
I shout stand up
be brave

to these starving mouths
to this tide of barefoot folk
I yell why don't you go away
to hell leave me in peace
to these tattered bodies
I screech drop dead you filthy beasts
go and fertilize the earth

to these skeletal hands
these imploring eyes
these tick-sheltering-feet[5]
to these half-witted mouths
I menacingly call commands
laugh dance jump
and make me laugh

but to those faces that drip with grease
        and jam
have chins that disappear and have thick necks
        I whisper be prosperous
        get fat grow big
        and rot
love power strength and wealth
        this is your lot
        So thrive on it.

The Wreck[6]

Buried inside time's lullaby
between two dreams

à ces yeux endormis
je dis veillez tard
réveillez tôt

à ces pieds ravinés
je crie debout
du nerf

à ces bouches affamées
à cette marée de va-nu-pieds
je hurle allez-vous-en
foutez-moi la paix
à ces corps loqueteux
je grince crevez sales bêtes
engraissez la terre

à ces mains squelettiques
ces yeux suppliants
pieds-gîtes-de-chiques
à ces bouches ahuries
j'intime menaçant
riez dansez sautez
faites-moi rire

mais aux faces dégoulinantes de graisse
        et de confiture
aux mentons croulants aux nuques épaisses
        prospérez je susurre
        grossissez enflez
        pourrissez
l'amour la puissance la force la richesse
        sont vos lots
        Profitez.

L'épave

Enfouie dans la berceuse du temps
entre deux songes

astride the mute interrogation
of dwarf crabs

arms stretched out in silent prayers
toward a forgetful god
laid out in its shifting tomb
spirit rust-eroded
meditating on the meaning of oblivion

destiny written on the pages of waves
secret spread by the song of the gulls
kingdom of Korah
home of Abiram
palace of Dathan[7]

the fragrant scents of springtime leave it
indifferent

it is a wreck of a
sigh
stranded in the depths of the Genocide sea.

Dina

    Dina
    daughter of the dawn
    fruit of hope
    my daughter
you weep when I sneeze
a bit too loud
but you smile when I scold you
when I am no longer there
to make you dance upon my chest
will you know
how to say
like others—though very few—
he was somebody

à cheval sur l'interrogation muette
de crabes nains

bras tendus en muettes prières
vers un dieu oublieux
dressée dans sa tombe mouvante
esprit rongé de rouille
méditant sur le sens de l'oubli

destin écrit sur les pages des vagues
secret colporté par le chant des mouettes
royaume de Qoré
maison d'Abirâm
palais de Datan

les effluves du printemps la laissent
indifférente

c'est une épave de
soupir
échouée au fond de la mer Génocide.

Dina

Dina
fille de l'aurore
fruit de l'espoir
ma fille
tu pleures quand j'éternue
un peu trop fort
mais tu souris quand je te gronde
sauras-tu
quand je ne serai plus
à te faire danser sur ma poitrine
dire
comme les autres—très peu—
c'était quelqu'un

Dina
I croon in your ear oh my much-beloved one
Dina my love
when I am no longer there
to drink in the sparkling burning
laughter of your shadowy eyes
after having grown breathless with you
under tables and chairs
in pursuit of happiness
will you in your turn know
how to read the one kiss
among the thousand kisses compressed into this poem
the one I've meant for you

Dina
pact of blood
my blood
I have made a vow
to never hate
as I've been hated and betrayed
I have promised Dina
that a blossoming star
a starry flower
plucked in future's field
will shine in the night of your hair
when I am no longer there
to read your face on the soot-blackened thatch
of the roof
to steal kisses from your angel's sleep
to suffer with happiness
as I listen to your crystalline babble
will you know
that I have given all of myself
for you
without a cry
without any regret.

Dina
que je roucoule à ton oreille ô ma bien-aimée
Dina mon amour
sauras-tu
quand je ne serai plus
à boire rutilant et brûlant
le rire de tes yeux d'ombre
après m'être avec toi
essoufflé sous les tables et les chaises
à poursuivre le bonheur
lire à ton tour
parmi les mille baisers appliqués à ce poème
celui que je t'ai destiné

Dina
pacte du sang
mon sang
j'ai fait voeu
de ne jamais haïr
comme j'ai été haï trahi
j'ai promis Dina
qu'une étoile fleurie
une fleur d'étoile
cueillie dans la prairie du futur
brillera dans la nuit de tes cheveux
sauras-tu
quand je ne serai plus
à lire ton visage sur la chaume noircie de suie du toit
à voler des baisers à ton sommeil d'ange
à souffrir de bonheur
en écoutant ton babil cristallin
que je me suis donné sans cri
ni regret tout entier
pour toi.

Dusk

The sky is nothing but an ulcer
in which
the piercing scalpel
goes on to perform a blank excision
a white excision

the guinea fowl's[8] song dies down plump pairings
in the meadowsweet

a latecomer adulterous bee
desecrates my temples
in its pollen-gathering playfulness
again

the shadow runs over the north-face
like an eyelid closing over a teardrop
the shadow lies waiting at the holy city gates
catlike
sublime in its unsightliness

some are hesitant
but the mango tree with its one hundred thousand fists
massive and serene
keeps watch
a partner in universal fusion that
lasts alas
no longer than a poem's time

soon
spirits come from elsewhere
will invade my sky
just like flies of steel that melt onto cadavers
putrefied by peace.

(Quatr'ams j'aime ça)

Crépuscule

Le ciel n'est qu'ulcère
dans lequel
le scalpel strident
continue à pratiquer une ablation à blanc
une ablation de blanc

le chant de la pintade expire par couples replets
parmi les ulmaires

une abeille adultère attardée
profane mes temples
par ses butinantes folâtreries
encor

l'ombre coule sur l'ubac
comme paupière qui se ferme sur une larme
l'ombre guette aux portes de la cité sainte
féline
sublime de hideur

quelques-uns hésitent
mais le manguier aux cent mille poings
massif et pacifique
monte la garde
complice de l'exogame universel qui
hélas
ne dure que le temps d'un poème

tout à l'heure
des esprits venus d'ailleurs
envahiront mon ciel
pareils à des mouches d'acier fondant sur le cadavre
putréfié de la paix.

(Quatr'ams j'aime ça)

Jean-Luc Raharimanana

(See the bio-bibliographical note in the "Short Stories" section.)

Crematorium Poems

There's peace when dust rises
Underneath the soldiers' boots
There's peace when the street child curls up
Against mute and silent doors
There's peace when on the convents' thresholds
Abandoned babies wail
There's peace when the bodies of those
They made you believe were alive
Lie rotting
In the soundness of sewers
A peace that kills you!
Exquisite the word that desecrates my mouth
I said: Kill, KILL!

* * *

My heart
Putrid meat
That discharges
The smell of every grave.

My soul
A battlefield
On which the shrieks of a myriad of words
Clatter and screech!

My life
A pool[1]
A madman laps up
In the middle of a storm!

Poems translated from the French by Marjolijn de Jager

Jean-Luc Raharimanana

(Voir la note bio-bibliographique dans la section "Nouvelles".)

Poèmes crématoires

Une paix quand s'éveille la poussière
Sous les brodequins des soldats
Une paix quand se love l'enfant des rues
Contre les portes muettes
Une paix quand du seuil des couvents
des bébés vagissent abandonnés
Une paix quand puent dans les égouts salubres
Les cadavres de ceux
Qu'on a fait croire vivants
Une paix qui te tue!
Exquise la parole qui viole ma bouche
J'ai dit: Tue, TUE!

* * *

Mon coeur
De la viande putride
Qui dégage
L'odeur de tous les caveaux.

Mon âme
Un champ de bataille
Où s'entrechoquent, où grincent
Les hurlements d'une myriade de paroles!

Ma vie
De la mare
Qu'un fou lape
Au milieu des orages!

I tumble
I slump
Into the somber
Tomb
They've dug for me!

* * *

Me!
Me too,
Me, I have a marble palace!
I own
Villas
And cars
And land
I sign agreements of cooperation
My wings merge with the blue of the sky.

I rule, I do!

Triumph of my secret dreams
My seat culminates
With the crests of hills
The Ankaratra[2] borrows majesty from me
Tsaratanana[3] begs me for a rock.

I know it all, I control all!

But I, sir,
Do not have blood on my hands!
Not one shudder of remorse
Not one torment of regret
In my muscles, in my flesh. . .

I, "Monsieur le Président"
Have a clear conscience!

Je tombe
Je sombre
Dans la sombre
Tombe
Qu'Ils ont pour moi creusée!

* * *

Moi!
Moi aussi,
J'ai un palais de marbre, moi!
Je possède
Et des villas
Et des voitures
Et des terres
Je signe des accords de coopération
Mes ailes se confondent au bleu de l'azur.

Je règne, moi!

Triomphe de mes rêves secrets
Mon siège culmine
Aux crêtes des collines
L'Ankaratra m'emprunte une majesté
Tsaratanana me supplie une roche.

Je sais tout, je contrôle tout!

Mais moi, monsieur
Je n'ai pas les mains rouges de sang!
Nul frisson de remords
Nulle torture de regret
Dans mes muscles, dans mes chairs. . .

J'ai, "Monsieur le Président"
La conscience tranquille!

* * *

Island!
Prostitute!
On your moist skin the scent of indecisive men
And I smash into you
Just someone among the thousands of the destitute
The wretched
The repulsive ones!

The outline of breasts, the softness of flesh
Have become objects of violence.
        Persistent in their caresses
        In their furtive pleasures
        On the run, as hands can grab
Blindly exploring forbidden places.

Your mouth in which kisses are devoured
Deep well in which to fling my fears
        Inexhaustible well
        Of wanting and desire
I'm killing off my memories
Oh no more empty belly, no more sodden soul
No more starving children, their dirty hands outspread!

* * *

And LONG LIVE the pot-bellied gentlemen
Long may you live heirs of the ages[4]
You the incarnations of kings
You who do not suffer
Over a few million death throes.

Viva!

But the Slave nation[5]
Adores you, venerates you
You are the kind
Before whom people kneel

* * *

Ile!
Prostituée!
Sur ta peau humide l'odeur des hommes indécis
Et je m'aplatis contre toi
Quelconque parmi les milliers de miséreux
De misérables
De repoussants!

Contour des seins, douceur de la chair
Devenus objets de violence.
        S'obstiner à des caresses
        A des voluptés dérobées
        A la volée, au hasard des mains
Qui aveugles explorent les lieux interdits.

Ta bouche où s'entre-dévorent les baisers
Puits profond où jeter mes terreurs
        Puits intarissable
        De vouloir et de désir
Je tue mes souvenirs
O plus de ventre vide, d'âme saturée
Plus de gosses affamés, de sales mains qui se tendent!

* * *

Et VIVE Messieurs les ventrus
Vive Vous les héritiers des âges
Vous les incarnations des rois
Vous qui ne souffrez
Pour quelques millions d'agonies.

Viva!

Mais la nation Esclave
Vous adore, vous vénère
Vous êtes de ceux
Devant qui l'on s'agenouille

People lie prostrate
Long may You live You who replace our houses of wood
With cellophane tents.[6]

Viva!

* * *

The habit of writing, once acquired,
prevents the mind from traveling
It strives hard to hurl you into the center
of a circle of words
Words that come back unendingly
to pester you
Kingly words: Destiny, Love, Joy,
Sadness
Princely words: Sun, Moon, Azure blue,
Dusk
Slavish words: weeping, despair
Blood and sweat, words that are slave to
The thirst for life
You take the blank sheet of paper
Kiss of ink
For a poem-child.

ECSTATIC

* * *

You see
I'm fed up with honeyed words
Uttered for an extravagant land
I refuse to sing the Ikopa[7]
I refuse to go to the spells of
Crevasses that return to Nothingness
My songs concealed among the memories
Of coastal spaces.

L'on se prosterne
Vive Vous qui remplacez nos maisons de bois
en tentes de cellophane.

Viva!

* * *

L'habitude d'écrire, une fois acquise
empêche l'esprit de voyager
Elle s'efforce de vous jeter au milieu
d'un cercle de mots
Mots qui sans cesse reviennent vous
harceler
Les mots-rois: Destin, Amour, joie,
Tristesse
Les mots-princes: Soleil, Lune, Azur
Crépuscule
Les mots-esclaves: larme, désespoir
Sang et sueur, mots qu'asservit
La soif de vivre
Vous prenez la feuille blanche
Baiser de l'encre
Pour un enfant-poème.

EXTATIQUE

* * *

Vois-tu
Ras l'bol des paroles mielleuses
Délivrées pour une terre extravagante!
Je me refuse à chanter l'Ikopa
Je me refuse à aller aux charmes
Des crevasses qui redonnent au Néant
Mes chants dérobés parmi les souvenirs
Des espaces côtiers.

But listen!

I will go and invoke the gods
For you on the lakeshores.
The elsewhere. . . the ELSEWHERE in our blood
Shall live again in our gestures.

Imagine just for now
Drunk geometer moths[8] challenging the daylight
—Our bodies enraptured and fever-filled.

And we shake ourselves and splash about
We've rid ourselves of Imerina's[9] dust
Suffused in our skins since childhood.

Tsaratanana[10] is far away Oh tender sister
The Sambirano[11] to our ears is but
A very gentle legend. . .

From the North these all too sweet dreams
Come to us to bring joy to our hearts.

Mais entends!

je t'irai au bord des lacs
Invoquer les dieux.
L'ailleurs. . . l'AILLEURS dans nos sangs
Revivra dans nos gestes.

Imagine un peu—
Des phalènes ivres défiant le jour
—Nos corps pleins de fièvres et extasiés.

Et l'on se secoue et l'on s'ébroue,
L'on se débarrasse de ces poussières d'Imerne
Qui ont imprégné nos peaux d'enfants.

Tsaratanana est loin ô tendre soeur
Le Sambirano n'est pour nos oreilles
Qu'une bien douce légende. . .

Du Nord nous reviennent ces rêves trop doux
Pour donner joies au coeur.

Jean-Claude Fota

(See the bio-bibliographical note in the "Short Stories" section.)

Island Cries

or the journey outside of oneself

Island Cries

Speak to me of your journeys oh frigate
Speak to me of islands
That lie close to the insular shores
Of regions hidden in one's most secret spaces
Speak to me of your fantasies beyond the endless seas
Farthest away from my words of distant islets
My winged words
Fearful of soaring into air
Speak to me of flights of geese on early morning river
  waters
Of swans taking off from watercourses glistening with
  ink
Speak to me of the mouths
Of wide deltas its shores strewn with cries
of worlds buried inside the confines of each word
My island cries drunken with travel
My loud cries raised in wrath against sorry destinies
Speak to me of narrow landstrips crossed
Of reefs that shred both skin and hulls of ships
Of passes and of straits cleared beyond any direction
Speak to me of this. . .
Speak to me of your beginnings.

(1989)

Poems translated from the French by Marjolijn de Jager

Jean-Claude Fota

(Voir la note bio-bibliographique dans la section "Nouvelles".)

Cris d'île
ou le voyage hors de soi

Cris d'île

Parle-moi de tes voyages ô frégate
Parle-moi d'îles
Qu'avoisinent des rivages insulaires
De contrées cachées au plus secret de soi
Parle-moi de tes envolées par-delà les mers immenses
Au plus lointain de mes mots d'îlots lointains
Mes mots ailés
Peureux de prendre l'air
Parle-moi de vols d'oies sur les eaux mâtinées des fleuves
De parages moirés d'encre d'où partent des cygnes
Parle-moi d'embouchures
De grands deltas aux rives ensemencées de cris
de mondes enfouis aux confins de chaque mot
Mes cris d'île ivres de voyage
Mes hauts cris enflés d'ire contre piètres destins
Parle-moi d'isthmes franchis
De récifs qui déchirent peaux et coques
de cols et de détroits frayés en deçà des sens même
Parle-m'en. . .
Parle-moi de tes naissances.

(1989)

Death to the Rats[1]

A rat is resting in my barn
A fringe of hay between its teeth
A young rat after a long fast
Now sleeps a heavy sleep
Like someone dead below the sheet
Remembers rest now rediscovered.
There you are! book-eating glutton.
And pilfering all my supplies!
I'll catch you who intrude through walls!
But only the fleas without a bed
Wordlessly jump to the ground
And burrow in low as under the trap
The assault dies, strangled
At the end of my long and shaky arm
My wasted joy at death to rats dissolves
A rat is dead here in my barn
A fringe of hay between its teeth
A young rat after a long fast
Now sleeps a heavy sleep.

(1987)

Sewers[2]

In the sewers you made me
Wait a long long time
And slowly
Like dirty water
My life drains off
My tasteless life
Rushes off beneath your steps
Drains away entirely
My body
Looking like black muck
Sullied by offerings impure
Withdraws below the city

Mort aux rats

Un rat se repose dans ma grange
Une frange de foin entre les dents
Un jeune rat après un long jeûne
Dort d'un profond sommeil
Comme un mort qui sous le drap
Commémore le repos retrouvé.
Te voilà! dévorateur de livres.
Et tous mes vivres volés!
Je t'attrape violeur de murs!
Mais seules des puces sans lit
En silence sautent à terre
Et se terrent comme sous la trappe
L'assaut meurt, étranglé
Au bout de mon bras long branlant
Ma joie ratée de mort aux rats s'en va
Rat est mort dans ma grange
Une frange de foin entre les dents
Un jeune rat après un long jeûne
Dort d'un profond sommeil.

(1987)

Les égouts

Dans les égouts longtemps
Tu m'as fait attendre
Et s'écoule lentement
Comme une eau sale
Ma vie
Sans goût
S'engouffre sous tes pas
S'écoule tout entier
Mon corps
Semblable à une boue noire
Souillée d'offrandes impures
Se retire sous la ville

So high so low
The lifeless water disappears
Submissive to its lot
That's me.

(1988)

Transes

Taboo,[3] today I violate you
In the wooded spot where you camp out
Every Sabbath evening
My incontinent body founders
Between your limbs in motion
Your dripping flesh in rut rejoices
When my lascivious claws are slashing
And your licentious chest ignites
When my muzzle consumed by fire
Sinks deeper down and wallows there outrageously
My head packed with obscene obsessions
In the admission of an inadmissible desire
Then I in turn rob you of the elixir
And all the lust you keep concealed from me
I drink your sap to the last drop
I taste your ripened fruits like Eve
In a spot in the accursed wood
Until my cankered soul has been consumed
Until my long blade is implanted
In your belly in its enraptured state
Then I absent myself with a small bite
A certain death you send
To run in my pursuit.

(1987)

Si haut si bas
L'eau qui sans vie s'en va
Docile à son sort
C'est moi.

(1988)

Transes

Interdit, je te viole aujourd'hui
Au coin d'un bois où tu bivouaques
Chaque soir de sabbat
Mon corps incontinent s'abat
Entre tes membres en branle
S'ébat ta ruisselante chair en rut
Quand mes griffes orgiaques déchirent
Et ta poitrine indécente brûle
Quand descend mon mufle en flamme
S'enfonce et se vautre à outrance
Ma tête étriquée d'obscènes obsessions
Dans l'aveu d'un désir inavouable
Je te vole à mon tour l'élixir
Et toute la luxure que tu me voiles
Je bois ta sève à la dernière goutte
Je goûte tes fruits murs comme Eve
Au coin d'un maudit bois
Jusqu'à consumer mon âme effritée
Jusqu'à planter ma lame longue
Dans ton ventre en transe
Puis m'en aller avec une morsure
Une mort sûre que tu envoies
Courir à ma poursuite.

(1987)

Advocates[4]

Advocates in toga
Prosper in my court
Very ripened advocates
Waiting
For us to come where these
So coveted fruits are picked
Of course they're advocates
Who from courtroom to courtroom
As might be expected eloquently plead
The cause of the starving
Who knowledgeably lend an ear
To the secrets of the epicures
My word, they are fine
Better than fines
Advocates as we love them
They are fat
Some are slimy
Some are slimier than others

They are all for sale

Odors[5]

Downspouts of latrines
I like to smell your dreadful wastes
And you, sweet stink of every recess
My daily bread
Nauseating and putrescent toilets
You are my sphere of comfort[6]
Rank decomposition of dead bodies piled
New companions of my senses
And my kisses without disgust
On the harmful mouths[7] of sewers
And my infected loves
In the fetid urinals of the capital

Avocats

Des avocats en toge
Prospèrent dans ma cour
Des avocats bien mûrs
Attendent
Que l'on descende sur les lieux
Cueillir ces fruits tant convoités
Des avocats bien sûr
Qui plaident avec éloquence
De palais en palais comme de juste
La cause des affamés
Qui écoutent avec science
La confidence des fines bouches
Ma foi, ils sont bons
Mieux que les amandes
Des avocats comme on les aime
Ils sont gros
Certains sont gras
certains sont plus gras que d'autres

Ils sont tous à vendre

Odeurs

Tuyaux de descente des latrines
J'aime sentir vos terribles vidanges
Et vous, douces puanteurs des recoins
Mon pain quotidien
Cabinets nauséabonds et corrompus
Vous êtes ma sphère d'aisance
Putrides décompositions des corps entassés
Nouveaux compagnons de mes sens
Et mes baisers sans dégoût
Sur de nuisantes bouches d'égouts
Et mes amours infectées
Dans les pissoirs fétides de la capitale

And the pungent smells of sisal
Under souring armpits
Smooth pestilences of the Other Ones
Let me sniff in you
The odor of my death.

(1987)

In My Image[8]

I like to see the image of God
Across my sweating face
I like to see me in his image
Slaving away under sacks of cement
At the hour of early morning mass[9]
Then in my eyes
Lodged as in two lakes
Worn out from innocuous praise
A traitor God depicted
Askew
I like to see the image of God
Across the hoarse hiccups
Of an old woman in rags
Whom I will soon assassinate
For a few banknotes
And see with my eyes close up
His image on the coins
I like to see the image of God.

(1988)

Et les piquantes odeurs de sisal
Sous les aisselles fermentées
Suaves pestilences d'Autrui
Laissez-moi humer en vous
L'odeur de ma mort.

(1987)

A mon image

J'aime voir l'image de Dieu
A travers ma face qui sue
J'aime me voir à son image
Trimer sous des sacs de ciment
A l'heure des messes matinales
Puis dans mes yeux
Logé comme en deux lacs
Lassés d'éloges anodins
Un traître Dieu portraituré
De biais
J'aime voir l'image de Dieu
A travers les rauques hoquets
D'une vieillarde en hardes
Que bientôt j'assassine
Pour quelques billets
Voir de mes yeux rapprochés
son image sur les monnaies
J'aime voir l'image de Dieu.

(1988)

Esther Nirina

Esther Nirina (Rabemananjara) was born in 1932. After a long stay in France, where she was a librarian, she returned in 1990 to live in Madagascar. A prominent literary figure in Madagascar, she has published several volumes of poetry: Silencieuse respiration *(Silent breathing, 1975);* Simple voyelle *(Simple vowel, 1980), for which she received the ADELF Grand Prix Littéraire de Madagascar;* Lente spirale *(Slow spiral, 1990); and, more recently,* Multiple solitude. *In search of universal values, her poetry often focuses nonetheless on the beauties of her native Madagascar.*

Silent Breathing

Tell me why did he choose
This corner of heaven to spread his fire
Is it a sunset
or the froth of time?

From the strong wind
A strange celebration
Shoots out onto this profusion of colors[1]

But alone. . .
A woman alone
Inside her bottomless abyss
Climbs an invisible ladder
On the beat. . .
Of her silent breathing.

(Simple voyelle)

Father, You who are present here
Lead me not into the temptation
Of "No longer believing" that He came
Also
For my people

All poems but "A buried and neglected history" translated from the French by Marjolijn de Jager

Esther Nirina

Esther Nirina (Rabemananjara) est née en 1932. Après un long séjour en France, où elle était bibliothécaire, elle est retournée en 1990 à Madagascar pour s'y fixer. Personnalité littéraire importante à Madagascar, elle a publié plusieurs volumes de poésie: Silencieuse respiration *(1975);* Simple voyelle *(1980), pour lequel elle a reçu le Grand Prix Littéraire de Madagascar (ADELF);* Lente Spirale *(1990); et tout récemment* Multiple solitude. *En quête de valeurs universelles, sa poésie n'en recherche pas moins les beautés de son île natale, Madagascar.*

Silencieuse respiration

Dis-moi pourquoi a-t-il choisi
Ce coin du ciel pour répandre son incendie
Est-ce un coucher du soleil
ou bien l'écume du temps?

Une célébration étrange
Jaillit du grand vent
Sur ces débauches de couleurs

Mais seule. . .
Une femme seule
Dedans son abîme sans fond
Monte une échelle invisible
Au rythme. . .
De sa silencieuse respiration.

(Simple voyelle)

Père, Toi qui es là présent
Ne me laisse pas succomber dans la tentation
De "Ne plus croire" qu'Il est venu
Aussi
Pour les miens

Lead me not
Into the temptation
Of "believing" that your will has
Wanted to create us
To be despised playthings
That it is You who stop us
From being more than half a man

But grant me
If only for a bit of time
The chance to whet
My faith
On solid rock
And fix my gaze
On the enduring sun.

(Simple voyelle)

Dadamanga[2]
(Blue-skinned father)

Often, on the fourth day of the week,[3] when the sun has awakened nature, and the courtyard of each house has been scratched lightly by the dried grass broom at sun's level.

A man with a tenor's voice would load the peddler's "Sobika"[4] on his shoulders.

He would bless The Eternal One before each opening door. Time enough to bestow the sign:

"Feed yourselves as the Children of Israel were fed while crossing the desert," he loved to repeat like a ritual phrase that came from the cavernous core of his throat.

—

Ne me laisse pas succomber
Dans la tentation
De "croire" que ta volonté est celle
De nous avoir créés
Pour être des jouets méprisés
Que Tu nous arrêtes
A l'état d'homme à moitié

Mais accorde-moi
Ne serait-ce qu'un temps
L'occasion d'aiguiser
La confiance
Sur la pierre solide
Et pouvoir fixer ma vue
Au soleil perdurable.

(Simple voyelle)

Dadamanga
(Père à peau bleue)

Souvent, le quatrième jour de la semaine, quand le soleil a réveillé la nature, et que la cour de chaque maison a reçu au ras du soleil les griffes légères de balais d'herbes sèches.

Un homme à voix de ténor chargeait sur ses épaules le "Sobika" du colporteur.

Il bénissait l'Eternel devant chaque porte qui s'ouvrait. Le temps d'une distribution du signe:

"Nourrissez-vous comme furent nourris les Enfants d'Israël durant la traversée du désert", aimait-il répéter comme une phrase rituelle venant de l'intérieur caverneux de sa gorge.

"How is it that you knew the Children of Israel?
"By what authority do you dare steal their history?"
my mother asked him.

Oh! woman blessed by Heaven!
May your descendants, too, be blessed.

Listen, there are those who are patriarchs from father to son.
There is One with the power to say: "This is my. . ."

But I, who am I? What do I know? my birth
comes from rumors alone. The hatching egg made me understand:

"God has chosen them."
So, without knowing who they were, my heart did choose them.

On my mother's face
I saw a tight smile begin.

Friends of my generation, which one of you, when opening your door to "Dadamanga" would have thought that he was nothing but a "Beggar of signals of the hand."[5]

Our neighborhoods formed his table.

That way he had of living as an echo, Love given to other peoples.

(Lente spirale)

When I see
Man
Set out to conquer a fly
Bring down the garden's trees
Without any hesitation

—Mais comment as-tu connu les Enfants d'Israël?
—De quelle autorité oses-tu subtiliser leur histoire?
lui demanda ma mère.

Oh! femme bénie du ciel!
Que tes descendants le soient aussi.

Ecoute, il y a ceux qui sont patriarches de père en fils.
Il y a Celui qui a pouvoir de dire: "Ceci est mon. . ."

Mais moi, qui suis-je? Que sais-je? ma naisssance vient de l'ouïe. L'oeuf en éclosant me fit entendre:
"Dieu les a élus".
Alors, mon coeur, sans les connaître, les choisit.

Je vis se dessiner un sourire ténu
Du visage de ma mère.

Amis de ma génération, qui de vous un jour, ayant ouvert sa porte à "Dadamanga", aurait cru qu'il n'était qu'un "Mendiant du Geste".

Nos quartiers étaient sa table.

Sa façon à lui de vivre en écho, l'Amour donné à d'autres peuples.

(Lente spirale)

Quand je vois
L'homme
A la conquête d'une mouche
Abattre sans hésiter
Les arbres du jardin

When I see
Woman
Add up the wounds
Distending inside her
Body filled with clotted blood

When I see
Children
Their stares piercing holes
Stretch out their rough and
palmless hands

I have nothing but a wisp of
Barely caught oxygen left.

When on the rebound I see
Man
Snore
Inside his blanket of pathetic
Vanity

When I see woman
Humiliated
At each step she takes

When I see the child
Struggle before
An obstructed exit

The father whose gaze
Has no sockets
The mother mute
From having shouted out
The day's existence

Do I still dare
Speak of love?

(Lente spirale)

Quand je vois
La femme
Additionner les plaies
Qui s'enflent
Dans son corps peuplé de sang caillé

Quand je vois
Des enfants
Aux regards térébrants
Avancer des mains rudes et
Sans paumes

Il ne me reste qu'un filet d'oxigène
Mal respiré.

Quand je vois par ricochet
L'homme
Ronfler
Dans sa couverture de vanité
Dérisoire

Quand je vois la femme
A chaque pas
Humiliée

Quand je vois l'enfant
Se débattre devant
Une issue murée

Le père au regard
Sans orbites
La mère muette
A force d'hurler
L'existence du jour

Oserais-je encore
Parler d'amour?

(Lente spirale)

Breath probes
As far as the bones of my spine
I make it into the flute
Of my conscience

But
For some
This barely audible voice
Has no place
In their orchestra

You alone
Oh silence!
Arrange the voice that
Speaks my mother's tongue
Inside your register.

(Multiple solitude)

Island
And islands
Fruits nourished by the oceans
Offerings
Destinies between the fingers
Of the early morning star
I salute you with clasped hands

Destined
To shine
Through the husk of grain
They cannot do
Without the book

Abundant
Drops of dew
That will give birth again
To an ancestral promise.

(Multiple solitude)

Le souffle pénètre
Jusqu'aux os de mes vertèbres
J'en fais la flûte
De ma conscience

Mais
Pour certains
Cette voix à peine audible
N'a pas sa place
Dans leur orchestre

Toi seul
O! silence
Disposes dans ton registre
La voix qui parle
Mon langage maternel.

(Multiple solitude)

L'île
Et les îles
Fruits nourris des océans
Offrandes
Destinées entre les doigts
De l'astre matinal
Je vous salue les mains jointes

Appelées
A luire
A travers bale
Elles ne peuvent se passer
Du livre

Multiples
Points de rosée
D'où renaîtront
Une promesse ancestrale.

(Multiple solitude)

Lovely woman
The bearing of a queen
In your train follow
Seven thousand seven hundred seven
Fields of rice
Over which
Time watches

With your smile of serenity
Bearer of mystery
From the height
Of the hill
You defy churchwardens
Who both classify and muddle up
The fabric of your history
From the other ocean
To this one here
For
All has been played out
In the flood tide of the sea

Your body fractured
By I know not what upheaval
Your majestic detachment
Renders you unrivaled
Lovely woman
Rampart of our progress
Your breath
Exhales
The Ode
To heaven.

(Multiple solitude)

Femme belle
Au port de reine
Tu as pour traîne
Sept mille sept cent sept
Rizières
Sur lesquelles
Le temps veille

Avec ton sourire serein
Porteur de mystère
Du haut
De la colline
Tu défies les marguillers
Qui classent et brouillent à la fois
Les trames de ton histoire
Depuis l'autre océan
Jusqu'à cet océan
Car
Tout s'est joué
Dans le flux de la mer

Corps craquelé
Par je ne sais quel séisme
Ton détachement majestueux
Te rend unique
Femme belle
Rempart de notre marche
Ton haleine
Exhale
L'Ode
A cieux.

(Multiple solitude)

A buried and neglected history. A past that murmurs across the ruins and inside the unassuming Amontana tree.[6] A hill surrounded by other hills. Its belly pregnant with blue granite and its sky a field of bees.

In this village, my village:[7] the reserve on the faces of simple, humble people; innocent children's faces frozen in a woeful look but each of which soon (?) will find its respectable mien. Taciturn peasants who think with their eyes, move in the rhythm of their natural dignity; the rice fields are their witnesses. Oh! life, water our life, green and golden valley.

Out of love I have learned to grasp the most truthful words in snatches, still crouching inside the darkness of their skins.

Who can give them the appropriate framework in which to help them think . . . without any great haste? help them coordinate their progress to the beat of their breathing. Do you hear the torrential waves of their hearts?

I say this: what is most pressing is a SMILE and I smile at them; the best light begins with a smile; a smile full of regard, a smile that awakens.

I come back here to put the imprint of my footsteps on these paths once again, paths my parents trod with their comings and goings, paths that have now become roads. All along the way, to find again today the inevitable, natural reproduction of the grasses of yesteryear, the same smoothness of the eucalyptus leaves and their old songs played by the fingering of the East wind. Oh! I do believe that my sense of smell alone could capture this region's identity. Look! I know you, you old wild rose bush of my childhood!

Histoire enfouie, méconnue. Passé qui bourdonne à travers les ruines et dans l'Amontana discret. Colline entourée de collines. Son ventre est enceinte de granits bleus et son ciel: champ d'abeilles.

Dans ce village, mon village: réserve de visages des gens simples, humbles; visages d'enfants innocents figés dans un aspect misérable, mais bientôt (?) trouveront chacun leur image respectable. Paysans taciturnes qui pensent avec leurs yeux, se meuvent à la mesure de leur dignité naturelle; les rizières en témoignent. O! la vie, eau notre vie, verte et or la vallée.

Par amour, j'ai appris à saisir bribe par bribe les paroles les plus vraies encore tapies dans les ténèbres de leur peaux.

Qui peut leur donner les éléments justes pour les aider à réfléchir. . . sans précipitation? les aider à coordonner leurs marches au rythme de leur souffle. Entendez-vous ces vagues torrentielles de leurs coeurs?

Moi je dis: le plus urgent c'est le SOURIRE et je leur souris; la meilleure lumière commence par un sourire; sourire qui considère, sourire qui réveille.

Je reviens remettre les empreintes de mes pas sur ces sentiers qu'avaient tracés mes parents avec leur va-et-vient, maintenant devenus chemins. Le long du trajet, retrouver aujourd'hui l'inévitable reproduction naturelle des herbes d'autrefois, les mêmes souplesses des feuilles d'eucalyptus et leurs vieux chants sous les doigtés du vent d'Est. O! Je crois bien qu'il n'y a que mon odorat pour capter l'identité de ce terroir. Tiens! Je te connais toi vieil églantier de mon enfance! Salut! honorable letchier, je me rappelle le bienfait de ton ombre. Te voilà enfin, "voara" providentiel, désormais, je prendrai soin de toi.

Hello! honorable lichee tree, how well I remember the benevolence of your shade. There you are at last, auspicious *voara*,[8] from now on I shall take care of you.

"Haody!"[9] little ancestral home where in earlier days the dusk's sweetness would prevail, rich with talk around the wood fire. Your call has always guided my direction. From here, underneath your roof, between your walls built by the hands and the sweat of my ancestors, I see the great crossroads of my universe . . . widen. The surrounding air spreads the cadence of your blessings[10] out over me. Inhaled by numerous gazes, I write so as not to leave the silence blank.

My body's timeless hour.

Outside, the silence of the soft drizzle murmurs across the windowpane. It permeates me. The thread that leads me as far as the farthest oceans guides me through the dense forest fraught with pitfalls and finally brings me onto the path that reaches the top.

My fingers intertwined with a beloved hand, I stand respectfully before this little hillock of stacked stones, the signature of an elementary artform, inside which reside bones whitened by time. Here is a wild rose I picked on my way up, for you who conceived me and who are there in part, a vibrant poem offered you by your daughter who remembers.

In listening, I've come to understand that melancholy is surprisingly close to happiness.

(Multiple solitude)

Translated from the French by Jacques Bourgeacq (The University of Iowa)

"Haody!" petite maison ancestrale où jadis régnait la douceur du crépuscule, riche de causeries autour du feu de bois. Ton appel a toujours guidé mon orient. D'ici, sous ton toit, entre tes murs bâtis avec les mains et la sueur de mes aïeux, je perçois le grand carrefour de mon univers. . . s'élargir. L'air ambiant me diffuse la modulation de vos bénédictions. Aspirée par de multiples regards, j'écris pour ne pas taire à vide.

Heure intemporelle de mon corps.

Dehors, le silence de la pluie fine, murmure à travers la vitre. Il me pénètre. Fil qui me conduit jusqu'au plus lointain des océans, me guide à travers la forêt touffue, semée d'embûches, pour tendre enfin vers le sentier des cimes.

Je me tiens debout respectueuse, les doigts entrelacés avec une main aimée devant ce monticule de pierres superposées, signature d'un art élémentaire, dedans lequel demeurent des os blanchis par le temps. A vous qui m'avez conçue et qui êtes là en partie, voici une rose sauvage cueillie sur mon chemin, poésie vibrante offerte par votre fille qui se souvient.

Dans l'écoute, je compris que la mélancolie voisine étonnamment avec le bonheur.

(Multiple solitude)

My hand beholds
My pen

My pen scoops
The echo
Of water
With a salty taste

The river
Creates its path
Between day and night

This
Pen
Rows
From one shore
To the other shore

The ocean will no longer frighten it.

(Multiple solitude)

Light would not be
If nights were not

I stand
Minuscule
In the visceral ebb of the world

Little by little
Enlarged
By the milk that cruises through
The royal blue high sea

My thirst for you
Ends up nurturing me

Ma main regarde
Ma plume

Ma plume fouille
L'écho
D'eau
Au goût de sel

Le fleuve
Crée son passage
Entre jour et nuit

Cette
Plume
Rame
D'une rive
A l'autre rive

L'océan ne lui fera plus peur.

(Multiple solitude)

La lumière ne serait
Si les nuits n'étaient pas

Je me tiens
Minuscule
Dans l'èbe viscéral du monde

Petit à petit
Agrandie
Par le lait qui traverse
La haute mer bleu-roi

La faim de toi
Finit par me nourrir

Lap up
Lap up my tongue
Swelling with thirst
Let us take all the needed time
For the bond
To regain the harmony
Of planned returns

(Multiple solitude)

Lape
Lape ma langue
Gonflée de soif
Prenons le temps qu'il faut
Pour que le lien
Retrouve l'accord
des retours prévus

(Multiple solitude)

Henri Rahaingoson

Henri Rahaingoson—also known as Di—was born in 1938. He is a professor and researcher in communication. Writing in both Malagasy and French, he gave himself this motto: "Andrianiko ny teniko; ny an'ny hafa koa feheziko" [I hold my Malagasy language sovereign; the language of the Other, I make it mine as well and master it]. His poems, in various styles, are still for the most part unpublished. They are often characterized by a scathing, almost Voltairian, humor. He has also produced a large number of translations of classical and modern authors, in both Malagasy and French.

Cacomany

Rock me Oh Cacomany[1]
In the anarhythm of your barbaric music
So that in a click
I will be unconformist
Away from all that old nun decency
The ceaseless refrain
of puppet-like[2] good kids
Of "as you ought"
For I am sick of it
Sick of hanging out with choirboys like this
In the contrivance of their eternal Mardi-Gras!

Let me then Oh Mascophobia
Fall in love
With a clown
But a real one
Who breathes the circus right down to his entrails
Yes . . . a close-up clown
Who mimics
The furtive smirks of ill-cloaked vices
That sometimes are betrayed
By a look's horizon
And the lips' frontiers . . .

Poems translated from the French by Marjolijn de Jager

Henri Rahaingoson

Henri Rahaingoson—connu aussi sous le nom de Di—est né en 1938. Il est enseignant et chercheur en communication. Ecrivant tant en malgache qu'en français, il s'est donné pour devise: "Andrianiko ny teniko; ny an'ny hafa koa feheziko" [Ma langue je la fais souveraine; quant à celle d'autrui, je la fais mienne et la maîtrise aussi]. Restée en grande partie inédite, sa poésie, d'inspiration variée, est caractérisée par un humour souvent grinçant, presque voltairien. On lui doit aussi nombre de traductions d'écrivains classiques et modernes dans les deux langues, malgache et français.

Cacomanie

Berce-moi O Cacomanie
Dans l'anarythme de ta musique barbare
Pour que cric et crac
Je me déconformise
D'avec cette pudeur vieille nonne
Que refrainent sans cesse
Les guignolesques bon-enfants
Des "comme il faut"
Car j'en ai marre
De frotter avec ces enfants de choeur
Dans la facticité de leur éternel Mardi-Gras!

Laisse-moi O Mascophobie
Tomber amoureux
D'un clown
Mais d'un vrai
Qui respire le cirque jusque dans ses entrailles
Oui. . . d'un clown en gros plan
Qui caricaturise
Ces grimaces furtives des vices mal camouflés
Que trahissent parfois
L'horizon d'un regard
Et les frontières des lèvres. . .

. . . For I would like to learn
How to be an anarchist
On the false melody
Of this paperpushing[3] life
So that I can sing and shout
My fill any old way
The hymn of garbage cans
The echo-tempered
Wordless choir
Of fat blue flies . . .

Oh! . . . let me sing the splendor of rankness!
And let me live in the intoxication
Of the garbage-confetti
That the attack and the hatred
Of the champions of order
And virtue's prizewinners
Will spit out on me! . . .

I will, of course, be told I am a killjoy
An anti-social madman or . . . quite simply . . . dumb!
Who cares . . . I'll just respond:
At least ugliness is true
"What is true is lovely"

So, I prefer it to all your faded finery!

(unpublished, 1963)

Don't Go

Often I see you motionless,
Your look vague . . . and always distant
Are you following a dream that pulls you
Toward other banks toward other islands?

Why does your soul stray
Toward other shores toward other skies?
. . . Futile flight and hollow hope
You still are of this world of ours!

. . . Car je voudrais apprendre
Comment on anarchise
La fausse mélodie
de cette vie paperasque
Pour que de bric et de broc
Je puisse chanter et crier tout mon soûl
L'hymne des poubelles
Que module en échos
Le choeur sans paroles
Des grosses mouches bleues. . .

Oh!. . . laisse-moi chanter l'éclat des puanteurs!
Et vivre dans l'ivresse
Des confétis d'ordures
Que cracheront sur moi la hargne et la haine
Des médaillés de l'ordre
Et des prix de vertu!. . .

L'on me dira, bien sûr, que je suis trouble-fête
Un fou anti-social ou. . . tout simplement. . . bête!
Qu'importe. . . je répondrai:
Au moins le laid est vrai
"Ce qui est vrai est beau"

Alors, je le préfère à tous vos oripeaux!

(inédit, 1963)

Ne t'en va pas

Souvent je te vois immobile,
L'air vague. . . et toujours lointaine
Suis-tu un rêve qui t'entraîne
Vers d'autres bords vers d'autres îles?

Pourquoi ton âme vagabonde
Vers d'autres rives vers d'autres cieux?
. . . Vaine évasion espoir creux
Tu es toujours de notre monde!

Oh nebulous and lunatic gaze
That gets you lost there on the moon
Be aware that adventure is a pocketful
Of holes where we stuff everything!

(unpublished, 1961)

By Way of Flowers

One evening she said to me
"I love you . . . , Dicky"
But I wouldn't believe her
Yes, she very simply told me so, as one sows seeds
Thrown out like that
Then she fell silent
Went away
And disappeared . . .
With hardly a last sigh
A final look
And when I was prepared to say:
"Me too" . . . it was too late . . .
. . . The following day
I learned
That she had died that night
In a railway accident.

(To the unknown woman of an October evening,
J.J.R. 1959 / E.N.; unpublished, 1963.)

There Is . . . You

There are faces the color of the dusk
That bear the imprint of some unfinished dream
There are eyes bottomless and vast
Like the ocean
And lost like the infinite gaze of the blind
Futilely scrutinizing the horizon
There are smiles of blue[4]

O regard vague regard fou
Qui te perds dans la lune
Sache que l'aventure est une
Poche trouée où l'on met tout!

(inédit, 1961)

En guise de fleurs

Elle m'avait dit un soir
"Dicky. . . , je t'aime"
Mais je ne voulais pas la croire
Oui, elle l'a dit, très simplement, comme on sème
A la volée
Puis elle s'est tue
S'en est allée
Et disparut. . .
Avec à peine un soupir
Un dernier regard
Et quand j'ai voulu lui dire:
"Moi aussi". . . il était déjà trop tard. . .
. . . J'avais appris
Le lendemain
Qu'elle était morte dans la nuit
Lors d'un accident de train.

(A l'inconnue d'un soir d'octobre,
J.J. R. 1959 / E.N. inédit, 1963)

Il y a. . . toi

Il y a des visages couleur de crépuscule
Qui portent l'empreinte de quelque rêve inachevé
Il y a des yeux profonds et vastes
Comme l'océan
Et perdus comme le regard infini des aveugles
Qui scrute en vain l'horizon
Il y a des sourires bleus

Like the sea in its lifeless azure
. . . Sometimes too there is . . . laughter cracked
Like breaking crystal
Bits of strayed stars the glimmer of a moment
There are women who have a moody soul
And the expression of a willow tree
And among these
There is . . . you!

(unpublished, 1961)

In-gra-ti-tu-de!

Oh! ungrateful homeless[5] one
Don't you see
That you still have
. . . the State . . .
That good daddy who loves you?

So then, Great God, Oh
What . . . you hadn't thought of that,
My poor pathetic madman!
. . . For he, he thinks of you . . . and wants,
Even against your will,
The State wants to make you happy
With all those safety nets[6]
For your own good!

Are these not yours, sidewalks and alleys?
And all these corners of the streets with their
perfume of trash . . .
. . . These food-protectors[7] open day and night,
Open indiscriminately to everyone who's homeless?
For . . . from there you may
Dredge up all that there is,
Collect . . . And nothing to pay,
As much as you want!

Comme la mer dans son azur sans vie
. . . Il y a aussi quelquefois. . . des rires fêlés
Comme le cristal qui se brise
Morceaux d'étoiles égarées lueur d'un instant
Il y a des femmes qui ont l'âme de la lune
Et l'expression d'un saule
Et il y a. . . toi
Parmi celles-là!

(inédit, 1961)

In-gra-ti-tu-de!

Oh! "4-Mi" ingrat
Ne vois-tu donc pas
Que tu as quand même
. . . L'Etat. . .
Ce bon papa qui t'aime?

Alors, O Grand Dieu,
Comment. . . n'y as-tu pas pensé,
Mon pauvre insensé!
. . . Car lui, il pense à toi . . . et veut,
Même contre ton gré,
Il veut te rendre heureux
Avec tous ces filets
Pour ta sécurité!

Ne sont-ils pas à toi, trottoirs et ruelles?
Et tous ces coins de rues au parfum de poubelles. . .
. . . Ces garde-à-manger ouverts jour et nuit,
Sans discrimination à tous les "4-Mi"?
Car. . . là tu peux
Tout puiser,
Ramasser. . . Sans payer,
Autant que tu veux!

Cram your insides full until you're satisfied!
. . . And then . . .
Then after that, my Friend,
You have . . . free time
To seek and choose
Places galore . . . in which to dream and sleep!

. . . Or else, you also may,
If such is to your liking . . .
Croak right away,
Go straight to Heaven
By T.G.V.[8] no ticket to be bought! . . .
That . . . for all the homeless ones
That too . . . is free of charge!

Oh! A fine bastard, he! Doesn't even say "Merci."

(unpublished, 1995)

Beggar's Refrain

Me, I have nothing,
Right, nothing at all,
It may be said just between us,
My pocket holds nothing but holes!

Me, I have nothing
Nothing I say,
Not even a crust or a small crumb of bread,
And later at night, when it is dark,
I devour with my eyes
The stars in the skies[9]
To sate my craving for food!

Me, I have nothing,
Right, nothing at all,
It may be said just between us,
That nothing is mine,
For . . . when sometimes it happens

Bourrer ton dedans jusqu'à satiété!
. . . Et puis. . .
Après ça, l'Ami,
Tu as. . . le loisir
De chercher et choisir
Des endroits à gogo pour. . . rêver et dormir!

. . . Ou bien, tu peux aussi,
Si tu en as l'envie. . .
Tout de suite crever,
Aller au Paradis
En T.G.V. sans billet!. . .
Car. . . pour tous les "4-Mi",
Ça aussi. . . C'est gratuit!

O! Le beau salaud! Ça dit pas "Merci".

(inédit, 1995)

Refrain d'un gueux

Moi, je n'ai rien,
Oui, rien du tout,
Soit dit entre nous,
Dans ma poche trouée désertée par les sous!

Moi, je n'ai rien,
Je n'ai rien,
Même pas de croûte ou une mie de pain,
Et le soir, quand la nuit vient,
Je dévore des yeux
Les étoiles des cieux
Pour satisfaire ma faim!

Moi, je n'ai rien
Oui, rien du tout,
Soit dit entre nous,
Rien à moi,
Car. . . lorsqu'il m'arrive parfois

That without knocking
I enter
Those places of prayer they call . . . Church,
Quickly, I realize, ever so quickly
How crude and how foolish I am!

. . . Lucky for me . . . they're always there,
The laymen, the clergy,
The fine-feathered folk!
Who, not a shade of unease,
Are kind and say gently
From the curve of a smile
With a simple swift gaze:

"Vagrant, you're lost,
The door is back there!"

. . . Yes, even there,
I don't have a roof to sleep under,
. . . I am . . . "without shelter,"
"S.D.F.[10] . . . and don't have a
home!"

(unpublished, 1964–1965)

D'entrer
Sans frapper
Dans ces lieux de prière qu'on appelle. . . Eglises,
Vite, très vite, je réalise
Ma grossière Bêtise!

. . . Heureusement qu'il y a. . . toujours là,
Laïcs et prélats,
Des gens chics et très bien!
Qui, sans l'ombre d'un rien,
Sont gentils pour me dire,
Dans le coin d'un sourire
Et d'un simple regard:

"Vagabond, qui t'égares
La porte est là-bas!"

. . . Oui, même là,
Je n'ai pas de toit pour passer
la nuit,
. . . Je suis. . . "4-Mi",
"S.D.F. . . sans abri!"

(inédit, 1964–1965)

LILA

(See the bio-bibliographical note in the "Short Stories" section [Lila Ratsifandriamanana].)

Close Your Eyes

Close your eyes
Plunge into unreality
Do not look back at this insane world!
The country is aflame,
Relentlessly preying on its land
Dregs of blood, bushfires, and ashes of misery.[1]
Down to its entrails
Blood-red flames.

Open your eyes
And return to reality . . .
With your hands revive the splendor of forests,
Behold the beauty
Of the white orchids
Flourishing in our hearts!

Artisan of happiness,
Protect from ruin
The lands of your Great Isle!

This Country of Mine

Could a country like mine
Hope for
A brighter tomorrow?
A country where Hunger
Is king.
Where Misery is queen!

Poems translated from the French by Jacques Bourgeacq, the University of Iowa

Lila

(Vior la note bio-bibliographique dans la section "Nouvelles" [Lila Ratsi-fandriamanana].)

Ferme tes yeux

Ferme tes yeux
Et plonge dans l'irréalité. . .
Ne te retourne pas sur ce monde insensé!
Le pays est en feu.
S'acharnant sur ses terres
Lie de sang, feux de brousse et cendres de misère.
Jusque dans ses entrailles
Des flammes rouges vermeilles.

Ouvre les yeux
Et retourne à la réalité. . .
De tes mains régénère la splendeur des forêts,
Apprécie la beauté
Des blanches orchidées
Fleurissant dans nos coeurs!

Artisan du bonheur,
Protège du péril
Les terres de ta grande île!

Un pays comme le mien

Un pays comme le mien
Pourrait-il espérer
Un meilleur lendemain?
Un pays où la faim
Est roi.
Reine est la misère!

A country where the law
Is mystery after mystery . . .
The law of all or nothing,
All for the powerful
And for the people . . . nothing!
A country where the Wrong
Sometimes has its reasons,[2]
Where life is torment

Yet a country like mine
Is indeed a treasure
In the Indian Ocean!

Un pays où la loi
N'est qu'un lot de mystères. . .
La loi du tout ou rien
Tout pour le plus fort
Et pour le peuple. . . Rien!
Un pays où le tort
A parfois ses raisons,
Où la vie est tourment.

Un pays comme le mien
C'est pourtant un trésor
Dans l'Océan Indien!

Rado

Rado—his real name is Georges Andriamanantena—was born in 1923, the heir of five generations of protestant ministers. He was thus educated in the religious literature developed in the Malagasy language by European missionaries. Malagasy ministers themselves carried this tradition over to profane Malagasy literature. Protestant intellectuals were also the fiercest "résistants," *defenders of Malagasy culture against French colonialism. Rado's poetry follows a double path: a political one urging "engagement" and an intimate one focused on daily life, nature, and love. Of all living Malagasy poets, Rado is the most admired by the contemporary public. He is also a figure in Malagasy cultural life today. He has written for many journals and is prized as a painter and composer of religious hymns as well. His main volumes of poetry are:* Dinitra *(Sweat, 1973),* Zo *(Rights, 1989) and* Sedra *(Ordeal, 1994). Malagasy schoolchildren know many of his poems by heart. Three of them are presented below, with each Malagasy poem followed by an English translation by Hanitra Raketokotany.*

Rado

Né en 1923 d'une famille de cinq générations de pasteurs protestants, Georges Andriamanantena—nom de plume Rado—a été formé dans la tradition littéraire religieuse des missionnaires européens. Ce sont les pasteurs malgaches qui étendirent ce savoir-faire à la littérature malgache profane. En outre, les intellectuels protestants furent les plus farouches "résistants" et défenseurs de la culture malgache face au colonialisme. La poésie de Rado se développe sur deux axes: d'une part une poésie engagée et d'autre part une poésie intimiste du quotidien, de la nature et de l'amour. De tous les poètes en langue malgache vivant aujourd'hui, c'est lui le plus apprécié du public. Rado est aussi une personnalité marquante de la vie culturelle du pays; il a collaboré à de nombreux journaux. Il est également peintre et compositeur de cantiques. Ses principaux recueils de poésie sont: Dinitra *(Sueurs, 1973),* Zo *(Les droits, 1989) et* Sedra *(Æpreuve, 1994). Les écoliers malgaches connaissent nombre de ses poèmes par coeur. Nous en reproduisons trois ci-dessous (dans la version originale). Une traduction en langue française par Voangy Andriamanantena suit chacque texte en malgache.*

Raha Mbola Misy

Raha mbola misy tsiky
azonao asetra ny ronjon'ny ankaso
Nahoana indrindra, iky
no dia laniana foana ny vongan-dranomaso!

Raha mbola misy ihany
kintana mamiratra azonao banjinina,
Nahoana no tomany
no andanianao ny alin'ny ririnina?

Raha mbola misy kalo
azonao hiraina anaty fahavaratra
Nahoana no himalo
mahita vodilanitra mosarena taratra?

(1970)

If You Can Still

If you can still give a slight smile
to face the mischances of life
Tell me why you are wasting
drops of tears away.

If you can still gaze at the stars
shining bright in the sky
Tell me why you are spending
winter nights crying away.

If you can still sing songs
in the midst of the rainy season
Tell me why you are so afraid
watching the lusterless horizon.

(1970)

Raha Mbola Misy

Raha mbola misy tsiky
azonao asetra ny ronjon'ny ankaso
Nahoana indrindra, iky
no dia laniana foana ny vongan-dranomaso!

Raha mbola misy ihany
kintana mamiratra azonao banjinina,
Nahoana no tomany
no andanianao ny alin'ny ririnina?

Raha mbola misy kalo
azonao hiraina anaty fahavaratra
Nahoana no himalo
mahita vodilanitra mosarena taratra?

(1970)

Tant que

Tant qu'un sourire
pourra te servir à braver les coups du malheur
Pourquoi donc
gaspilles-tu les grains de tes larmes!

Tant qu'il y aura encore
des étoiles scintillantes que tu peux contempler,
Pourquoi à des pleurs
gaspilles-tu les nuits d'hiver?

Tant qu'il y aura une chanson
que tu peux chanter au plus fort de l'orage
Pourquoi cette crainte
devant le spectacle d'un horizon sans éclat?

(1970)

Fotsiny

Tiako fotsiny ianao
Tsy asiana hoe "nahoana"
na tovonana "satria"
Fa tiako fotsiny amin'izao
Tsy amerana fotoana
Tsy fotsiny doria.

Ny "satria" sy ny "nahoana"
mety ho takatry ny saina?
tetika ikendrena laka. . .
haingon-teny babangoana,
rindram-bolam-bery maina,
ravina tsy misy faka.

Tsy ny teny izay tononina
no hahafeno ny fitia
efa feno rahateo.
Tsy ny toky izay foronina
mora rava sy malia,
fa ny fo tsy manam-peo

(1974)

Simply

I simply love you
No need to ask why
No use adding because
I just simply love you
With a feeling stronger than time
More eternal than eternity.

Questions and answers
Are tools of the mind
Nothing but weapons to rule a kingdom over
Void and meaningless words
Elaborate but dry
Like unrooted fallen leaves.

Fotsiny

Tiako fotsiny ianao
Tsy asiana hoe "nahoana"
na tovonana "satria"
Fa tiako fotsiny amin'izao
Tsy amerana fotoana
Tsy fotsiny doria.

Ny "satria" sy ny "nahoana"
mety ho takatry ny saina?
tetika ikendrena laka. . .
haingon-teny babangoana,
rindram-bolam-bery maina,
ravina tsy misy faka.

Tsy ny teny izay tononina
no hahafeno ny fitia
efa feno rahateo.
Tsy ny toky izay foronina
mora rava sy malia,
fa ny fo tsy manam-peo

(1974)

Simplement

Je t'aime simplement
Sans demander "pourquoi"
Ni ajouter "parce que"
Je t'aime tout simplement
Sans durée limitée
Je t'aime à jamais.

Les causes et raisons
que l'on puisse imaginer
ne sont que manières de séduire. . .
vide préciosité
vaine éloquence
feuille sans racine.

Words are expressed
To fully describe a love
But my love is already full
So useless it will be to utter them
As well as make up weak temporary promises
A silent heart is enough to speak to me.

(1974)

Laingalainga. . .

Laingalainga! Fa raha misy sombin-kalon'ny fahiny
natopan'ny kisendrasendra. . . Aiza ianao no tsy fanina
Raha miverina ny lasa ka manako ankehitriny
Mikimpy ianao. . . Toa mitadidy, dia manaraka ka manina!

Laingalainga! Fa raha misy sombin-tsoratra tsy may
noheverinao ho kila, kanjo hay tsy kila akory. . .
Aiza ianao no tsy hahatsiaro 'lay nanoratra azy indray:
Maka sary ny salovany tsy maty fa matory!

Laingalainga! Fa raha misy topi-masom-pahagola
mampiserana ny lasa izay nilaozanao nifindra. . .
Tsy helokao ny valin-tsiky mbola mamimamy angola
Satria ny nisy nefa rava: ireny no tadidy indrindra!

(1977)

You May Lie in Vain

You may lie in vain, but if you happen to hear the pieces
of a melody
Springing up from the past unexpectedly . . . You can't
help feeling dizzy
When echoes of the past ring back in the present, you
close your eyes
As if you remember, then sing along yearning after by-
gone times.

Ce ne sont pas les paroles
qui vont combler l'amour
en soi déjà comblé
Ni non plus les promesses inventées
si fragiles et si frêles,
C'est plutôt le coeur silencieux.

(1974)

Laingalainga. . .

Laingalainga! Fa raha misy sombin-kalon'ny fahiny
natopan'ny kisendrasendra. . . Aiza ianao no tsy fanina
Raha miverina ny lasa ka manako ankehitriny
Mikimpy ianao. . . Toa mitadidy, dia manaraka ka manina!

Laingalainga! Fa raha misy sombin-tsoratra tsy may
noheverinao ho kila, kanjo hay tsy kila akory. . .
Aiza ianao no tsy hahatsiaro 'lay nanoratra azy indray:
Maka sary ny salovany tsy maty fa matory!

Laingalainga! Fa raha misy topi-masom-pahagola
mampiserana ny lasa izay nilaozanao nifindra. . .
Tsy helokao ny valin-tsiky mbola mamimamy angola
Satria ny nisy nefa rava: ireny no tadidy indrindra!

(1977)

On a beau mentir

On a beau mentir si un petit air d'autrefois
déferlait par hasard. . . Comment pourriez-vous ne pas
vous émouvoir
Si le passé revient et résonne aujourd'hui
Vous fermez les yeux. . . et comme il vous revient, vous
fredonnerez dans la mélancolie!

You may lie in vain, but when you see unburnt frag-
ments of writings
You meant to burn, but which you failed to burn out
You can't help remembering the one who wrote them,
The one who died once is now asleep in your heart.

You may lie in vain, but whenever tender stealthy eyes
Look at you from a past you moved out
Do not feel guilty to smile back with sweet wheedlings
For what was is no more. They are what you remember
the most.

(1977)

On a beau mentir! Car si un fragment de lettre qui, non consumée,
fut supposée détruite, bien qu'elle l'ait été. . .
Comment pourriez-vous ne pas vous rappeler celui qui l'a écrite:
Imaginant ainsi son visage immortel, endormi!

On a beau mentir! Car si une oeillade d'antan
ranime un instant de passé, auquel vous avez déjà renoncé. . .
Vous n'aurez aucun tort de lui rendre un sourire encore doux de tendresses
Car ce qui existait mais qui ne l'est plus: cela sera le mieux gravé dans la mémoire!

(1977)

Notes

Introduction

1. *Kabary:* A kind of speech in prose, filled with proverbs, given at official or solemn occasions. Formerly, it was through *kabary* that the king or queen pronounced his or her edicts. Today, the *kabary* is used in major events of family life (weddings, initiations, funerals, etc.).

2. *Hainteny* (literally, "words of knowledge"): A poem in the form of a sparring dialogue on the theme of love (declaration, rejection, jealousy, etc.), laden with proverbs, and establishing comparisons between phenomena of nature and exemplary human situations. The tone is often mocking or lyrical. Such poems were—and sometimes still are—frequently applied to any daily life situation.

3. *Antsa:* Originally, chants to celebrate royal glory, often after a military victory.

4. *Angano:* A tale or legend in prose. As in much of Africa, such tales are still told for the young and old alike at evening gatherings.

5. In fact, unlike that of Africa, this traditional literature was already in written form before colonization: the royal *kabary* as early as 1825 and the other types, collected and transcribed by European missionaries, from 1860 on. The French writer Jean Paulhan and the Malagasy poet Jean-Joseph Rabearivelo were the first to translate them into French in the early twentieth century.

6. Jean-Louis Joubert, *Littératures de l'Océan Indien* (Vanves: Edicef/Aupelf, 1991), 39.

7. These Protestant missionaries established Christian journals and a whole network of schools, where information and education were provided in Malagasy. This situation would ultimately lead to a

written literature in Malagasy strongly grounded in religious inspiration, themes, and forms (hymns, psalms, nativity scenes, etc.).

8. Joubert, *Littératures,* 44–45.

9. Daniel Defoe, *Life, adventures and pyracies of the Famous Captain Singleton* (London: J. Brotherton, 1720). In fact, medieval Europeans and even ancient Greeks were already fantasizing about the Indian Ocean: see Jacques Le Goff, "L'Occident médiéval et l'Océan Indien: Un horizon onirique" (The medieval West and the Indian Ocean: An oneiric horizon), in *Pour un autre Moyen Age,* edited by Jacques Le Goff (Paris: Gallimard, 1977).

10. Among them: *18 degrés latitude sud* (1923); *Capricorne* (1930); *Océanides* (1937); *Du côté de chez Rakoto* (1938); and *La revue de Madagascar* (1946).

11. Jean-Joseph Rabearivelo was one of the three Malagasy poets presented in Léopold Sédar Senghor's *Anthologie de la nouvelle poésie nègre et malgache de langue française* (Paris: Presses Universitaires de France, 1948). More recently, on the occasion of the fiftieth anniversary of his death (1987), an international colloquium was held at the University of Antananarivo (see note 15).

12. His personal drama is illustrated by the title of his recently published novel, *L'interférence* (written in 1928; reedited by Jean-Louis Joubert [Paris: Hatier, 1987]). However, in the novel, *interférence* refers primarily to the demise of a decadent Malagasy ruling class under early French colonization.

13. This novel was published by Hatier (edited by Jean-Louis Joubert) on the occasion of a colloquium held in Madagascar on the fiftieth anniversary of Rabearivelo's death.

14. Abeona was a minor Roman divinity, invoked for simple daily matters. She was also the occult power propitiated before a trip. At a time when his material life had taken a turn for the worse, is Rabearivelo anticipating his suicide here?

15. The proceedings of this colloquium were published in a volume entitled *Jean-Joseph Rabearivelo, cet inconnu?* (J.-J. Rabearivelo, unknown?) (Marseille: SUD, 1989).

16. This single volume in French was published again in 1995 by Editions du Centre Albert Camus in Antananarivo, a French tribute to a poet whose main production was not in French.

17. Jacques Rabemananjara, *Oeuvres complètes,* Paris: Présence Africaine, 1978, 139–141.

18. Flavien Ranaivo, *L'ombre et le vent* (Shadow and wind) (Tanan-

arive: Imprimerie Officielle, 1947); *Mes chansons de toujours* (Forever my songs) (Paris: Author); and *Le retour au bercail* (Returning home) (Tananarive: Imprimerie Officielle, 1962).

19. Ranaivo stated that it was while reading Jean Paulhan's French translation of *haintenys* that he experienced the "esthetic shock" that induced him to write poetry.

20. Joubert, *Littératures*, 90.

21. Preface to *Chants capricorniens* (Antananarivo: Editions du Centre Albert Camus, 1995), p. 5. Dox began writing these poems in the early 1970s. They were not published as a volume until almost twenty years later.

22. The poet Jean-Joseph Rabearivelo is the perfect prototype of this bicultural, bilingual scholar.

23. Serge Henri Rodin and R. Rakotoarivelo, "Littérature malgache d'expression française," in *Notre Librairie* 110 (July–September 1992).

24. Ibid., 51.

25. Régis Rajemisa-Raolison, *Les poètes malgaches d'expression française* (Antananarivo: Imprimerie Catholique, 1983), 47.

26. See, for instance, *Notre Librairie* 104 (1991), *Dix ans de littérature 1980–1990: Caraïbe-Océan Indien* (issue title).

27. During this period, the capital city of Antananarivo saw a tremendous increase in the number of homeless people, in particular children abandoned by parents who could no longer feed them. These children were called *quat'mi*, from the French *quatre murs* (four walls), which ironically they do not have (see Henri Rahaingoson, note 5). From 1991, the economic situation gradually collapsed and eventually led to the demise of the Ratsiraka government.

28. Contemporary literature written in Malagasy is said to have retained something of the inspiration and conservative tone of its early religious origins. Through the French language, on the other hand, this generation of writers has felt free to vent its frustrations and revolt.

29. Liliane Ramarosoa, *Anthologie de la littérature malgache d'expression française des années 80* (Anthology of Francophone Malagasy literature of the eighties) (Paris: L'Harmattan, 1994), 19 (my translation).

30. An initiatory quest in the perspective of Arnold van Gennep and Mircea Eliade.

31. This French project is headed by Michèle Rakotoson, who is one of the foremost contemporary Malagasy writers. Jean-Luc Raharimanana, Jean-Claude Fota, and David Jaomanoro, whose texts appear in this anthology, are among the laureates of these contests.

32. Although *L'interférence* was recently published, the other novel, *L'aube rouge* (The red dawn), is yet unavailable in print. Between the 1950s and 1980s, none of the following novelists made an impact in Madagascar or elsewhere: Aimée Andria, Robinary, and Pelandrova Dreo.

33. It is interesting to know that Rafenomanjato wrote the latter novel at the same time as her essay *La marche de la liberté* (The march for freedom) (Paris: L'Harmattan, 1992), which gives a detailed account of the recent political events in Antananarivo that led to the massacre of August 1991: the people of Antananarivo, demonstrating against President Ratsiraka's politics and economics, marched peacefully toward the presidential palace located some ten miles from the center of the city. An order was given to fire on the demonstrators as they neared the palace.

34. D. N. Andrianjafy, "Le théâtre," *Notre Librairie* 110 (July–September 1992): 69–75.

35. In Imerina (home of the Merina people, where Antananarivo is located), the ancestral tomb, a grandiose monument of granite, is adjacent to the house of the living, sometimes a modest shack in comparison. Although families are often poor, huge sums are spent for the periodic exhumations (*famadihana*, literally, "turning of the dead;" the changing of the shrouds ceremony) and for the maintenance of the tomb, in which everyone knows that his or her place is reserved for eternity. In *Le Tsiny et le Tody dans la pensée malgache* (The *Tsiny* and the *Tody* in Malagasy thought) (Paris: Présence Africaine, 1957), Richard Andriamanjato describes the paralyzing effect that fear of displeasing the ancestors has on society. This fear, caused by a sense of guilt *(tody)* and personal insignificance *(tsiny)* is often invoked to help explain Madagascar's past and present stagnation.

36. On the one hand, Madagascar is almost entirely Christianized; the Malagasy landscape is literally spiked with church steeples. On the other hand, witchcraft, divination, communication with the dead through dreams, etc. are vigorous survivals of the ancient past.

The Pioneers

1. *Papango:* A large bird of prey with the reputation of a thief *(Milvus aegyptius).*

2. *Farahantsana* (From Malagasy *fara* = last + *antsana* = cascade, abyss): Is it the name of an actual waterfall or a symbolic image? At any rate, one does not exclude the other.

3. Note the argumentative dialogue between two lovers (as shown by the alternating masculine and feminine forms in French), a specific feature of the *hain-teny* poem.

4. *Vahiny:* Malagasy word for a passing stranger receiving hospitality.

Short Stories

Funeral of a Pig:

1. Kalachs: Unruly gangs or brigades of adolescents, organized by the government to fight popular opposition, who often intimidated the population and sometimes committed crimes, especially in Diego-Suarez (cf. note 3).

2. *Ampango:* The crust of rice that sticks to the bottom of the pot after cooking. Mixed with sugar as a dessert, it is considered a treat.

3. Diego-Suarez (Malagasy name: Antseranana): A major port city at the Northern tip of Madagascar, the home region of the author of this short story.

4. *Tamango:* In the Northern dialect, the word refers to a coffin, sexualized as in the text. Elsewhere in the country, the word designates an ornament worn at initiation ceremonies. Perhaps the new beginning represented by death is connected here to initiation.

5. Eighty thousand francs: This sum, in Malagasy francs, is the equivalent of about twenty U.S. dollars; it is no great fortune, even in Madagascar!

6. *Ziva:* Abbreviation of *mpiziva*, a member of a "joking kinship." This form of kinship, found also in some parts of Africa, links two distinct social groups in a privileged relationship involving mutual duties and rights: e.g. attending the other clan's funerals; "insulting" the other clan to relieve the tension that often builds up in close communal living; and, during such trying times as death, taking charge of the burial ceremony. "Pig" is indeed a frequent insult, the epitome of impurity and the object of many taboos.

7. Njoaty: The dead boy's clan, a people of the coastal town of Vohémar, in the North of Madagascar. In this same region, the Makoa, a tribe of African origin, are also called Morima.

8. Antankandrefa is the name of the other clan. In this context, it is a joking kinship (cf. note 6). The comparison with an animal (here a pig) is probably a verbal strategy used to divert the attention of eventual

evil spirits. The destabilized, vulnerable soul of the recently deceased person needs a smooth road to the realm of the ancestors. This strategy of exorcism is misunderstood by the young boy, Ntsay.

9. *Boutre:* The traditional boat with a triangular sail, used to transport merchandise and passengers along the coasts of the island.

10. Morima: See note 7.

11. "Disgrace" is in fact the opposite of the meaning of this ritual and thus corresponds to the verbal strategy explained in note 8. Furthermore, death is not named directly, but rather through euphemisms such as "disgrace." Dead uncircumcised children are said to have "returned to water."

12. *Kigny:* A *kabary*, or public speech, of the type given at funerals.

13. The final rest—or rather the change of ontological condition—of the dead person occurs when the flesh has completely decomposed, the clean bones being the "eternal" remains of the deceased. During decomposition, the soul is thought to be at a vulnerable stage, subject to potential evil forces. In some areas of Madagascar, decomposition is activated so that the soul can more quickly reach the safe realm of the ancestors. The harsh treatment inflicted on the body may be an incentive for the soul to depart without delay on its last journey and never to want to return.

14. During funerals, death and its objects and manifestations are mocked, as a form of exorcism. Thus the dead person is often verbally and physically abused. Straddling being a gesture of domination, death is thus symbolically conquered and derided.

15. *Gouma:* A rhythmic dance for funeral ceremonies.

16. The Federals (French Fédérés) were government supporters who organized to suppress the people's opposition (numerous demonstrators and strikers in the streets of the capital and other main cities). The youth brigades, or *Kalachs,* were part of their armed forces (cf. note 1).

17. The 4L, a small car made by Renault, is quite economical to run and maintain. It is thus found in large numbers in Madagascar.

18. Drinking blood is a practice associated with witchcraft in Madagascar.

Little Bone:

1. House of Cold: Probably a literal translation from a Malagasy periphrase referring to the tomb.

2. Dancing Women: These dancing women *(mpandihy)* or sorceresses *(mpamosavy)* come out at night, especially when a funeral is in preparation. Their role is the destruction of social harmony, perhaps as a ritual prelude to the renewal of order. The short story "Grandma" by Christiane Ramanantsoa (page 76) describes further the behavior of these dancing witches (see also "Grandma," note 2).

3. *Mosavy:* This type of witchcraft is specifically related to casting spells.

4. Holding old score: The French is *garder des restes,* an expression literally translated from Malagasy; it means something like "to hold a grudge" (against someone).

5. The final sprinkling is part of the funeral rite.

6. To break the taboo of the Cold means to enter a tomb, obviously a literal translation of a Malagasy expression. Entering a tomb can only be done as part of a specific ritual (burial or the "turning of the dead"); otherwise it is a profanation.

7. Whenever honey is associated with the female body, it is an image of sexuality in the Indian Ocean region.

8. *Sojabe:* Grandfather, and by extension, the village sage. Among the Tsimihety in Northern Madagascar where the story is situated, the *sojabe* is the clan's chief.

9. *Gouma:* Chants and dances for funerals and other family ceremonies.

10. The dead are supposed to depart from the land of the living once and for all, although they still have input in their family's destiny.

11. *Masevy:* Traditional dance in Northern Madagascar.

12. These are ingredients for a potion, probably a love potion (common practice in Madagascar) for ensuring her husband's fidelity in the future.

13. Witches are said to wander at night without their clothes. Naked, Masizara will fool the witches into believing that she is one of them and will thus manage to return home safely.

14. *Habobo:* Malagasy word for curds.

15. *Kitoza:* A type of dried meat, like a jerky.

The Rich Child:

1. *Valiha:* A traditional stringed instrument made of bamboo.

2. Rova: The queen's palace, built on the highest hill of Antananarivo. It was destroyed by fire in November 1995. Only the stone frame remained standing.

3. *Gitane* (French for "Gypsy"): The reference is to a famous advertisement for the French cigarettes of the same name which portrays a Gypsy woman draped in a spiral of smoke.

4. 100 fmg: Malagasy francs, worth less than three U.S. pennies.

5. *Lamba:* The traditional, elegant Malagasy shawl or toga, sometimes made of silk, wrapped around the body or folded on the shoulder.

6. A full-size, deluxe Peugeot.

7. *Mpihira gasy:* A troupe of itinerant singers and dancers.

Case Closed:

1. *Boutre:* A sailboat (cf. "Funeral of a Pig," note 9).

2. There was in Madagascar a class of slaves *(andevo)*. The term is still abusively associated with the black race, although there exists in Madagascar a noble caste that is black. Merina nobility can also be demoted to the slave caste in the case of serious social transgressions. Today, the old class and caste systems still exist, alongside of the modern social structure inherited from the West. The woman in this text belongs to the slave class because of her color and her own self-image. Indeed, her "surgical" job links her to witches, who are said to rip out the hearts of their victims; hence the associations in her own mind with zombies and evil spirits *(djinns)*. Her dementia is aggravated by this awareness.

3. Red is indeed the color of royalty in Madagascar. The evocation of Madagascar's glorious past is in sharp contrast with this macabre traffic. If one considers the high intrinsic value placed on children in Malagasy traditional society, the author's irony is all the more scathing.

4. This ending suggests the complicity of the police, who quickly close the case after the elimination of this cumbersome, loquacious criminal!

Grandma:

1. In Madagascar, according to Jorgen Ruud, "the phases of the moon . . . influence many things and undertakings" (*Taboo: A study of Malagasy Customs and Beliefs* [Oslo: Oslo University Press, 1970], 64). For instance, burial during the full moon phase in certain lunar months, or in conjunction with certain individual or family destinies *(vintana)*, is taboo.

2. "In olden days midnight was called: 'When the witches go out.' . . . The witches are often old women. They undress and make a bundle

of their clothes, which they put on their heads. They smear their bodies over with pig's fat, which is taboo to other people. Unseen they steal out of the hut and start their dancing outside, mostly on the graves. If someone is mortally ill in the village, or if a wake is being held, these witches are very active and in high spirits . . . [their laughter] jeers at the grieving and anxious people, and acclaims the victory of death" (Ruud, 150–51).

3. This behavior is reminiscent of the representations of the primordial disorder (or Chaos) during rites of renewal, as described in the works of Mircea Eliade.

4. This violent attack seems to be part of the above ritual.

Grandmother:

1. This description of a French-style marriage ceremony and a family of only two children suggests the extent of the brother's westernization.

2. The Malagasy often take on a new name. As a child can incarnate a revered ancestor and thus take his or her name, the parents may change their names to include the child's name, generally the firstborn. This custom has also a practical side: since children are often known by all in their neighborhood, identifying the parents by way of the child is thus made easier.

3. *Falafa:* Latticework made from palm fronds of the *falafa* tree.

4. Beef (in this case, zebu meat): Zebus are killed at funerals and the meat is shared by the family and friends at a sacrificial meal.

5. Although it should be abundant, sacrificial meat must not be gastronomically appreciated; consequently flavoring with salt, a stimulant for taste, is avoided. Any verbal reference to the meat as tasting good is also taboo.

6. Traditional funerals are also rites of eternal return and, as such, stress the regenerative dimension of death. As in many societies, sexual exuberance enhances the celebration of life: life goes on and its resulting effect, birth, is an antidote to death in an ancestor-oriented society.

7. Insult is probably part of a diversion strategy: pretending indifference or hostility toward the dead person detracts evil forces from harming his/her soul (see "Funeral of a Pig," note 8).

8. *Brèdes:* Cooked greens, much like our spinach. There are many different *brèdes* in the Malagasy culinary tradition. They are often used to accompany meat dishes and rice. The grandmother's exclusive

taste for traditional food is all the more significant if one considers the fondness of the Malagasy westernized elite for French food.

9. As seen in David Jaomanoro's short story "Funeral of a Pig," sitting on a coffin is a part of the funeral rite.

Wretched Sun:

1. As we have seen, names in Madagascar have a meaning, defining, as our Western nicknames do, the identity and character of the person. A Malagasy name can be changed by its bearer and will thus often reflect the personality or refer to a life occurrence of an individual. The patronymic (clan's name) does exist, but is used less often. The author has chosen to weave into his French text this important Malagasy cultural feature.

2. Boots (French *brodequins*): The word is used metonymically to designate soldiers or police.

3. *Pagne:* A cloth, usually several meters in length, used as a toga for men or as a dress for women (see "The Rich Child," note 5).

4. The word "blue" (Malagasy *manga*), often used affectively, means beautiful, good, heartwarming. Thus it may not be taken literally here, but rather figuratively.

5. Captives: Another word for slaves *(andevo)*, members of the lower social class in Madagascar. The noble *(andriana)* and the free *(hova)* are the other classes (see "Case Closed," note 2).

6. There is nothing unusual about this bargaining: almost everything is negotiable in Madagascar, as in many other parts of the world. In fact it may be used here, as suggested later in the text, as a spying strategy.

The President's Mirror:

1. *Lamba:* In general, the traditional toga worn by Malagasy (see "The Rich Child," note 5). A type of *lamba*, made of fine silk and called *lambamena*, serves as a shroud and is changed at exhumation ceremonies *(famadihana*, or "turning of the dead").

2. Red is the traditional color of royalty, fertility, and nurturing. Madagascar is the "Red Island" of the Ancestors. Ironically, the pauper leaves on the plush carpet marks of the red earth that his bare feet have dragged in from a land turned sterile under the current political regime.

3. Naming in Madagascar, as in Africa, can be an unending pro-

cess, since a name is never a simple label, but accounts for a reality; and realities do change. Similarly, an individual will acquire, as we have indicated earlier, new names in his/her lifetime. Serge Henri Rodin's short story provides examples of the importance of naming (see "Wretched Sun" in this anthology).

4. The old nurse probably belongs to the slave *(andevo)* caste.

Walk no Work:

1. Diviner (Malagasy *ombiasa*): An astrologer and medicine man, who reads individual destinies *(vintana)* and has the power to modify them. Here, the main protagonist's future is predicted.

2. School benches, another way of saying that the son is going to acquire a Western-style education.

3. *Hachélème:* In the French text, this invented word reproduces the pronunciation of "H.L.M.," an acronym for H*abitation à* L*oyer* M*odéré* (literally, "Moderate Rent Lodging"; more idiomatically, "Government-Subsidized Housing").

4. *Ombiasa:* Malagasy for a diviner (cf. note 1).

5. *Soubique* (Malagasy *sobika*): This word for a specific shopping basket is well known throughout that region of the Indian Ocean.

6. Refers to a particularly trying period in recent Malagasy history, both politically and economically.

7. It is as if Job's word game were a parody of the *ombiasa*'s divination techniques, namely the writing of figures with sand or seeds *(sikidy).* The *ombiasa*'s "writing of destiny" is not to be placed in just anybody's hands. Might as well "whip a crazed horse." The hero learns this the hard way!

8. Old Micheline: A motorized railcar, originally equipped by the Michelin Tire Company.

9. *Récit/Ecrit:* French words for Narration/Script. These two words lend themselves to an anagram in French.

10. The French is *Lorsque les poules auront* du répondant. This is a pun on a French saying: *Lorsque les poules auront* des dents (When chickens have *teeth*).

11. *Tanrec:* An insect-eating mammal of Madagascar.

God Will Come Down to Earth Tomorrow!:

1. The extent of deforestation in Madagascar is well known. The island, seen from the air, now appears more red than ever before.

2. A reference to Malagasy forests destroyed by fire for the production of charcoal.

In the Top of the Aloalo:

1. *Aloalo:* A sculptural pole marking a grave in Southern Madagascar; it marks the grave as an expression of ideal values, and often as a reconstruction of the most important features of the life of a deceased person.

2. Tulear (Malagasy Toliari): A major port city in southwest Madagascar.

3. Bush-taxi (French *taxi-brousse*): A station-wagon, minivan, or car used as long-distance transportation throughout Madagascar. Their schedules are often unpredictable and the vehicles prone to breakdown.

4. Taboos regarding days of the week, and time in general, are tied to traditional astrology, and are still taken very seriously in Malagasy life, even in urban society.

5. *Dahalo:* Local bandits who in the old days stole cattle. Now they no longer specialize in cattle, mugging road travelers as well.

6. In Madagascar, private telephones are still rare and people go to the post office to make their calls.

7. A small town on the west coast, Ifaty is known also for its scuba diving facilities for tourists.

8. A narrow dug-out canoe, used for all sorts of transportation: freight, passengers, and even cattle. It is equipped with a lateral floater for stability.

9. A small town on the coast, some fifteen miles south of Tulear.

10. These lakes are situated some sixty miles inland from Tulear, along the Onilahy River. Lying on beautiful terraced ground, they are considered sacred and attract many tourists. Some are taboo to foreign visitors *(vazaha).*

11. An indigenous plant of Madagascar discovered by the explorer Grandidier.

12. All are practices, either Christian or Animist, aimed at "rectifying" Marielle's behavior.

13. Madagascar was Christianized as early as the beginning of the nineteenth century. Today, much of the population, even in rural areas, is Christian. This does not, however, preclude the simultaneous existence of Animist beliefs and occult practices.

14. Imerina, where Antananarivo is located, is one of the regions of Madagascar practicing periodic exhumation of the dead *(famadihana)*, a joyful celebration designed to revere and maintain contact with the ancestors. The *famadihana*, a very costly ceremony, plays an essential role in Merina life, as it brings the whole family together, strengthens the clan's bonds, and assures its survival.

15. During the *famadihana*, the family members hold in turn in their hands the remains of their dead kin (often those they once knew), showing them signs of affection.

16. Marielle's vision is ironic, insofar as the *aloalo* is a sculptural reconstruction of the most important features of the deceased's life history. The *aloalo* is placed on the grave as a concrete representation—not a mere figment of the survivors' imagination.

Poetry

David Jaomanoro:

1. One of two tunnels in Antananarivo, close to the *Zoma*, the busy marketplace.

2. The French, *fait l'entrée du tunnel*, is an expression coined from *fait le trottoir* (is a streetwalker; literally, "does," that is, "paces" the sidewalk). The expression ironically points to the Malagasy way of being a hooker!

3. Five francs: Five Malagasy francs, too insignificant a coin to buy anything at all.

4. A customary endearing term in French for a child. The name also evokes the shrewd character of La Fontaine's fables.

5. Tiny Malagasy ticks (French *chique*) penetrate the skin, especially under toenails, where they lay eggs and trigger infection. In the long run, feet are deformed by repeated infections.

6. The French word *épave* can be applied, as in English, to a human being. The description of an old ship on the shore of the Indian Ocean suggests the human wrecks of Malagasy cities, especially Antananarivo. It also evokes the island of Madagascar itself, beached along the African coast, seemingly forgotten by History.

7. Korah, Abiram, Dathan: All Biblical names of leaders of ancient Israel who, having revolted against Moses, perished with their peoples by God's fire.

8. This bird is often associated with one of the astrological signs

(vintana), Alahamady (the most prestigious one), according to Louis Molet (*La conception malgache du monde, du surnaturel, et de l'homme en Imerina* [Paris: L'Harmattan, 1979], 1:65).

Jean-Luc Raharimanana:

1. See Raharimanana's short story "The Rich Child" in this anthology, in which the pool takes on a symbolic dimension.

2. Ankaratra: A mountain range some fifty miles south of Antananarivo.

3. Tsaratanana: A large mountain range in Northern Madagascar.

4. Probably a reference to the Merina noble class *(andriana)*, still wealthy and powerful in Madagascar.

5. The word slave *(andevo)*, although suggesting the disadvantaged class, may also include people from all classes and walks of life, nearly the whole nation, who are barely surviving the current economic stagnation.

6. Possibly a reference to the government surveillance to which people were subjected during the eighties.

7. Ikopa: A river flowing in central Madagascar and through the city of Antananarivo. To "sing the Ikopa River" may refer to the poems of the previous, post-independence generation of writers who celebrated the Grand Isle, newly liberated from French colonialism.

8. Geometer moths: *Phalènes*, in the original poem, are nocturnal butterflies that seek light and are believed to host the souls of the dead.

9. Imerina: The central region where Antananarivo is situated, home of the Merina people, of Indonesian ancestry.

10. Tsaratanana: See note 3. This mountain range is not yet totally explored, although it is well known for its unique flora and fauna.

11. Sambirano: A river that flows in northern Madagascar through the Tsaratanana Mountains.

Jean-Claude Fota:

1. The original French *(mort aux rat)* refers to Mort-aux-Rats, a type of rat poison in France.

2. This poem is indeed a strikingly accurate representation of the many open sewers of the capital city.

3. Malagasy contemporary life is still governed by numerous social and religious taboos. The "violation of a taboo" is described here in literal, graphic terms, probably in violent reaction to a tyrannical and paralyzing traditional order.

4. The title in the original text is *Avocats.* The whole poem is con-

structed on a pun: the French word *avocat* means both lawyer and avocado (the tropical fruit). Due to a resulting series of other ironic double entendres (mature/ripe; courthouse [*palais de justice*]/palate; fine, fee/kernel; for sale/for bribe; etc.), the poem can be read at two distinct levels that, oddly enough, coincide linguistically!

5. This graphic description corresponds all too closely to the realities of the Malagasy capital city.

6. Another pun: when tied to the word *sphere*, the French word *aisance* means comfort, ease. But *lieux d'aisances* (literally "place of ease") means water closet, toilet.

7. Another pun on the French *bouche d'égoût* (literally the mouth of a sewer, for manhole).

8. The poet sees the world through the eyes, in turn, of several poor, marginalized citizens, with whom he identifies.

9. This description is accurate: throughout the capital city, whether on weekdays or on Sundays, numerous construction workers are at work from daybreak, building houses for the rich. The latter do find time to attend church services.

Esther Nirina:

1. Madagascar is known for its spectacular sunsets, especially during the rainy season.

2. *Dadamanga:* The subtitle is provided by the poet; *dada*, "father"; *manga*, "blue." The word *manga* often has positive connotations: good, beautiful, heartwarming.

3. Although it has its taboos, the fourth day of the week, Thursday *(alakamisy)*, is considered a day of good destiny *(tsara vintana)*, "filled with optimism and expectation" for those who wish to undertake new projects (cf. Ruud, 34).

4. *Sobika:* peddler's basket (*soubique* in French). See "Walk No Work," note 5.

5. Beggar: Since he had nothing, except the sacerdotal gesture.

6. *Amontana:* A name given to a type of fig tree in Imerina (author's note).

7. My village: The name of this village is Ambohimifangitra. Located some thirty miles east of Antananarivo, it boasts two churches, a Protestant and a Catholic, as well as an elementary school. Esther Nirina pays frequent visits to her village and her ancestors' tomb.

8. *Voara:* A kind of fig tree with red fruit.

9. *Haody:* A courteous, discrete call from the threshold of someone's

house, equivalent to "Anybody home?" Perhaps early missionaries used this dialectal English greeting in their daily life: "Howdy!"

10. Blessings: The Malagasy believe that the ancestors bestow their blessings on the living, often in the form of health, fertility, and prosperity.

Henri Rahaingoson:

1. Cacomany: A neologism coined from "cacophony." The poet has confided that he wrote this text in his youth, as a response to a high school teacher who had called him a "rebel," a "non-conformist."

2. Puppet-like: The poet used the term *guignolesque* in French, an adjective coined from Guignol, a famous traditional French puppet character, who symbolizes the plebeian, revolutionary spirit.

3. Paperpushing: The poet used the term *paperasque* in French, yet another neologism built on the French *paperasse* ("red tape," "bureaucracy") and the adjectival ending —*que*. The word also evokes *fantasque* ("unpredictable," "whimsical").

4. Blue: This color often means good, heartwarming, beautiful in Madagascar. (See Esther Nirina, note 2).

5. Homeless: The term used in the original text is *4-Mi*, a homeless person in Madagascar. The expression may be based on four Malagasy verbs expressing forms of violence, each beginning with the prefix *mi-*. This is, however, a fairly common prefix of Malagasy verbs. Another, more plausible, explanation is that it comes from the French *4 murs* (4 walls), pronounced with a Malagasy accent and of course ironic, as *4-Mi* have no home.

6. Nets may also refer to the wire netting along the arcades of Avenue de l'Indépendance in the center of town (the poet's window happens to open on to this avenue). The question is, safety for whom? Indeed, these fences keep the numerous homeless people on the sidewalk, away from the stores and restaurants of the wealthy. Thus the poor are ironically kept "away from trouble."

7. Food-protector (French *garde-à-manger*): A meat safe equipped with a screen. The word refers here to garbage cans and city dumps scattered around town. Another irony might be that such resources are not so easily available as one may think: they constitute territories among the homeless, off limits to intruders. So, in reality, the abundance described by the poet is quite limited!

8. T.G.V.: French acronym for "T*rain à* G*rande* V*itesse,*" a high-speed train.

9. Stars in the skies: This gesture of gazing at the stars is not without significance, if one remembers the importance of stars for the calculation of individual destinies in Madagascar: one's fate is written in the stars.

10. S.D.F.: French acronym for "S*ans* D*omicile* F*ixe,*" meaning without permanent residence.

Lila:

1. Madagascar is the scene of numerous brush fires purposely set to make firewood, among other reasons. Deforestation has remained to this date a most serious problem.

2. Reasons: An allusion to a famous aphorism by seventeenth-century thinker Blaise Pascal: *Le coeur a ses raisons que la raison ne connaît point* (The heart has its reasons that reason knows not), parodied here to stress the unreasonable, unpredictable behavior of the powerful in Madagascar.

Selected Bibliography

I. Social Sciences and History

Andriamanjato, Richard. *Le Tsiny et le Tody dans la pensée malgache.* Paris: Présence Africaine, 1957.

Baré, Jean-François. *Pouvoir des vivants, langage des morts: Idéo-logiques sakalava.* Paris: F. Maspero, 1977.

Bloch, Maurice. *Placing the Dead: Tombs, Ancestral Villages and Kinship Organization in Madagascar.* New York: Seminar Press, 1971.

Boiteau, Pierre. *Contribution à l'histoire de la nation malgache.* Paris: Editions Sociales, 1958.

Chaigneau, Pascal. *Rivalités politiques et socialisme à Madagascar.* Paris: CHEAM, La Documentation française, 1985.

Colin, Pierre. *Aspects de l'âme malgache.* Paris: Editions de l'Orante, 1959.

Deléris, Ferdinand. *Ratsiraka: Socialisme et misère à Madagascar.* Paris: L'Harmattan, 1986.

Delivre, Alain. *Histoire des rois d'Imerina: Interprétation d'une tradition orale.* Paris: Klinsieck, 1974.

Deschamps, Hubert. *Histoire de Madagascar.* Paris: Berger-Levrault (4e édition), 1972.

Ellis, Stephen. *The Rising of the Red Shawls: A Revolt in Madagascar, 1895–1899.* Cambridge: Cambridge University Press, 1985.

Haring, Lee. *Verbal Arts in Madagascar: Performance in Historical Perspective.* Philadelphia: University of Pennsylvania Press, 1992.

Huntington, Richard. *Gender and Social Structure in Madagascar.* Bloomington: Indiana University Press, 1988.

Koenig, Jean-Paul. *Malagasy Customs and Proverbs.* Sherbrooke: Editions Naaman, 1984.

Kottak, Conrad P. *The Past in the Present: History, Ecology, and Cultural Variation in Highland Madagascar.* Ann Arbor: University of Michigan Press, 1980.

Le Goff, Jacques. "L'Occident médiéval et l'Océan Indien: Un horizon onirique." In *Pour un autre Moyen Age,* edited by Jacques Le Goff. Paris: Gallimard, 1977.

Little, Henry W. *Madagascar, Its History and People.* Westport, Conn.: Negro Universities Press, 1970.

Mack, John. *Madagascar, Island of the Ancestors.* London: British Museum Publications, 1986.

Molet, Louis. *La conception malgache du monde, du surnaturel, et de l'homme en Imerina.* 2 vols. Paris: L'Harmattan, 1979.

Ottino, Paul. *L'étrangère intime. Essai d'anthropologie de la civilisation de l'ancien Madagascar.* Paris: Editions des Archives Contemporaines, 1986.

Rafenomanjato, Charlotte. *La marche de la liberté.* Paris: Azalées/ L'Harmattan, 1992.

Rajoelina, Patrick. *Madagascar, la grande île.* Paris: L'Harmattan, 1989.

Ravololomanga, Bodo. *Etre femme et mère à Madagascar.* Paris: L'Harmattan, 1992.

Revel, Eric. *Madagascar: L'île rouge: Les remords d'un président déchu, Didier Ratsiraka.* Paris: Balland, 1994.

Ruud, Jorgen. *Taboo: A Study of Malagasy Customs and Beliefs.* Oslo: Oslo University Press, 1970.

Sharp, Lesley. *The Possessed and the Dispossessed: Spirits, Identity, and Power in a Madagascar Migrant Town.* Berkeley: University of California Press, 1993.

Tronchon, Jacques. *L'insurrection malgache de 1947: Essai d'interprétation historique.* Paris: Karthala, 1986.

II. Literary History and Anthologies

Bavoux, Claudine. *Devinettes de l'Océan Indien.* Paris: L'Harmattan, 1993.

Chevrier, Jacques. *Littérature africaine*. Paris: Hatier, 1987.

Joubert, Jean-Louis. *Littératures de l'Océan Indien*. Vanves: Edicef/ Aupelf, 1991.

Paulhan, Jean. *Les Hainteny merinas. Poésies populaires malgaches*. Paris: Guentner, 1913.

———. *Les hainteny*. Paris: Gallimard, 1960.

———. *Hain-Tenys merina*. Antananarivo: Foi et Justice, 1992 (reedition).

Rajemisa-Raolison, Régis. *Les poètes malgaches d'expression française*. Antananarivo: Imprimerie Catholique, 1983.

Ramarosoa, Liliane. *Anthologie de la littérature malgache d'expression française des années 80*. Paris: L'Harmattan, 1994.

Senghor, Léopold Sédar. *Anthologie de la nouvelle poésie nègre et malgache de langue française*. Paris: Presses Universitaires de France, 1948.

III. Criticism

1. Books and Articles:

Aly, Jacques. "Où en est la littérature malgache depuis 1960?" In *Reflections on the First Decade of Negro-African Independence*. Paris: Présence Africaine, 1971.

Adrianjafy, Danielle N. "Le théâtre." *Notre Librairie* 110 (July–September 1992): 69–75.

Andriantsilaniarivo, E. "Où en sont les lettres malgaches?" In *Reflections on the First Decade of Negro-African Independence*. Paris: Présence Africaine, 1971.

Davies, Wendy. "The Lost Generation." *Index on Censorship* 14 (October 1985): 45–47.

Fox, Leonard. *Hainteny, the Traditional Poetry of Madagascar*. Lewisburg, Pa.: Bucknell University Press, 1990.

Gérard, Albert. "The Birth of Theatre in Madagascar." *Educational Theatre Journal* 25 (1973): 362–65.

Mantoux, Thierry. "Regard sur la littérature malgache." *L'Afrique Littéraire* 30 (1973): 8–12.

Ranaivo, Flavien et al. "Writing in Madagascar." *Contrast* 7, no. 4 (1972): 40–50.

Rodin, Serge Henri and R. Rakotoarivelo. "Littérature malgache d'expression française." *Notre Librairie* 110 (July–September 1992).

Shafik, Maher. "Translations from the Night." *Lotus: Afro-Asian Writings* 29 (1976): 146–48.

Valette, J., ed. *Flavien Ranaivo: Textes commentés.* Paris: Fernand Nathan, 1968. (poetry and criticism)

Wake, Clive. "Modern Malagasy Literature in French." *Books Abroad* 38 (1964): 14–19.

———. "J.-J. Rabearivelo: A Poet before Negritude." In *The Critical Evaluation of African Literature,* edited by Edgar Wright, 149–72. London: Heinemann, 1973.

2. *Journal Issues:*

Notre Librairie 104 (1991). *Dix ans de littérature 1980–1990: Caraïbe-Océan Indien.*

Notre Librairie 110 (July–September 1992). *Madagascar: La littérature d'expression française.*

Notre Librairie 116 (January–March 1994). *2000 titres: Océan Indien.*

3. *Colloquium Proceedings:*

Jean-Joseph Rabearivelo, cet inconnu? Marseille: SUD, 1989.

IV. Literary Works

Andrianarahinjaka, L.-X. M. *Terre promise. Présence Africaine* 2ème série n° special 57, 1er trimestre 1966, pp. 150–58.

Bemananjara, Zefaniasy. *Contes de Madagascar.* Paris: Cilf/Edicef, 1979 and 1980.

Dox. *Chants capricorniens.* Antananarivo: Editions du Centre Albert Camus, 1995. (poetry)

Fota, Jean-Claude. "Marche et chôme." (short story, unpublished, n.d.)

———. *Cris d'îles.* (poetry, unpublished, n.d.)

Jaomanoro, David. "La retraite." Morlanwelz: Editions Lansman, 1990. (play)

———. "Le petit os." Paris: RFI, 1991. (short story)

———. "Funérailles d'un cochon." Paris: RFI, 1993. (short story)

———. *Quatr'ams j'aime ça.* (poetry, unpublished, n.d.)

Lila. *See* Ratsifandriamanana, Lila.

Nirina, Esther. *Silencieuse respiration.* Orléans: Editions Serjent, 1978. (poetry)

———. *Simple voyelle.* Orléans: Editions Serjent, 1980. (poetry)

———. *Lente spirale.* Antananarivo: Editions Revue de l'Océan Indien, 1990. (poetry)

———. *Multiple solitude.* Antananarivo: Tsipika, 1997. (poetry)

Rabearivelo, Jean-Joseph. *L'aube rouge.* (novel, unpublished, 1925)

———. *Translations from the Night.* London: Heinemann, 1975. (poetry)

———. *L'interférence.* Paris: Hatier, 1987. (novel; written in 1928)

———. *Vieilles chansons du pays d'Imerina.* Paris: Orphée/La Différence, 1990. (translation of hain-teny)

———. *Poèmes.* Paris: Hatier, 1990. (poetry)

Rabemananjara, Jacques. *Antsa.* Paris: Présence Africaine, 1956.

———. *Oeuvres complètes.* Paris: Présence Africaine, 1978. (poetry)

———. *Rien qu'encens et filigrane.* Paris: Présence Africaine, 1987. (poetry)

———. "Agape des dieux. Tritriva." Paris: Présence Africaine, 1988. (play)

Rado. *Dinitra.* Author, 1973. (poetry)

———. *Zo.* Author, 1989. (poetry)

———. *Sedra.* Author, 1994. (poetry)

Rafenomanjato, Charlotte. *Le pétale écarlate.* Antananarivo: Société Malgache d'Edition, 1980. (novel)

———. *Le cinquième sceau.* Paris: L'Harmattan, 1993. (novel)

Rahaingoson, Henri. (selected poems, unpublished, n.d.)

Raharimanana, Jean-Luc. *Lucarne.* Paris: Le Serpent à Plumes, 1996. (short stories)

———. *Poèmes crématoires.* (poetry, unpublished, n.d.)

Rakotoson, Michèle. *Dadabe et autres nouvelles.* Paris: Karthala, 1984. (novel; short stories)

———. *Le bain des reliques.* Paris: Karthala, 1988. (novel)

Rakotozafy, Mathilde. *Les chaînes de la liberté.* Antananarivo: Author, 1990. (poetry)

Ralambo, Bao. "Le miroir du président." (short story, unpublished, n.d.)

Ramanantsoa, Christiane. "Grand-mère." (short story, unpublished, n.d.)

Ranaivo, Flavien. *L'ombre et le vent.* Tananarive: Imprimerie Officielle, 1947. (poetry)

———. *Le retour au bercail.* Tananarive: Imprimerie Officielle, 1962. (poetry)

———. *Poèmes hain-teny.* Paris: Publications Orientalistes de France, 1975. (poetry)

———. *Mes chansons de toujours.* Paris: Author, n.d. (poetry)

Randriamirado, Narcisse. "Grand-mère." Bulletin of the Alliance Française in Madagascar, *Variété* 2 (1990). (short story)

Ratsifandriamanana, Lila. "Dieu descendra sur la terre demain!" (short story, unpublished, n.d.)

———. Selected poems, unpublished, n.d.

Ravoson, Alice. "Aux cimes des aloalo." In *Nouvelles.* Antananarivo: Editions du Centre Culturel Albert Camus, 1995.

Rodin, Serge Henri. "Chien de soleil." *Recherches et Cultures* 5 (1990). (short story)

Valette, J., ed. *Flavien Ranaivo: Textes commentés.* Paris: Fernand Nathan, 1968. (poetry and criticism)

BAKER & TAYLOR